CW00694906

Rising from the Ashes

ROAD TO BANGLADESH SERIES

Rising from the Ashes

Women's Narratives of 1971

Editorial Board

Shaheen Akhtar, Suraiya Begum,
Meghna Guhathakurta, Hameeda Hossain
Sultana Kamal

Translated by

Niaz Zaman

Ain o Salish Kendra (ASK)

The University Press Limited

The University Press Limited, Red Crescent House, Level 6
61 Motijheel C/A, G.P.O. Box 2611, Dhaka 1000, Bangladesh
Phone: 9565441, 9565444, 9565443
E-mail: info@uplbooks.com.bd
Website: www.uplbooks.com.bd

Original Bangla edition by Ain o Salish Kendra, Dhaka, February 2001
First English translation, The University Press Limited jointly with
Ain o Salish Kendra, Dhaka, 2013

Credits:

Front cover concept, Najib Tareq. Design and graphics by Amal Das.

Photo on the front cover, Naibuddin Ahmed (DRIK).

Back cover: Poster by Pranesh Kumar Mandal, in the poster series printed by the Ministry of Information and Broadcasting, Government of Bangladesh during the War of Independence 1971, and later reprinted by the Liberation War Memorial Museum, Dhaka.

ISBN 978 984 506 044 8

Published by Mohiuddin Ahmed, The University Press Limited, Dhaka. Book design by Ashim K. Biswas and printed at the Elora Art Publicity, 635 North Shahjahanpur, Dhaka, Bangladesh.

Contents

Contributors

Hasina Ahmed is Associate Editor of *The Journal of Social Studies, Shomaj Neerikhon,* and Assistant Editor of *Bangladesh Chorcha.* Currently working at the National University in Bangladesh, Gazipur as a deputy Controller. Her publications include *1971: Muktijuddher Patra-Patrika,* collected essays titled *Gonomadhome Bangladesher Muktijuddho,* and a collection of translated essays titled *Bangladesher Naree o Onyanno Probondho.*

Shaheen Akhtar is an award winning novelist and currently Editor of Ain o Salish Kendra (ASK) publications. Her published Bangla novels are *Palabar Poth Nei, Talaash and Shokhi Rongomala.* Her collected stories include *Srimotir Jeebon Dorshon, Boner Shonge Amarloke, 15 ti Golpo* (published from Kolkata), and *Abaro Prem Ashche*. She is the co-editor of *Zanana Mahfil/ Bangali Musalman Lekhikader Nirbachito Rochona* 1904-1938, published jointly from Dhaka and Kolkata. Her novel, *Talaash,* based on the Liberation War in Bangladesh, won the *Prothom Alo*'s Best Book of the Year Award in 2004. Its English translation *The Search* was published by Zubaan in January 2011.

Suraiya Begum, Assistant Director at Research Initiatives, Bangladesh (RIB) is also Associate Editor of *Samaj Nirikkhon* and *The Journal of Social Studies.* Her publications include *Paschim Banglar Rajnoitik Ongshogrohone Grameen Nari : Ekti Samikkha,* and *Nari, Muktijuddhao O Desh: Ontorloke Anneshon* as well as research writings on women's participation in political development and governance in both Bangladesh and West Bengal.

Manzurul Ahsan Bulbul, Chief Executive Officer of Boishakhi Television.

Salma Choudhury was a Research Officer at Ain o Salish Kendra (ASK).

Meghna Guhathakurta is a former professor in the Department of International Relations in the University of Dhaka is currently executive director of Research Initiatives Bangladesh. She is an active participant in the post war rehabilitation of Bangladesh, development, and women's liberation, Meghna's work ranges from international development, South Asian politics to gender studies. She has also contributed to research and activism for the rights of the indigenous communities of Bangladesh. She is currently member of the executive committee of Ain o Salish Kendra (ASK), and trustee of Protichee Trust, amongst a number of other organisational involvements.

Mofidul Haq is a Trustee of the Liberation War Museum and the Publisher at Shahitya Prakash.

Hameeda Hossain is chairperson and founder–member of Ain o Salish Kendra (ASK). She was editor of ASK's annual publication *Human Rights in Bangladesh* from 1996 to 2007 and has written extensively on human rights and women's rights. Her PhD thesis from Oxford University was published under the title of *The Company Weavers of Bengal* (Dhaka: UPL, 2010). She has also co-authored *No Better Options?: Women Workers in Dhaka* (Dhaka: UPL, 1990) and co-edited *From Crisis to Development: Coping with Disaster in Bangladesh* (Dhaka: UPL, 1992). She is also vice chair of Research Initiatives Bangladesh (RIB).

Sultana Kamal is the Executive Director of Ain o Salish Kendra (ASK), Chairperson of the Board of Trustees of Transparency International Bangladesh and a former Adviser to the Caretaker Government. She is a lawyer and strong campaigner for human rights and women's rights. Sultana Kamal was a participant in the war of liberation during which she worked in a hospital at Agartala for the war wounded. She was awarded the John Humphrey Freedom Award in Canada in 1996. Her publications include *Manobir Nihshonko Mon,* a book on women's legal and customary rights in Bangladesh published by Women Living under Muslim Laws.

Amena Mohsin teaches in the Department of International Relations, University of Dhaka. She is the author of *The Politics of Nationalism: The Case of Chittagong Hill Tracts,* Bangladesh (Dhaka: UPL, 1997), *The*

Chittagong Hill Tracts, Bangladesh: On The Difficult Road To Peace (Lynn Rienner Publishers, 2002) and *Ethnic Minorities of Bangladesh: Some Reflections on the Saontals and Rakhaines* (Programme for Research on Poverty Alleviation, 2002). She has co-edited *Women and Militancy: South Asian Complexities* (Dhaka: UPL, 2011). Amena has received several national and international fellowships, including the East-West Center Graduate Fellowship, CIDA International Fellowship, Commonwealth Staff Fellowship, SSRC Fellowship and Freedom Foundation Fellowship. She has written extensively on rights issues, State, Democracy, Civil-Military relations and human security.

Qurratul Ain Tahmina is a journalist and works for *Prothom Alo* – a leading daily newspaper in Bangladesh. She is the co-author of *Bangladeshe Jounota Bikri: Jeeboner Daame Kena Jeebika* and *Sex Workers in Bangladesh: Livelihood-at What Price* (Dhaka: UPL, 2004).

Niaz Zaman is Professor of English at University of Dhaka. She is the author of *The Art of Kantha Embroidery* (Dhaka: UPL, 2012), the first book on this folk craft. She has translated and edited important literary works from Bangla to English, including *Laal Shalu* (Tree without Roots) by Syed Waliullah (Dhaka: writers.ink, 2010). Her creative writing is influenced by her interest in folk traditions as demonstrated by her prize-winning short story, "The Dance," and her novella, *The Baromashi Tapes* (Dhaka: writers.ink, 2012), based on the local tradition of the *baromashi*. She has edited and supervised the translation of this volume.

Foreword

In 2001 Ain o Salish Kendra published oral histories of 22 women, who recounted their experiences during the war of independence in 1971 – accounts of loss, sexual violence, displacement, desertion, escape. We learnt from these accounts how their pain and trauma had not ended with the war. On the contrary, their recollections illustrate their fortitude in coping with deprivation and isolation after 1971, in facing personal tragedies, economic want and social exclusion as a consequence of the war.

Although there had been many references to rape and other forms of war crimes in the press and public pronouncements, women survivors had found little space to record their stories, to share their trauma, and even to locate themselves in the national narrative. Government and non-government initiatives had concentrated on providing social and economic support to the survivors, but these initiatives had given little space for their self expression. Apart from Dr. Nilima Ibrahim's accounts *(Ami Birangana Bolchi)* of women victims of rape in 1971, ASK's publication was one of the first few to break the silence of women who faced the war and its aftermath.

ASK engaged in these conversations, so as to collect testimonies of violence inflicted upon women from the beginning of the military operation in March as a record of war crimes. Within the country demands for trials of war criminals, voiced after 1972, had gathered momentum during the movement for democracy and against military rule in the eighties. Internationally too, gendered violence in conflict situations had emerged as a central issue of human rights at Vienna in 1993 and it was one of twelve concerns universally acknowledged in the Platform for Action in Beijing. A strong feminist campaign led by a gender caucus at discussions on the Statutes on International War Crimes led to the recognition of rape as a war crime. The trial of war criminals in former Yugoslavia and Rwanda set some standards for an accounting of sexual violence in war.

These developments had raised some expectations that the crimes committed in Bangladesh would receive attention, even if many years later. As human rights defenders ASK took on the task to bring the evidence to the attention of governments and the public and perhaps at trials for war crimes. As the 19 survivors talked they raised questions of justice: revenge, retribution, restoration. Each story identified how gendered power relations in times of war and post war mediate issues of justice, peace and human dignity.

While there was some concern that public exposure may revictimise the survivor, many feminists argued that women needed to share their pain as part of the national narrative, to seek not only retribution for the past, but restoration of their human dignity. Justice also demanded that these stories of war crimes become warning signals against the violence in our societies.

ASK's publication of an English translation of *Narir Ekattor o Juddhoporoborti Kothokahini* is a much needed initiative that will, by informing a wider audience beyond Bangla readers, help to break the silence on crimes against women committed in Bangladesh in 1971 and interrogate contemporary narratives of justice from feminist perspectives.

This publication would not have been possible without the cooperation of the 22 women who were persuaded to reveal their experiences. It took considerable courage, fortitude and patience. A few of them have become open campaigners for trials of war crimes, others formed bonds in sharing their experiences. They may not be present at the trial courts, but their voices will find a resonance amongst those who speak out against the brutality of the war and actively demand peace. In some cases pseudonyms have been used.

ASK acknowledges the contribution of many persons who joined us in this exploration. Foremost among them were Dr. Meghna Guhathakurta, Advocate Sultana Kamal, Dr. Amena Mohsin, Suraiya Begum, Qurratul Ain Tahmina, Hasina Ahmed. Some of them had also worked in the field, recording the oral histories. Gita Sahgal has been a source of inspiration. Shaheen Akhtar, who edited the Bangla edition, has been instrumental in putting together this volume. Niaz Zaman with her team of translators, Mahbubar Rahman, Muhammad Saiful Islam and Shahidul Islam Khan – has given us a sensitive translation.

Others whose assistance ASK would like to acknowledge include – Shajedur Rahman for designing the cover, Rakhee for compiling and documenting newspaper reports. Babul Dhar for its production.

Hameeda Hossain

Preface

There are multitudes of ways in which women are inscribed into nationalist struggles. Yet most nationalist histories tend to relegate them into specific roles: victims, mothers who send their sons to war or symbolically etched in the notion of a motherland to be defended. The historical construction of the Bangladesh Liberation War was no exception. The dominant image that one gets through the mainstream literature and media (be it novels, poems, drama or personal accounts) is the plight of women as war widows, rape victims or upheld in the symbol of *Matribhumi* (motherland) under siege. Only recently has this trend been interrogated by scholars and activists rediscovering and foregrounding women as soldiers in the battlefield (e.g. Taramon Bibi), the widow or mother's own autobiography, in-depth scholarly research e.g works of Nayanika Mookherjee and Bina D'Costa. In these interventions, women's own perspectives of the war have come through and these have not only encouraged a more holistic sense of nationalist history, but have gone beyond the object of mere inscription of women into the history of nationalist struggles to interrogating power relations embedded in that struggle. This has often led to the contestation of nationalism itself! Feminist studies have stated that this is almost inevitable because women's lived reality leads them to negotiate male dominant power relations at all levels, domestic, local and national. The nationalist project valorises the nation and the people of the nation in ethnic, religious, linguistic or racial terms that simultaneously tend to invisibilise other kinds of oppression such as those based on class or gender. Women's perspectives of the struggle unearth such oppression and feminist studies seek to reclaim the nationalist space aiming thereby to transform it. When *Narir Ekattorer o Juddhoporoborti Kothyokahini* was first published in Bangla (February 2001), it was the aim of the editors and researchers to do just that.

The title itself hinted that it was not the aim to merely inscribe women's stories into the canvas that was 1971. Therefore it was not

Ekattorey Nari (Women *in* 1971) but *Narir Ekattor* (Women's 1971). Furthermore it did not stop at 1971, as the title also implied (*Juddhoporoborti Kothyokahini* meant the stories after 1971), but followed these women in their day-to-day struggles in the post-independence phase implying that women's struggles did not necessarily end with the attainment of nationhood.

Narir Ekattor locates women in Bangladesh within a specific historicity of struggle which had inspired them to address various layers of oppression. For example how women, who took a proactive role in 1971, were previously exposed to a culture of resistance e.g. the 1952 Language Movement, the uprising against the military regime of Ayub Khan, etc. Names like Ashalata Sen, Monorama Bosu, Hena Das, Sufia Kamal, Laila Samad, Nadera Begum, Hajera Mahmud, Kamrunnahar Laily come to mind.

It also locates women in everyday resistance within and outside the home, which has informed and shaped women's responses during the conflict as well as after it. But mostly it talks of women's aspirations and expectations in a socially transformed world which they wished to see at the end of their struggles. Many of their accounts bear testimony to the fact that such aspirations often fell far short of what an independent Bangladesh state could offer them. But even then their dreams and aspirations continue to ignite them to struggle for a socially transformed world, which would uphold those notions of freedom which they cherished so dearly in their hearts, even in times of darkness.

Women's struggles in Bangladesh both individually as well as in the form of social movements have historically been located in the civil rights discourse accompanying the process of democratisation, which included struggles against military regimes, national liberation struggles and anti-fundamentalist struggles.

In post-partition East Pakistan, one could see women get involved in various social reconstruction projects, formation of neighbourhood committees, championing girls' education and participation in politics and culture. As a result of this we saw Bangali Muslim girls taking active part in the social life of a polity that was struggling to set up liberal democratic institutions in the face of traditional conservatism. This space in which women gained some freedom alongside the struggle for Bangali identity as opposed to the Islamic identity being promoted by the Pakistan State, did not gain favour in the Pakistan establishment. As a result many women joined the resistance against some of the impositions by the state such as forbidding the broadcast of *Rabindra sangeet* (Tagore songs) in the Government media, or the wearing of *teep* (*bindis*) on the forehead of Bangali women as it was thought to resemble Hindu culture. As a result of such social resistance, women became more visible when the struggle for Bangali identity took on national proportions as in the 1952 Bangla Language Movement, the 1969 uprising against the Ayub military regime, culminating of course in the 1971 Liberation War.

From the Pakistan military crackdown on March 26, 1971 to the surrender of the armed forces on December 16, women participated in many ways in the Liberation War: from fund raising, looking after the sick, hiding arms, acting as messengers in reconnaissance activities to even directly participating in armed struggle. These stories had largely remained untold in the mainstream war literature. It was only after two decades had passed that women and women's organisations started unfolding their stories through autobiographies and other activities. The autobiographies of Jahanara Imam, Mushtari Shaffi, Panna Kaiser, Shyamoli Nasreen Chowdhury, Basanti Guhathakurta and Nilima Ibrahim's anthology of the stories of rape survivors in *Ami Birangona Bolchhi* were landmarks in this trend. These narratives had a twofold impact on their wide readership. First, they succeeded in conveying the message that women had very important roles to play in the war, and second, they told of the impact that violence has had on their personal lives and how far it had transformed them.

As a research collective, the work on *Narir Ekattor* was conceptualised keeping both these strands in mind. But our thinking also evolved as we confronted the challenges of taking up such a task almost 25 years down the road.

The primary focus of our research was to look at rape as a war crime and how the Pakistan Army used it as a form of torture and as a weapon of war against the whole nation. We hoped that such a research would contribute to the gathering of solid evidence in the event that war crime procedures were taken up by the state. But we encountered problems on the way. Even 25 years down the road from 1971, people were not willing to talk of rape. Those who were marginalised and poor had their testimonies used in a peoples' tribunal *(Gono Adalat)*, organised by civil society to pressure the then BNP[1] Government to try war criminals, but without the sensitivity or preparation on the ground that was needed to probe the issue. As a result the witnesses who returned to the village faced mockery and blame from their families and society who held them responsible for bringing them shame. In trying to overcome this challenge, we decided to broaden our focus to include women victimised through different circumstances: forced eviction, widowhood, rejection by society, defending family and home, etc. This helped us to find our second objective of the research, which was to see how women even in a hostile environment defended the hearth and home, looked after their children, and above all upheld their hopes and aspirations for a peaceful future. In this warlike situation, women faced not only the common enemy, i.e., the Pakistani forces and their collaborators, but also those whom they considered close to them, neighbours who induced them to flee and later grabbed their properties, villagers who mocked at them, parents who refused to accept them or the child they gave birth to, so-called friends who averted their eyes when they saw them on the streets. The third objective was to understand and learn through the experiences of these women in the form of oral histories, the different strategies and language of oppression used by the Pakistani occupying forces as means of creating evidence for war crimes.

This was also a time when, in the backdrop of the Vienna and Beijing conferences, the case for including sexual violence against women during conflicts as a war crime got highlighted. Over the years, feminist legal researchers had brought up this issue in the international legal discourse through rigorous studies that were both grounded and sensitive. We derived a lot of information from this work and from the fact that one of us was able to represent women war victims of 1971 in a tribunal at the Beijing Conference.

At the more official level, the Tribunals set up by the UN on Rwanda and Bosnia helped to project women's perspectives on war crimes in a broader way. Following these trends, the case of "comfort women" or sexual slavery was brought to light in the Tokyo Tribunal of 2000 where one of our interviewees, Ferdousi Priyobhashini, also participated.

1 Bangladesh Nationalist Party hold office from 1991-1996 and 2001-2006.

It is because of the importance of these testimonies in the international sphere that we thought of translating the accounts into English. The original *Narir Ekattor o Juddhoporoborti Kothyo Kahini* in Bangla and its current English version contain oral histories of 22 women who had to cope with violence during 1971 in all its dimensions: rape, torture, murder, arson, eviction and displacement. Their testimonies have been preserved in 48 cassettes. They came from different parts of Bangladesh: Dhaka, Narayanganj, Savar, Sherpur, Nalitabari, Kushtia, Kumarkhali, Satkhira, Khulna, Barisal and the Chittagong Hill Tracts. Out of these 22 women, 18 are Muslims, two are Hindus and two Buddhists. At the time of taping the interviews, 15 were housewives, one a cultural activist, and six were working women. About ten lived in Dhaka, three in suburbs, and nine were from rural areas. Out of the 22 interviewees, nine were rape victims, the rest spoke of their trials and tribulations after members of their families were killed. Out of the nine rape victims eight were raped or systematically raped by Pakistani soldiers and one by a Bangali collaborator.

Outwardly, the majority of these women led ordinary lives before and after the war. One exception is the case of Ferdousi Priyobhashini who underwent such a transformation as a self-made artist that she became a national figure. Incidentally, she was one of the first among the middle-class who had the courage to come out with her story. It is with heartfelt thanks and gratitude to her patience, courage and perseverance that we can say that though published much later, her story first came out through a process that we recorded in this book. But, aside from her, the lives of the other women too had changed, although that process is not as visible to the public eye as in Ferdousi's case. The experience of violence and the accompanying trauma affects one's life in different ways. Those who have a relative degree of support from family and friends find it easier to overcome the hatred and anger with which the experience leaves them. Others take the refuge of forgetting. Very few can overcome their immediate feelings of hurt and victimhood and channelise it in creative ways of self-transformation. Often such a process takes a whole life-time! But whatever individual ways of coping these women had recorded in their interviews, one thing was common to all. They had great expectations from a nation whose freedom they had helped to secure, with their tears, toil, and the blood of their dear and loved ones. But many were disappointed at the result, and some continued to struggle for the peace and harmony they so earnestly desired in their personal lives and in the society and nation in which they lived. It is this aspiration, which we wanted to bring to the attention of our national leaders and international community. Since the present Government of Bangladesh has been elected on the promise of a trial of war criminals of 1971 and an official process is under way, we feel it is necessary for officials, civil society and the international community to revisit the issue of sexual violence and war crimes. We hope that the interviews in this book will provide a starting point in this effort.

Dhaka and Narayanganj

Introduction

Mofidul Hoque

Any oral history project has its strengths and limitations. Oral account can probe deeper into human experience that remain outside the purview of formal history, but the broad perspective of historical events cannot be fully explored by oral accounts only. Morever, there is a limitation on the number of oral accounts one can collect and analyse. As every oral account is unique and reflects the depth of human experience, it incorporates multiple layers of reality and is not only about what the participants have witnessed and gone through, but also how he or she percieved the reality. Thereby oral accounts always have very significant features that can become an important tool in understanding history. In this chapter focusing on Dhaka and its neighbourhood oral accounts of two women (Zebunnessa Begum and Rasheda Khanom) and four sisters of a single family (Nilufa, Rumana, Sharmin and Farzana) have been put together. They in a way also highlight the experiences of the families. In fact most of the accounts in the anthology ultimately became family accounts as in our society it is difficult to separate the women's narratives from the story of her family.

The reality as reflected in the oral accounts could be used to construct the broader picture in human terms, specially in our understanding of the genocide and the crimes against humanity perpetrated by the Pakistan Army in 1971. The experiences of the families from Dhaka and its suburbs depicted two incidents of brutal murder when Zebunnessa Begum's husband was killed by non-Bangali 'Biharis' in front of his house. The parents of four sisters (in fact of five daughters and one brother), affluent businessman Jasimul Haq and his wife Laila Hasina Banu, a famous woman athlete in Narayanganj, was brutally killed by the Pakistan Army on the night of 27 March as they were entering Narayanganj town. These three senseless killings of unarmed civilian men and women were not isolated or accidental acts but part of the killing spree which went unabetted for nine months and reflected the widespread and systematic killing by Pakistan Army. In the definition of crimes against humanity the International Criminal Court (ICCI) stated, "Crimes against humanity means any of the following acts when committed as part of a widespread and systematic attack directed against any civilian population, with knowledge of the attack."

Various other narratives in the book highlighted the genocidal nature of the attack and killing when Pak Army specially targeted the Hindu population and the intellectuals in order to annihilate them in whole or in part. ICC defined 'genocide' as, "any of the following acts committed with the intent to destroy, in whole or in part, national, ethnical, racial or religious group."

Right from the beginning, the genocidal intent of the Pakistan Army was reflected in the brutal nature of the attack and ethnic targeting. The massacre at Jagannath Hall, attack on the Hindu dwellings at Shankhari Bazar, killing of Professor G.C. Dev and others, Dhaka university canteen manager Modhu (affectionately known as "Modhu Da" to teachers and students alike) alongwith his family members, etc. are blatant evidences of the genocidal intent of Pakistan Army. It is interesting to note that one of the first persons to identity this genocidal intent of Pakistani attack was Archer K. Blood, the then US Consul General in Dhaka. As early as March 28 , 1971 in his secret cable to the State Department he used the word 'Selective Genocide'. Later on in his memoirs Archer K. Blood wrote, "On March 28 I sent a telegram captioned 'Selective Genocide'. As far as I know, it was the first time that term had been used, but it was not to be the last."

Interestingly the genocidal intent and elements of crimes against humanity, specially targeting the civilian population, had also been reflected in the military doctrine 'Operation Searchlight', prepared by the GHQ as their action plan. The Pakistan Army aimed at a Blitzkrieg operation and the target, mostly composed of civilian population was identified after very careful observations. Even the military target, the Bangali members of the Armed Forces, East Pakistan Rifles and Police Forces cannot be considered as military as at that time there was no mutiny, no all-out war had been declared against the State of Pakistan, neither was there an armed conflict. All the targets were soft ones and the Pakistani Armed Forces unleashed the attack with full military might. As a basis for the sudden attack the plan openly stated that, "As A.L. has widespread support even amongst the E.P (East Pakistan) elements in the Army the operation has to be launched with great cunningness, surprise, deception, and speed combined with shock action." The Army was given the task of interpreting the meaning of the words, 'great cunningness', 'deception' and 'shock action' in real terms. How they started to implement it had, been reflected in the brutal killing of the members of Zebunnessa Begum's family and Nilufa's sisters. It was neither unintentional nor unplanned.

'Operation Searchlight' was a chilling document which could be compared with Wansee Declaration, the Nazi plan for the final solution of the "problems" of European Jews. Even more chilling than the text of the document was what happened in reality, with so many deaths, thrown out of their homes and country and women being made victims of sexual violence. Zebunnessa Begum and Nilufa sisters narrated their sufferings in detail. For them and millions of others, the ordeal did not end in 1971; rather for the female survivors a new struggle started immediately after the tragic event. In many cases the death of the male member in the family suddenly put a great burden on the female head. How they coped with this totally unforeseen and unprepared situation showed their determination, courage and composure.

Such heroics of the women have remained out of our focus and one can get a glimpse of that from the life and struggle of Zebunnessa Begum who took the role of the bread-earner and protector of the family or of Nilufa sisters in their struggle for survival from an early age in a world not supportive of them and hostile in many cases.

The survivors of extreme violence had to struggle against external difficulties as well as internal complexities which has been recognised of late as Post-Traumatic Stress Disorder (PTSD). This psychological syndrome is very common in societies that experience violent clashes. It became a focus of attention for justice and rehabilitation since the 1990's in the discourse of various tribunals like ICTY, ICTR and finally with the International Criminal Court (ICC). In the frank accounts given by Nilufa and Rumana they lay bare their psychic condition, the dark dreams that haunt them, lack of sleep, depression, fear psychosis, mental and physical anxiety, loneliness, etc. All these are glaring examples of PTSD which need proper counseling and support from experts that our society does not lack. What is lacking is the attention of the society to address the needs of survivors of extreme violence, the large number of such victims of 1971 tragedy is still coping with the problem all by themselves.

The psychological and social complexities found another kind of reflection in the account of Zebunnessa Begum. Her husband, a local Awami League leader, became the target of attack at the very beginning of the military operation, an example of 'Operation Searchlight' in action whereby it was stated that, "A.L. (Awami Leage) action and reactions to be treated as rebellion and those who support [A.L.] or defy M.L. (Martial Law) action be dealt with as hostile elements." Mohammad Salimullah, father of ten children, had established himself through a long struggle. He was an Inspector at Kidderpore Dockyard in Kolkata and migrated to Dhaka after the 1950 riots. He was alloted a plot at Mohammadpur and built his house in a neighbourhood which was mostly inhabited by non-Bangali Bihari refugees from India. The Government of Pakistan had a deliberate policy to extend all out cooperation to the Bihari settlers with an aim to raise their support group in the then East Pakistan. After the military attack on March 25 the house of Mohammad Salimullah at Tajmahal Road became a kind of shelter for local Bangali people as they took refuge there. On March 26 with the lifting of curfew Mohammad Salimullah went to the mosque to attend the Jumma prayer. The 'Biharis' unleashed their attack after the prayer was over and Salimulla's house became a prime target. He was brutally killed by the Biharis in front of his house, before the eyes of his own sons. The house was looted and put on fire, the family members thrown out on the street. How Zebunnessa Begum managed to survive and kept together the scattered members, her young siblings, was a story of great shock and pain. While describing the Bihari atrocities in detail, the nameless faceless butchers in their frenzy, she also narrated how other non-Bangalis, individuals with empathy and sensibilities, came to their help, even risking their own lives. These are other humans in her narrative with a face and a name in contrast with the Bihari community.

Zebunnessa Begum held the Biharis and Pakistanis responsible for what happened to her family and to the nation in 1971. She refused to offer alms to Bihari beggars if they came to her door. On the other hand she went out of her way in post-independent Bangladesh and provided shelter to other Biharis who helped her and her family including a Punjabi family, who had rendered assistance to her during their days of ordeal. While she nurtured a deep-seated hatred towards the Biharis, she also helped the distressed Bihari families who rendered assistance and she narrated that experience with gratitude.

Zebunnessa Begum had little education but she had a deeper perspective of life, which she acquired through her struggle for existence. She was a strong supporter for trial of war crimes, and held on to the belief that Pakistan should formally and officially offer apology for what they have done in 1971. She can never forget and forgive the Biharis for the atrocities they committed. At the same time she also recognised the support rendered by the 'Bihari' individuals and did her best to help them in time of their crisis. That Zebunnessa Begum could keep her human values alive even in the face of extreme violence she had to go through and rekindle that in other people's heart, had found eloquent reflection in her narrative. She may be one among the million ladies, but she represented the human spirit and the strength of the liberation struggle of the Bangalis, a struggle that did not end on December 16, 1971, rather it continued throughout her life, in raising her family and in the effort of keeping the flame of human spirit alive.

Such are the narratives of the women of 1971, that tell us much more than what we know about 1971.

Zebunnessa Begum

A Mother's Struggle for Her Family

Qurratul Ain Tahmina

Introduction

The independence of Bangladesh was declared on March 26, 1971. On that same day Mohammad Salimullah, a businessman and President of Awami League, Mohammadpur, was killed by non-Bangali[1] residents [Biharis], in front of his residence in Mohammadpur, on the north-western fringes of Dhaka. His attackers then set his four-storeyed building on fire. Mohammad Salimullah's wife, Zebunnessa Begum, their ten children and a few other relatives survived and managed to escape. The effects of this catastrophe lasted long after the creation of Bangladesh.

A housewife in a conservative family where women observed purdah, Zebunnessa Begum had been entirely dependent on her husband. However, after her husband was killed, she was obliged to assume responsibilities as the head of the family. During the war she had to support her family as they ran from village to village seeking refuge. She secretly helped her eldest son who was a freedom fighter. When the war ended, she was helped by her friends and relatives and, through her own efforts, earned enough to support her family. She managed the household with a firm hand and brought up her ten children with vigil and care.

We have attempted to narrate the story of Zebunnessa Begum's struggle for survival. We have tried to find out what happened to the family members in March 1971, their experiences during the nine-month period of the war, and how they recovered after the war and became self-reliant. We have tried to find out how the personal losses she suffered during the Liberation War changed Zebunnessa Begum's life.

---

[1] Subsumed under the generic term "Bihari," Zebunnessa Begum used the term in her narrative.

Methodology[2]

Zebunnessa Begum travelled down memory lane and recounted the events vividly and in great detail as if they were happening before her.

Though her eyes did not betray any tears, her voice often became choked and faint. The manner of her narration, her listless tone, her singular way of speaking made it clear that it was excruciatingly painful for her to rummage through those past events time and again. She could not continue speaking for a long time. While talking she would look away and would abruptly fall silent. At other times she would make excuses and slip away on the plea of some housework. After we had interviewed her for three days, she made it clear that she had nothing more to say. No matter how long she spoke, her narrative, even were she to continue, would never end.

Five of Zebunnessa Begum's ten children live in Dhaka, the rest are abroad. Of those in Dhaka, her fourth son and fifth child, Shibli Mohammad Enamullah, and her youngest daughter, Farida Yasmin Banu, were present during the interviews and gave us a lot of information. Both of them, particularly Farida Yasmin, were quite young in 1971. Shibli spoke mostly from memory. Farida and Shibli's accounts were corroborated by other members of the family as well.

Jahanara Khatun, the closest neighbour of the Salimullah family, also gave us more details. Mrs. Khatun's family had been staying in a house opposite Mr. Salimullah's, on Tajmahal Road. Mr. Harunur Rashid, Mrs. Jahanara's husband, a Subedar Major in the Pakistan Army Medical Corps [since 1969], was one of the accused in the Agartala Conspiracy Case and had been in custody for eleven months. With the release of Sheikh Mujibur Rahman and the collapse of the Agartala Conspiracy Case, he too had been released. In February 1971, Harunur Rashid was posted to West Pakistan. Jahanara continued to stay in their Tajmahal Road house with her eight children. On the night of March 25, 1971, she and her family sought shelter in Mr. Salimullah's house. Towards the end of March, they again took shelter in Mr. Salimullah's village home in Shalmashi (Shyamalapur) under Savar Police Station near Dhaka, on the other side of the Buriganga. We talked to Jahanara because she was the

2 This account is based on three long [and exclusive] interviews with Zebunnessa Begum, taken in the middle of 1997, 26 years after the war, in the same house where Mohammad Salimullah and his family had been attacked by Biharis on March 26, 1971.

closest non-family witness to the tragedy that befell the Salimullah family.

The Salimullah Family

Before relating details of the incidents, we will give a brief introduction to Mohammad Salimullah and Zebunnessa Begum. We also tried to find out what each of their children had been doing at that time.

Mohammad Salimullah was born most probably in 1929. He grew up in the village of Sachar under Kachua Police Station in Comilla District (the present Chandpur District). The family was not well off, and Mohammad Salimullah had to pursue his studies by working as a house tutor, getting free board and lodging as remuneration. After he passed his Matriculation examination from Comilla, Mohammad Salimullah moved to Kolkata to work as an Inspector in the Khidirpur Dockyard. After the communal riots in 1950, he returned to East Pakistan and worked in the Jute Board, Narayanganj for some time. After that he worked as a Section Officer for fourteen years in the Home Ministry. He left the job to become an enlisted contractor with the Public Works Department. He also had some extra income as he owned three auto rickshaws and a truck. These were sold before 1971. He was active in politics. During Ayub Khan's rule, Mohammad Salimullah contested for a seat in the Provincial Assembly as an independent candidate from Kachua Police Station but did not win the election. In 1968-69 he joined the Awami League.

In 1947, while working in Kolkata, he married Zebunnesa Begum who was from Nalai village under Chandina Police Station in Comilla District. Their first child was born in Kolkata.

Notwithstanding his preoccupation with politics and business, Salimullah pursued his studies. In 1971, before the war, he appeared for the M.A. examination in Islamic History. Results of his success in the exams were announced after his death. He was due to appear in the LLB. (Final) examination in May 1971.

In addition, he had two brick fields and some landed property in the village of Shalmashi (Shyamalapur), west of Dhaka, in Savar Police Station. He also owned a four-storied building in Mohammadpur. When he died on March 26, 1971 at the age of 42, he left behind his wife and ten children. He was then the President of Awami League, Mohammadpur.

Zebunnessa Begum was born in Chandpur. She was 18 years old when she married Mohammad Salimullah. She had studied up to Class Seven in Lady Protima Girls' School at Chandpur. Her father was an *imam* in the local mosque and owned a considerable tract of landed property. Before she was widowed in 1971, she was a housewife, busy looking after her children and household chores. She was also interested in sewing, and, after moving to Dhaka with her husband, she did a diploma course at Singer's in tailoring and embroidery.

Of the ten children born to Mohammad Salimullah and Zebunnessa Begum, their eldest son, Shahjahan Mohammed Safiullah, also known as Shanu, and their eldest daughter, Maleka Parvin Banu, were studying for the B.A. degree in 1971. Their third child (second son) Sami Mohammad Naqiullah was then in secondary school. Their fourth child (third son), Sadi Mohammad Taqiullah (a noted Tagore artiste) was due to appear in the Matriculation examination. The other children, Shibli Mohammad Enamullah (a noted dance artiste), Khaleda Nasrin Banu, Shoeb Mohammad Tarikullah, and Sohel Mohammad Ekramullah were studying in Classes 6, 5, 4 and 1 respectively. The youngest were twin sisters, Laila Nazmin Banu and Farida Yasmin Banu, then about two and a half or three years old.

The Locality

Mohammad Salimullah and his family strongly supported the cause of Bangladesh. They had close links with the leaders of the Awami League and the Chhatra League, the student front of the Awami League. But they were living in an area of Dhaka where a pro-Pakistani, non-Bangali population formed a majority. In 1971 the Mohammadpur area of Dhaka was not safe for any Bangali, and, particularly, not for any one from the Salimullah family.

Mohammadpur Residential Area on the north-west of Dhaka, was home to mainly non-Bangali Muslims from different Indian provinces such as Bihar, the Punjab and Uttar Pradesh. It had been built after the creation of Pakistan in 1947. Dhaka Improvement Trust (the present Rajdhani Unnayan Kartripakkha or RAJUK) had allotted plots of land there to many non-Bangali refugees from India. A small number of Bangalis too managed to get allotments there where they subsequently built houses. Salimullah constructed his house on Tajmahal Road in 1963 and moved there with his family.

Mohammadpur Police Station lies on the west of Mirpur Road. Salimullah's house was almost in the centre of the locality, which is on the western fringe of Dhaka city, not far from the Buriganga. On the south lies Lalmatia Residential Area. Further down, on the southwest, lie Rayer Bazar, Madhubazar, Jhigatola, Hazaribagh, and Dhanmondi. Sher-e-Bangla Nagar is on the northeast of Mohammadpur. On the south are Sukrabad and Kalabagan, on the north are Shyamoli, Kalyanpur and Mirpur.

Quite a number of plots in Mohammadpur were lying vacant in 1971. At the time, the locality was dominated by well-to-do and powerful non-Bangalis, popularly known as Biharis. Very few Bangalis lived there prior to 1971. Thus, there were no other middle-class Bangali families where Zebunnessa Begum lived, except those of Jahanara Khanum and Golap Mia, owner of a ration shop in the vicinity. A few poor Bangali families lived in the slums nearby.

Although Zebunnessa Begum stated that she did not notice any symptoms of animosity between Bangalis and Biharis before March 26, some of her comments reveal that rivalry, clash of interests and political and cultural differences had already divided the two communities quite distinctly. Their neighbour Jahanara Khanum thought that there was hostility between Bangalis and Biharis in Mohammadpur well before 1971. She recalls that in 1970 her third son, who was returning from a local mosque after his Arabic lesson, said that he heard some Bihari students whisper amongst themselves, "We will kill all the Bangalis, and you will cease to exist." Jahanara Khanum commented, "Children were saying these things. They must have heard their elders talking in such a way." After she completed her house in Tajmahal Road in 1969, Jahanara Khanum had become used to hearing that Biharis were given preference in the allotment of plots in the Mirpur-Mohammadpur area and that Bangalis were not allotted land in this area. By March 1971, the Bangali-Bihari tension became acute on the Pakistan-Bangladesh issue.

1971: Flag Hoisting on March 23

Even in the last week of March 1971, Zebunnessa Begum was not afraid of Biharis and did not apprehend any danger from them. However, because of frequent strikes and other protests, she had been stocking sugar, molasses, rice and lentils. She had also stocked wheat, flour and mustard oil harvested from their own fields in the village. She had felt confident that the Bangalis were going to win. "The students were united like a rock under the command of Sheikh Saheb." Her eldest son, commonly known as Shanu, was a close associate of Chhatra League leaders Abdur Rab, Abdul Quddus Makhon, and Nur-e-Alam Siddiqui.

On March 23, Zebunnessa's son informed her about the decision to hoist Bangladesh flags on all buildings. He gave her a piece of cloth to make a flag. She started making a flag on her sewing machine. Her third son Sadi used a yellow pencil to draw the map of Bangladesh inside the red coloured sun in the flag. Zebunnessa said, "I made the flag happily. I felt very strong." She recalled making small festoons for the motor bikes of her eldest son and the student leader Rab. In the morning, the family hoisted the Bangladesh flag on their roof. It never occurred to anyone that before the dawn of March 26, the flag would have to be brought down. In fact, on the evening of March 25, Salimullah tried to diffuse the tension by arriving at a compromise between the Biharis and Bangalis.

March 25, 1971

A meeting of local Biharis and Bangalis was convened at Mr. Salimullah's residence on the evening of March 25. Zebunnessa Begum remembers that student leaders A. S. M. Rab and Abdul Kuddus Makhon also attended that meeting. Before this the Bangali student leaders had decided that, in order to compel the Biharis to support Bangalis, the supply of ration, electricity and water to Mohammadpur would be stopped. Salimullah and his eldest son were apprehensive that this decision would endanger the handful of Bangalis living there. "We are just a few Bangalis, they [the Biharis] will smash us like ants." They convinced the student leaders that it would be wiser to compromise with the Biharis rather than disconnect electricity and water. It was to resolve this issue that a meeting was convened on the evening of March 25. At the meeting Biharis of the locality declared that they too would hoist the Bangladesh flag. Zebunnesa Begum remembers that at the end of the meeting the Biharis shouted slogans such as "Biharis and Bangalis are brothers, we live and eat together."

Zebunnessa Begum's neighbour, Jahanara Khanum, too recalled this slogan, and added that the Biharis were feeling insecure and held another meeting at the same time. Zebunnessa Begum's sons, who had gone to the newspaper offices to report the news of the Bihari-

Bangali entente, returned home late at night. By that time the road to Nilkhet had been barricaded. They reported that Iqbal Hall,[3] one of several residential halls at the University of Dhaka, had been attacked and several places had been set on fire. Troops were patrolling the city.

Late that night, several Bangalis of the locality took shelter in Mohammad Salimullah's four-storeyed building. The third floor of the house was occupied by Mr. Salimullah's family, Jahanara Khanum and her eight children, her brother's family, Golap Mia's nephew Chinu Miah, her 70-year-old uncle, a grand nephew on her husband's side, the son of her husband's elder brother, an eleven-year-old girl Rupban, (who was brought up by Zebunnessa Begum) and her brother Malek. Rupban's parents lived in a slum; her father sold *paan* and the mother worked part-time in different homes. When the Bangali slums were set on fire, they took shelter in Mr. Salimullah's house.

On the third floor, in front of the rooms, there was an open space. Everyone spent a sleepless night there, walking up and down. Zebunnessa Begum said she saw that several places had been set on fire. The Biharis were marching in groups on the streets, setting fire to the slums and shouting, "*Nara-e-Takbir, Allahu Akbar*." They were cursing the Bangalis. She recalls the sight of Biharis carrying pipe guns and daggers. Zebunnessa Begum's eldest daughter was crying in fear. According to Zebunnessa Begum, "My daughter, after doing her *wazu* (ablution for prayer), spread the prayer mat on the floor, and kept praying and crying at intervals, 'What's going to happen, Amma? What's going to happen to us, Amma?' Words failed us and we were all dumb with fear. We realised that we were in a very difficult situation. It was impossible to hope that we could escape alive. What a dreadful night that was!"

March 26, 1971

That is how March 26 dawned. Zebunnessa Begum clearly remembers that morning. "I could see as far as Mirpur Bridge through the window. I saw lines of people crossing the fields, some carrying baskets on their heads. The scene resembled the pictures

---

3 Renamed Sergeant Zahurul Huq Hall after Liberation.

shown in the movie *Muktir Gan.*[4] People were fleeing in terror, with whatever belongings they had crammed into baskets on their heads, some holding their children by their hands, some leading their cows, some carrying their chickens.

"By then the Biharis' anger was clear. We could not leave the building and escape. It then struck us that the flag had to be lowered. But how could we do this? I got Rupban's father to bring it down. When he was bringing it down, there was a big commotion all around. We were all terrified." Jahanara mentioned later in her interview that she had heard that the Biharis were particularly angry with them because they had hoisted the flag.

Zebunnessa Begum's narration was remarkable for its detail. She described everything that had happened that day: what was eaten for breakfast, what was cooked for lunch, who had eaten, and who had not. Neither she, nor her husband nor her eldest son were able to eat anything that day. "Nothing would go down our throats. Words fail to describe the plight we were in. We wondered whether we were human beings at all, and if so, what kind of human beings – human beings like we see today or what? My old uncle watched what was happening through the window and wept uncontrollably."

"It was a Friday. Even in that situation my husband left the house for the mosque opposite our house to offer Friday prayers. He did so, confident that nobody would touch him. He believed that whatever happened to thousands of Bangalis would happen to him. Obviously, neither he nor anyone else ever imagined what was in store for Bangalis. Hardly had the prayers ended, when the Biharis alleged that gun shots were aimed from our house at the mosque." Actually, there were a few shots aimed at the mosque during the prayers, but these were not from Salimullah's house. Salimullah somehow managed to escape to the third floor. His house, which the Biharis had encircled, was under continuous gunfire. Zebunnessa Begum said that these gun shots sounded like thunder on a tin roof.

Jahanara and her relatives returned to their own homes that morning. When the shooting started at noon that day, 17 persons, including Salimullah's family, were prostrated in prayer in a room on the third floor. Their old uncle, who had gone to the mosque, was

4 *Muktir Gan* (Song of Freedom) was a movie made by Tareq and Catherine Masud from archival footage taken by Lear Levin in 1971.

unable to climb up, as he had been shot at and received injuries on his knees. Zebunnessa Begum learnt later that nine Bangalis among those who had taken shelter on the ground floor died that day. An innumerable number of bullets were sprayed onto the third floor room. Their mouths were dry with thirst and fear. One of them somehow managed to crawl into the bathroom and get a mug of water, with which they moistened their lips.

By four in the afternoon the firing ceased, but the lower floors of the house were ablaze. There was a knock on the door. Salimullah and Zebunnessa, thinking death was inevitable, opened the door. Three Bihari boys entered. They had come to rescue the family, while the others were searching the premises for arms and money. The boys tried to assist them downstairs. But fire had engulfed the stairs, so it was impossible to go that way. The boys then held their hands and assisted them down over the balcony.

Zebunnessa Begum's second son had already slid down the sanitary pipe, offering himself as a target to the attackers so that they could slake their desire for revenge. As soon as he reached the ground, a Bihari doctor pulled him away. Zebunnessa Begum learnt this later. "While we all were being helped down, we failed to notice that Mohammad Salimullah had come down and had been taken away by the Biharis. Earlier, they had tried to throw him down the stairs, but my children and I had foiled their attempts. Then they commanded him, 'Come down.' Before he could go down, they started asking for his eldest son. 'Give us Shanu.' At that point, my husband and I held Shanu tightly. A struggle ensued. They had pipe guns and shining daggers in their hands. It seemed strange that they did not use these weapons but simply asked us to hand him over. They failed to catch Shanu but they succeeded in taking Salimullah away."

The last to come down from the third floor were Zebunnessa Begum and her eldest son Shanu. As soon as Shanu reached the railing of the first floor veranda, he jumped down and escaped into the neighbouring house at the back. Zebunnessa Begum too followed him and jumped. However, she fell down on the roof of the garage and hurt her legs so badly that she could not get up. Her nephew later helped her down into the courtyard of the house behind theirs. It was full of people. It too was a Bihari house. She noticed Salimullah surrounded by several Biharis who were arguing. Some wanted to save him, while the others wanted to kill him. She caught a brief glimpse of her husband's head and face, but then her nephew pushed her towards the veranda. Her three small daughters were with her. "Then the Biharis tried to push us women into a room. As soon as we were inside, we saw my husband being pushed in by the same people who had pushed us in. When he was about to join us, someone else – not one of those who had pushed us in – appeared suddenly and thrust a dagger into his back. That much I could see, and nothing more. Then he was taken away. Sadi tried to pull my husband back, but they took him away. My husband was bewildered. He said, 'I have done nothing wrong. Why did they stab me?' "

Zebunnessa Begum was unable to walk. Two Bihari boys, about 18 years old, separated her from the group and made her accompany them. She did not know where she was being taken. Nor did she have the strength to think about it. She could just utter, "If you have to kill me, kill me here. Why are you taking me away?" There was no reply. While crossing the road, she saw Salimullah lying on the road face down, his body still. "I begged them not to take me further, and implored them, 'Kill me here.'" (Zebunnessa Begum's fourth son Shibli recalls how his father was lying on the road, and how a few Biharis were pressing his throat down with iron rods).

The Bihari rescuers took Zebunnessa Begum, her five children and Rupban to a single-storey structure nearby and vowed that they would not allow any more killing because they considered them innocent. Zebunnessa Begum did not know what had happened to the other five children, including her eldest daughter.

Meanwhile, one of the three rescuers recognised Zebunnessa Begum's eldest daughter on the road. He took her back to her mother. She had been hiding all this time in the Bihari house behind the one where Zebunnessa Begum had taken shelter. Zebunnessa Begum's old uncle, who had been shot in the legs, was also in that house. Zebunnessa's fifth son Shoaib was there with him. He too was brought back to his mother. (The old uncle continued staying there, and there was no news about him for several months. Towards the end of the war he was found at the Lalbagh mosque.)

One of the three rescuers, Iqbal, took Zebunnessa Begum and the others to his own house. They dressed her eldest daughter in a *burqa* so that she would not attract unwanted attention. Meanwhile, Zebunnessa Begum's feet had become painfully swollen. While they were waiting in Iqbal's house, they noticed that the same persons who had rescued them were also busy looting other houses. They also noticed bullets stored in a bag in Iqbal's room.

Zebunnessa Begum requested Iqbal to send for Mr. Rafi, a Bihari friend of Salimullah. When he arrived, she requested him to look for Salimullah, whom she had seen lying on the road, and to arrange medical treatment for him. Mr. Rafi left without saying anything. He returned along with Zebunnessa Begum's third son Sadi, and advised her to rest content and express gratitude to Allah for those who were alive. Zebunnessa Begum understood from this remark that her husband was dead. She and her children, except for the eldest and the second son, were then in Iqbal's house.

Departure from Dhaka

From the morning of March 27, Biharis surrounded Iqbal's house where the Bangalis had taken shelter. The Bihari boys who had rescued the Salimullah family took them in a car belonging to a non-Bangali doctor to the house of a Punjabi gentleman, Mr. Mujahidi. When Mrs. Mujahidi saw them, she burst into tears. She gave them food, clothes, and also a *burqa* for Zebunnessa Begum. Zebunnessa Begum told Mr. Mujahidi that he was like her brother and requested him to arrange for them to go to their village Shalmashi (Shyamalapur) on the other side of the Buriganga, where they had land. However, they were unable to cross the river because its bank was guarded by Pakistani troops. Mr. Mujahidi then took them in his car and dropped them in Madhu Bazar, which was a Bangali locality. Mr. Mujahidi did not think it safe for him to stay there too long and he hurried back.

Zebunnessa Begum's younger sister and her husband lived in Madhu Bazar. They all spent the night together in a Bangali house on the other side of the river. In the morning they hired a boat and reached Shalmashi. The village of Shalmashi in Savar Police Station was about 3 km west of their house on Tajmahal Road, on the other side of the Buriganga river. By now, Zebunnessa Begum was totally incapable of moving because her feet were swollen, and had turned black and blue. From her account it is obvious that a vast multitude of people had gathered on the river bank and were attempting to cross over to the safety of the villages. When they reached the other side, they came across many known faces. Zebunnessa Begum was carried to her village home on a plank bound to bamboo poles, like a palanquin.

In the village Zebunnessa Begum finally found her missing sons and nephew. About 50 persons known to them from Dhaka, including Jahanara Khanum and her brother's family, had taken shelter in their home at Shalmashi. These two families had escaped by different routes. Zebunnessa Begum stayed in Shalmashi for five days. There she had the rice harvested and ground into flour. She also sent people to Dhaka to look for Mohammad Salimullah at all possible places and different hospitals but all in vain.

Jahanara Khanum was all praise for Zebunnessa Begum's forbearance during this time and remarked, "I was impressed with her immense patience and endurance. She had so many children dependent on her, her husband had died. She was immobile herself. Still she managed everything so well. It is remarkable. She was numb like a stone, but did not lose her sense of duty. Even today she shows the same kind of efficiency and calm."

Towards Comilla

Within five days of their coming to Shalmashi, there was an army raid nearby in Kamrangir Char. That made Zebunnessa Begum decide to move further away. Along with her children and other helping hands, her sister, her sister's husband and his brother, in all about twenty of them, they started moving westwards, with Zebunnessa Begum being carried on a plank as before. Others carried head loads of cans containing flour, rice and lentils. Although unable to move because of her painful legs, Zebunnessa Begum continued to make all the arrangements. It took them a day to reach the Dhaleshwari river. They crossed the river and stayed overnight in a stranger's house in Mohonpur village. Next morning they boarded a large country boat and reached Sherajdikhan, south of Munshiganj, and from there proceeded to Taltola on their way to Shaitnol. Their final destination was Comilla. At Shaitnol her sister's family parted from the group as they were going to Daudkandi. Zebunnessa Begum and her children changed to another boat in order to go to her father-in-law's home at Sachar in Kachua Police Station in the district of Chandpur. Starting in the morning, they reached Sachar the following night.

Meanwhile, Zebunnessa Begum's two brothers came to Dhaka to look for them. Learning that they were not there, they went to Sachar. By this time Pakistani troops had been Sachar three times. Zebunnessa Begum and her family stayed at Sachar for three months. Then her brothers took her and her children to her father's home in Lonai village under Chandina Police Station in the district of Comilla. The family stayed there for about three months. Meanwhile, her eldest son Shanu and her two younger brothers joined the Liberation War.

Soon Lonai became unsafe. Zebunnessa Begum did not know what to do. She was not able to move to Sachar because the army patrolled the river, while the road to and from Lonai was frequented by the army. She thought it might be safer to go to her maternal uncle's home in Daudkandi which was quite deep in the interior.

Around this time, her eldest son and her younger brother came from Agartala to take them to India, but she refused, thinking that it would be too risky to cross the border with so many children. Eventually, they made up their mind to go to her uncle's home at Daudkandi. But half-way there, they stopped at her maternal aunt's home in the village of Bargaon in Matlab Police Station, and stayed there for a month. In late October, when the river was almost dry and Sachar had become safe from raids by the Pakistani soldiers, she decided to proceed to Sachar along with her small children. She had decided to earn her living, no matter what the nature of the work. Her eldest son was away fighting and her second son had been taken by her eldest brother to Narayanganj to work in a ration shop.

With the help of her nephew, she stocked some food – paddy, rice and *muri* (puffed rice). She took some utensils, and then moved with her eight small children and Rupban, to Sachar. They stayed in a part of her father-in-law's house, which they owned. Her husband's brothers offered to take responsibility for their board but she declined. She had decided that she would make her own arrangements for food. Her logic was, "How could we be a burden on them? It might be all right for them to entertain us for a day or two, but if this were to continue too long, it would certainly hamper our relationship. That is why I decided to make separate arrangements for food. Though I had no son who was earning, I felt we could manage simple meals of rice and lentil or spinach." It is interesting that with so many children she never stayed for long in any relative's house, even though the money she had brought with her was fast depleting.

She had very little money left after paying their boat fare and other expenses. She had about Tk. 600 of her own which she had brought from Dhaka, Tk. 300 which her second son had given her, Tk. 200 which Abdul Quddus Makhon had sent through her eldest son, and Tk. 500 which her elder brother used to give her every month. She was also able to save by rotating her stay in different houses. Her decision not to depend on anyone was because she did not know how long the war would last. "There was no certainty about when the country would be free. There was no certainty about when my sons could start working and earn money. So under such uncertain circumstances, I needed to stand on my own two feet."

Working for Freedom Fighters

In spite of being in this uncertain and stressful situation, Zebunnessa Begum helped freedom fighters. Her eldest son was the Thana Commander of the freedom fighters in Kachua Police Station. At times he would come with a full complement of 25 to 30 fighters to Sachar and Lonai. It was difficult to accommodate so many in one place for fear of attracting the attention of *razakars* (collaborators). So they were quartered in different houses of the locality, one in each house. Zebunnessa Begum said, "The girls used to be with me. Each family of the village had the responsibility of providing food and shelter to one freedom fighter. If they hadn't, how would the young men have the strength to fight? My father was particularly prompt in meeting these requirements. My mother too used to prepare basketfuls of *muri* (puffed rice) mixed with molasses and shredded coconut. The coconuts were from her own trees. She used to tell the freedom fighters, 'Eat this and you will get some strength to fight.' The poorer families, unable to provide anything substantial, also tried their best to provide whatever they could to the freedom fighters."

Towards the end of November, when the country was at the point of being liberated, her eldest son left for Dhaka with his troops. The whole contingent came to show their respect and saluted her before leaving. She gave them packets of food to take along.

Zebunnessa Begum recalls how she had to devise cunning ways to hide weapons brought by the boys. "Guns, dynamite, rifles, revolvers, Chinese rifles, SLRs, LMGs, all these used to be carried in light boats and ferried secretly into my father's premises. Covered chicken coops would be removed and pits would be dug underneath overnight. There were cautious guards around the village, keeping watch so that *razakars* or other villagers were unable to sense what was happening and leak information. Wooden planks were laid on the bottom of pits, and bamboo mats and hay were then spread over these to store guns." Extra guns were used to train young village boys and girls in the courtyard of her father's home. The guns and the bullets used to be in the custody of the girls. "We used to work during the night, rather than in the day, in the rooms where the firewood was stored, lest some village women saw us and talked. After all, you could not trust everyone. You never knew who was on which side. Fuel wood was removed at night to store bullets in cooking utensils, big tin canisters, and earthen jars filled with rice husk. The husk was used to prevent weapons becoming damp in the rainy season. In those days Allah showed us dynamite and mines which I had never seen or even heard of before. We had to hide these tin canisters in the holes which we dug under the chicken coops. All this digging and covering the place with firewood meant that we had to work all night long. Also we needed to take out items as and when required. "We were afraid of the Pakistan army and the *razakars*. Ordinary villagers and even the Bangali officers of Chandina Police Station sided with the freedom fighters."

Return to Dhaka after Liberation

Zebunnessa Begum was in Sachar when Bangladesh was liberated. Her two sons Sadi and Shibli were in an aunt's house in Daudkandi. When they were nearing Sachar, they learnt that the country had become independent. People in Comilla were moving around excitedly, carrying Bangladesh flags. The news of independence was being announced over radio and loud speakers. Zebunnessa Begum's two sons returned home and informed her that the country was now free.

In January 1972 her eldest son brought them to Dhaka by car. They came to the house of Shoeb Babu, a non-Bangali friend of her eldest son, at Chandina Ghat-Lalkuthi in old Dhaka. Shoeb Babu's family was originally from Delhi. During the war the Bangalis had killed one of Babu's maternal uncles. Many of his family then left for Pakistan.

Zebunnessa Begum and her children remained with this non-Bangali family till 1974. Her eldest daughter got married from here in 1972, with their help. Shoeb's family supported them during their stay with them. They have an excellent relationship even today.

After the war, when Zebunnessa Begum returned to Dhaka, she couldn't get back her husband's business. His two brick fields too. Referring to her days of hardship, she continued, "With ten children, our condition was so pitiful that even if we had been on the streets there wouldn't have been enough place for us. Somehow we were saved because we had this house." During the nine months of war, the Tajmahal Road house had been occupied by some Biharis. In 1972, it was empty. It had been left completely uninhabitable: it was just an empty brick shell, without doors or windows. A chicken coop and a stove in each room indicated that poor Bihari families had been occupying these rooms. In the garage, there was a four to five-inch thick layer of dried blood.

"There were cracks in the dried layers. We informed the police, who visited the spot and collected the dried blood. Some people told us that the garage had been converted into a slaughter house, which meant that our garage had been used to slaughter Bangalis. People who were killed were thrown into the manhole nearby. I came across a large number of skulls in the garage. In 1974 we sent a sweeper down into the manhole and had it cleared of bones. All this was done before we moved back into the house."

Earlier, in 1972, she had learnt from the imam of the mosque opposite their Tajmahal Road house that her husband along with two others had been buried in the mosque premises without the religious ritual bath and final prayer. The men who had killed him had justified their action with the remark, "*Kafirs* (non-believers) do not deserve such religious rites." The Biharis had handed over the dead bodies to the imam for burial. The imam pointed out a spot in the mosque area and identified it as the grave of Mohammad Salimullah.

"With the help of the family from Lal Kuthi and other relatives, we had windows and doors made of tin and mango wood, and re-entered our own house in 1974. The roof had been cracked by the fire. During the rains, water used to leak through the roof and flood the floor, and the electricity had to be switched off. It took two years to set everything right. To start with, we had to depend on assistance and loans from relatives, and on an annual income of Tk. 15,000 from our landed property at Shalmashi. At times there was nothing to cook. We had to borrow money, sometimes as little as Tk. 20 from neighbours to buy rice, lentils and fuel to prepare meals on mud stoves. We had to undergo a lot of hardship. If we try to remember all our suffering, and start talking about each incident – things that we cannot talk about, things we do not talk about – it impossible."

While they were staying at Lal Kuthi in 1972, she had her three sons admitted to school with their host's help. While they were still there, her third son Sadi passed his Matriculation examination.

After they moved to their Tajmahal Road house, she got her two young daughters admitted to school. The Government had waived their tuition fees and education was free. After he returned home from war, her eldest son Shahjahan, alias Shanu, did not continue his studies. He set up a small shop, but his family hardly got any financial help from him. This was because after his return from the war, he had started drinking heavily. Zebunnessa Begum thinks that the Liberation War and his father's death were too traumatic for him. Among her personal losses, Zebunnessa Begum includes the change in her eldest son.

After they shifted to their own house in 1974, her second son, Sami Mohammad Naqiullah, started looking after the family. He took a job in 1975 in the sales department of Biman Bangladesh Airlines. He also continued his studies. Zebunnessa Begum was very careful about spending her son's earnings on household necessities. For instance, when there was only one pair of shoes or a shirt (there was hardly ever more than one good shirt) the three brothers had to use them in turn. The good shirt was reserved for the brother who had to visit some special place. The children were bright students. When they did well in their examinations, their relatives used to give them gifts of clothes and shoes. Their mother used to wash their clothes at night, so that they would be ready for use the next morning. Her elder brother used to help them regularly upto 1972 with money, clothes and other things. His assistance in different forms continued much later too. After coming to their Tajmahal Road house, Zebunnessa Begum repaired the first floor and rented it for Tk. 250 per month. This became another source of income. Even under great financial strain, Zebunnessa Begum was very particular about her children's education. She would not allow her children's education to suffer even in their straitened circumstances.

Government Help, Recognition and Struggle for Existence

In 1972 Quaid-e-Azam Road adjoining Tajmahal Road was renamed Shahid Salimullah Road. However, the family received no recognition beyond this, nor any help from the Government. Immediately after independence, Zebunnessa Begum asked for some help, but in vain. "I addressed a letter to Sheikh Saheb, and gave it to Tofail Ahmed to deliver. Sheikh Saheb expressed his inability to help, saying that the Bangladesh Government did not have funds." With great difficulty, she managed to have half of the House Building loan of Tk. 80,000 waived. She was often unable to pay their electric bills, and the electric supply was disconnected a number of times. She regretted the lack of Government help; no matter who was in power, the family received no help. They had a small tract of land at Savar. She sold it to pay off the House Building loan. She managed somehow to repay her loans to others. "With what my second son earned from Biman, we could not manage even three simple meals of rice and lentil or spinach and mashed potato. Of course, I had to cook rice for those who couldn't go without it; for instance the small children, who otherwise would start crying. If I was able to cook fish for one meal, a piece had to be kept aside for my youngest son for the next meal. The elder children volunteered to save a piece because they knew he would start crying. If meat was cooked one day, I would put aside a bit for the young one for the next two or three meals. Otherwise he would start crying and would not eat. That is how I passed those difficult days."

In 1978 the eldest son got married and moved out. Shortly before that, Zebunnessa Begum devised a way to earn some money. She wasn't very educated so she could not get a job. All along she had been fond of sewing and had made her children's clothes herself. Her training in tailoring and embroidery proved useful. In 1976-77 she started selling her embroider items such as handkerchiefs and napkins. Her daughters took them to school and sold them there. When an NGO for family planning in the locality opened a sewing course for skill development of elderly women, she started teaching sewing there.

Zebunnessa Begum selected six or seven women from there, and started sewing on a large scale. She used to sell her products keeping a minimum of profit. She went around different shops with her products. She sold directly from home as well. Her eldest son had bought her a sewing machine. She was able to get orders for her products from big handicraft shops like KARIKA. She used to work till the small hours of the morning to meet her orders.

In describing those difficult days, Zebunnessa Begum said that it was the thought of her children that kept her going. "I had to live for them. They had to be brought up well. They had to have a good environment to grow up in. Hence my efforts." Today she is free from any want. Her children too are well established in their own professional fields.

Her eldest son Shahjahan, who Zebunnessa Begum said had gone astray after 1971, was given US citizenship through the DV programme in 1997 and is now leading a reasonably stable life abroad with his wife and children.

All her daughters are graduates, married and settled. Her eldest daughter, who was married in 1972 while she was still an undergraduate, lives with her husband in Chittagong. Her other daughters have their own establishments in Dhaka. Her youngest daughter, Farida Yasmin Banu, has done her Master's in Child Psychology, and is now teaching in a school. She got married in 1996.

Her second son Sami Mohammad Naqiullah, alias Shamim, has been looking after the family. While working in Bangladesh Biman, he continued his studies. He did his Master's in Commerce and later set up an advertising firm. In 1994 he was diagnosed with cancer. He along with his wife and son migrated to the US, where he underwent treatment. Zebunnessa Begum visited him during this time.

Her fifth son, Shoeb Mohammad Enamullah, is a major in the Bangladesh army. Her sixth son, Sohel Mohammad Ekramullah, is a citizen of Denmark and lives there with his family.

Zebunnessa Begum lives in her Tajmahal Road house with her third and fourth sons. While still a student of Engineering, her third son, Sadi Mohammad Taqiullah, left for Shantineketan to study music. After getting his Master's Degree in music from the Vishwa Bharati University, he joined the Government Music College as a teacher. He is now a well-known singer of Tagore songs.

Her fourth son, Shibli Mohammad Enayetullah, after doing his Honours in Physics from Jahangirnagar University, went to India to study classical dancing. He was a student of Birju Maharaj in Delhi and has a diploma in *kathak* dance. He also has a diploma in ballet from England. He is now a well-established dance artiste in Bangladesh and a dance instructor at the Bangladesh Shilpakala Academy.

As we have seen, Zebunnessa Begum's second son had all along been a great support to her and the family. Her other children too, after they became established, tried their best to contribute to the household. They have helped her repay many of her loans. Zebunnessa Begum was particularly touched when her fourth son Shibli handed over his entire earnings, a handsome sum, from his first dance performance abroad, to help his mother repay the loans incurred for repairing the house.

Zebunnessa Begum feels very happy that her family is well knit and the children are close to each other. She also feels content that all her hard work and sacrifices for her children have borne fruit. She further believes that since her children have grown up in the midst of hardship, they are able to appreciate the sufferings of other people, are devout, and sympathetic and kind to fellow human beings. She takes particular pride in these qualities of her children.

Now her children have shouldered the responsibility of their mother. She no longer needs to work. Nevertheless, she has not given up her sewing business, and is able to give work to 40 girls. Her products have a large demand in big concerns like Aarong. Many people come to her house to buy her products. After meeting various expenses, she has a net monthly profit of about Tk. 5000. On being asked why she still works, she replied, "People say, 'Since your sons are now earning, why do you still take the trouble of sewing clothes?' But you see, I do not consider it any trouble at all. It was this work that helped me to survive and to hold my head high. How can I give it up?"

At one point of this lengthy discussion, I asked Zebunnessa Begum when she felt her husband's absence the most. She replied that she missed his presence in all the everyday practical problems of running a household: bringing up the children, providing for the family, maintaining the house in good order, in everything. She felt that the loss of her husband in 1971 had changed the whole pattern of her life. "I had a different life when my husband was alive. How happy I used to be with him! My children are grown up now. But they are still my children. They can never take his place. They cannot fill the vacuum that was created by his loss. That deep love, affection, and sympathy those things are lost forever."

Memories of 1971: A Nightmare

Zebunnessa Begum was asked which incident among the many that occurred in 1971 was the most painful. "The fact that we had to leave my husband's dead body behind!" was her reply. She also thinks about the "trouble" she caused people for over three months because of the injuries she had sustained to her legs on March 26, 1971. We enquired whether the nightmares of 1971 recurred in her dreams. She replied, "Often I dreamed that those Biharis were running around with daggers and guns to kill people. That made me wake up abruptly with a loud cry. For the last five or six years, however, I have not had such dreams." She would often recall the scene of the Pakistani soldiers raiding the villages, jumping out of their trucks and jeeps, attacking one house after another, setting them on fire, shooting indiscriminately and hurling bombs. The firing and bombing sounded like hailstorms. They mostly fired guns; bombs were used much less. "All these scenes float clearly before my eyes even today – the soldiers jumping out of their transports, the people slumping to the ground as they were shot. When we saw them coming from a distance, we used to flee with our young children to the next village in fear."

During her narration of the incidents of 1971, she seemed to choke and her voice grew faint. "These memories still recur, but I try to keep calm. Often in the past I spent sleepless nights. At times I still have sleepless nights. I could not speak. I would get thirsty at night which meant I had to drink water, and I had to go to the toilet several times. I would stay awake till the early hours. And then maybe around 3 am or 4 am, I would fall asleep. In the past I could not sleep at all. Now I am able to sleep. These days I do not have a sleeping problem. Before, if anybody asked me to tell them what happened during those days, I was unable to speak. Nowadays when I speak, many people shed tears, but there are no tears in my eyes. I have grown hard."

Effect of 1971 on the Children

When asked whether the turmoil of 1971 had left any permanent mark on any of her children, she replied, "The younger of my twin daughters was quite strong, but the elder one was so panic-stricken that she used to cry aloud in her sleep. I was unable to calm her down even while walking about with her in my arms in the dead of night. She used to sob and cry continuously. Then she used to go into hiccups and only slowly dropped off to sleep. She was filled with such terror. This condition persisted for quite a few years after independence."

In addition, after taking part in the War of Liberation, her eldest son had gone astray and had started drinking. He has lost his peace of mind, suffers mentally, and talks of his loss. Till today he has not been able to regain his normal state of mind and is unable to work properly.

Even after all that has happened, Zebunnessa Begum has no grievance against the Almighty. She believes strongly that Allah has been kind enough to spare her from a bigger catastrophe and has helped her in getting over her losses. She does not resent the personal losses she incurred in the Liberation War but she feels she should have got more help and facilities in a free country. Nevertheless, she feels happy that the country has become independent and that we are living now in a free country.

Attitude towards Biharis and Pakistanis

Zebunnessa Begum holds Biharis and non-Bangalis responsible for what happened to her in 1971. Although she refuses to give alms to any Bihari beggars, she acknowledges that there are many good people among the Biharis. She has never forgotten Mr. Mujahidi, the Punjabi gentleman who befriended her. Immediately after independence, she sent her eldest son to look for Mr. Mujahidi, and helped to get his release from Comilla Cantonment and brought him to her house. She made her sons arrange some protection for him and his wife. She said, "The situation was reversed. Just as we had been afraid of the non-Bangalis, they were now afraid of the Bangalis. Night after night, the Bangalis looted the houses of the Biharis and assaulted them. The Bangalis were more interested in grabbing their cash and property than in killing them." Zebunnessa Begum also looked for Iqbal, who had rescued them on March 26, but could not trace him. She learnt later that he had been killed by freedom fighters.

Zebunnessa Begum not only arranged board and lodging for Mr. Mujahidi's family, but also arranged, through her eldest son, to send them to Pakistan at an opportune moment. She recalls that when they were stuck here in Bangladesh, Mr. Mujahidi's father wrote a letter to him, praising the family for what they had done. He said, "If ever the route to Bangladesh reopens, I will, if I am still alive, go to see those Muslims who, in spite of being beaten and losing their father, have done so much for you. I would like to see those true Muslims who have done so much for the Pakistanis at whose hands their father had been killed."

Zebunnessa Begum has not forgotten the services rendered by Mr. Mujahidi. Her sufferings have not clouded her sense of judgement that all human beings are not evil and that there are good people everywhere. This attitude led Zebunnessa Begum's family to save a few other families as well. But in general she feels a lot of anger towards Biharis and Pakistanis. She gets upset and angry at the attitude of Bangladeshis towards Pakistan. "I see that the people of Bangladesh have a good relationship with the people of Pakistan. I grieve and feel hurt that even our Prime Minister has a cordial relationship with Pakistan. She gives them a red carpet treatment. My whole body burns when I see this. Pakistan has not apologised to Bangladesh! So how can we have a relationship with Pakistan? But we not only have personal relationships with Pakistanis, our Government too has a relationship with Pakistan."

Although 25 years have passed since the war, there has been no apology from Pakistan. Zebunnessa Begum said, "Haven't the Japanese apologised to the Koreans, after so many years? In the same way the Pakistanis should also ask forgiveness. The way they brutally killed people, the way they made mothers and sisters like me suffer in such an inhuman manner .... Had I been educated I would have dedicated myself to a movement like Jahanara Imam has done. Unfortunately, I am unable to speak like her and move about like her, with educated and cultured people. And so I did not go forward." She continued that if she had the power to write and to express herself well, she would have taken up a pen and vented her anger.

Zebunnessa Begum has had no opportunity to take part in any social struggle or movement. As a result of the upheaval in 1971, which ravaged her life, the years have passed with her trying to keep her head above water, bringing up her children, holding her family together, struggling to keep alive. When she thinks about her pain and loss, she strongly feels that Pakistan must offer an apology for the incidents of 1971. Even today Zebunnessa Begum thinks that if Pakistan apologised to Bangladesh, many who had suffered like her might find a little consolation. Many grieving hearts might be filled with some sense of peace.

Nilufa, Rumana, Farzana and Sharmin

Residents of Nirala But Nowhere to Go

Hasina Ahmad and Moushumi Rahman

Site

Narayanganj, a commercial centre and the third largest port of the country, stretches along both sides of the Sitalakhya river. This township ten miles southeast of Dhaka. Five thanas and 61 Union Parishads are situated within this 450-square-mile area. In 1974 it had a population of 176,879.[1]

On March 27, 1971 the Pakistan occupation army faced its first opposition in Masdair, a small town just outside the jurisdiction of Narayanganj Municipality. Located in Enayet Nagar Union within the jurisdiction of Fatullah Thana, south of the Dhaka-Narayanganj highway just before Narayanganj, Masdair was slowly taking on the shape of a township as rich families started building houses there. The majority of residents of this area, however, earned their living by farming, trading or doing odd jobs. The population of Masdair was about 20,000 in 1971. Muslims, Hindus and Christians dwelt in harmony as evidenced by the juxtaposition of a Muslim graveyard, a Christian cemetery and a Hindu crematorium. It was here that Jasimul Haq, owner of Jamil Dockyard, lived with his family in 1971.

The Liberation War

What happened after the Pakistani forces entered Narayanganj can be found in *Narayanganjer Itihash* (History of Narayanganj). From the early morning of March 26, the residents of Masdair were apprehensive of an attack. To stop the movement of Pakistani forces from Dhaka to Narayanganj, the Chhatra Sangram Parishad

1 *Bangladesh Bureau of Statistics*, September 1994.

(Students' Resistance Association), along with political activists and ordinary people had dug up the rail line from Fatullah to Chashara Rail Station. Narayanganj became a town of barricades as people took their positions along the Dhaka-Narayanganj highway.

At ten in the morning on March 27 news of the army advance, with heavy artillery and tanks, reached Narayanganj. Road barricades had slowed their pace. The first confrontation took place at Fatullah as the occupation forces had to stop several hundred metres west of the Masdair mosque. On their way from Tikatuli they engaged in heavy shelling. Cannon fire was heard at irregular intervals. A group of students and workers took up positions at Masdair in a few houses and high lands west of the house of Mr. Khair. Another group of students took up positions in the graveyard. The students retaliated with the weapons they had: small arms and one-barrel and two-barrel rifles. The first shot fired by the students resulted in the death of a Pakistani soldier. Nevertheless, as two-barrel rifles proved useless against tanks and cannons, the strong resistance was forced to subside. The army occupied the Government Girls College between about noon to one in the afternoon.

In the afternoon near Masdair, Pakistani soldiers shot and killed unarmed civilians and set fire to their houses. They killed the elder son of M. A. Sattar, a businessman, who later was appointed an adviser by General Ershad, and his friend, Rana. They broke into Jasimul Haq's house, which was at the end of the village, and where many had taken shelter. Amongst those who in the house were Mr. Akhter, his wife, his brother, and Bakul, their domestic help, Mr. Sattar of Grindlays Bank, Jasimul Haq, Laila Haq, their cook and Amin, another helper. The armed forces killed Ali Akhter and his brother Ali Ahmed (both non-Bangalis), Abdus Sattar, Jasimul Haq and his wife. Several civilians who had taken shelter inside the mosque, were dragged out and forced to stand in a line. Then the soldiers gunned down 15 or 16 of them. Even this was not enough to appease the soldiers, and they set fire to the place. A day later, on March 28, the Pakistan army finally entered Narayanganj.[2]

Methodology

We interview of the four surviving daughters of Jasimul Haq during two months, from December 1996 to January 1997. Two of the

2 *Narayanganjer Itihas* (Narayanganj: Sudhijan Pathagar, 1985), 209.

daughters had witnessed their parents being killed. Two women relatives of the family were also interviewed; one of them was an eyewitness and the other, a free-lance journalist, was a freedom fighter. Two neighbours were interviewed. The interviews were very traumatic for the interviewees even twenty five years after the incident and they often broke down in tears and took time to recover before they started talking again.

The Family

Jasimul Haq and his wife Laila Hasina Banu used to live in an unfinished one-storey building called Nirala, which stood on five bighas of land in south Masdair. They had been living there since 1967 with their children. Laila Hasina Banu, a former athlete, was from Narayanganj. Her father, Moulvi Ahmad Mia, was the first Muslim chairman of Narayanganj Municipality in 1938. The family was well known in the town. Though Jasimul Haq was from a rich family of farmers in Jamalpur, he had settled in Narayanganj after his marriage and was a first-class contractor of Narayanganj Dockyard and the proprietor of Jamil Dockyard.

As a student of Dhaka Medical College, he had once been imprisoned for his involvement in the Language Movement. The couple had five daughters and a son. The eldest child was fourteen and a half years old and the youngest only a year and three months in 1971. The couple was sociable and progressive in their political views.

The Present Condition

At the time of the interview, Jasimul Haq's children were not living together but in different places. However, the eldest daughter, Nilufa Selim Shelly, had kept the family together. From a very young age, with little knowledge and almost no experience of the realities of life, through a hundred difficult situations, she had assumed the responsibility of looking after her younger siblings. The story of Jasimul Haq's eldest daughter forms the core of this interview. Nilufa was only fourteen in 1971. Now she is a housewife of 40 years and the mother of two. She had studied up to the higher secondary level. In 1978 she married her cousin, a businessman. They live in their own house in Segun Bagicha. She does not belong to any political party.

The second daughter of Jasimul Haq, Nasrin Ahmad, married a businessman in 1978. They migrated to the US in the eighties and have settled there. They have one son. She works for a business agency in the US.

Jasimul Haq's only son, Jamilul Haq, had a speech and hearing impairment, the result of typhoid shortly after his birth. For some time he was enrolled in a special school for the speech and hearing challenged, and has learned to write a little. He lived alone in an apartment in Segun Bagicha, which was paid for with his inheritance money.

Rumana Rahman was the third daughter of Jasimul Haq. Married and the mother of two, a son and daughter, she worked as a secretary in a Japanese car company. Her husband was a businessman and they lived in their own house in Gulshan. At the time of the interview, she was 34 years. Rumana completed her Intermediate from Lalmatia College. She couldn't continue her studies because of her job and family responsibilities. She is a member of *Projonmo Ekattor*[3] and has written a few articles for the organisation. She wants to write a book on her experiences of 1971.

Jasimul Haq's fourth daughter was 29 years at the time of the interview and unmarried. A graduate from Home Economics College, she was employed in an American company in Dhaka and stays at the Working Women's Hostel in Nilkhet. Jasimul Haq's youngest daughter, Farzana Hasnat, was 28 years. She was only a year old in 1971. She graduated from Eden College and was employed as a secretary in the Project Transport and Logistic Concept Company. She too stay at the Working Women's Hostel in Nilkhet.

March 27, 1971

Nilufa Selim Shelly and Rumana Rahman Polly recounted the brutal killing of their father and mother on Saturday, March 27, 1971. Shelly was fourteen at the time and Polly only eight.

The killing took place in Jasimul Haq's house, Nirala, in southern Masdair. As the house was only about 400 to 500 metres from the Dhaka-Narayanganj highway, one could see what was happening on the highway from the house. The land between the house and the

[3] *Projonmo Ekattor* was formed by the children of Bangalis who were killed in 1971.

highway consisted of low-lying paddy fields. The freedom fighters took their positions on either side of the highway as well as in Jasimul Haq's house from where they fired several shots. This infuriated the occupation forces at the inmates of the house. The Pakistani soldiers could not enter the area from the northern side, where the graveyards and crematorium were located, so they advanced up the southern alley that faced Nilufa's house. There were about 21 persons inside the house: Nilufa's parents, five children, a distant grand aunt, a maternal cousin Heera, Amin, Raisuddin, a cook, Bakul, and another domestic help, and Mr. Sattar, a neighbour.

Nilufa Selim Shelly gave the following account of what took place on the day: "On the previous night, that is March 26, Major Nawab Ali, an army doctor who was a friend of my father's, telephoned and told us to leave the house. He said it would be difficult to flee during the day, as soldiers would shoot us or bombs would be hurled from helicopters. It was therefore better not to wait for daylight but to leave during the night. Abba did not leave. He said, 'If we have done nothing wrong, why should we be afraid of something happening to us?' The night passed in this way. The next morning nothing happened; there was no news. We tried to listen to the radio. But there was no news on the radio either. At about noon, Abba said, 'I'm going to Fatullah Thana to deposit my gun.' The students of Tolaram College had barricaded the road. Nevertheless, Abba tried to go towards the thana. However, he noticed that people were streaming out of their houses. He learned that the army had come up to Pagla Ghat. When Abba heard this, he returned home."

Rumana said, "Abba had wanted us to finish our baths and have our lunch. He thought there would be time enough if we left in the evening. Those were the instructions he had given mother. Mother was more or less prepared to leave. We had also packed some clothes and other essentials. Things in the house were also more or less tidied up. We were waiting for Abba to return. Our next-door neighbour, Mr. Khair, a political leader of some standing wanted us to leave with his family. He was so insistent that we finally gave in. But, as we were about to leave, Abba returned. He prevented us from leaving. He said, 'It is not necessary to leave now. Let the Khairs leave. We will join them later.' Because of Abba, Amma changed her mind and we went back inside our house. Mr. Akhtar, his two sons and two daughters, his younger brother, his male domestic help, and

Mr. Sattar stayed back with us. Mr. Sattar had sent his family away to his village earlier. Mr. Khair went away leaving us behind. He regretted our decision and felt that we were endangering ourselves by staying behind. He thought that this was the right time to leave. We might not be able to escape later. He realised this as he was closely associated with the Awami League. He knew that there would be an attack on Narayanganj. After Mr. Khair left, we started preparing lunch. Abba had just spread the prayer rug to say his prayers. It must have been around twelve or twelve-thirty, time for *zohr* prayers. Abba had completed his ablutions and was getting ready to say his prayers. Amma was in the kitchen, preparing to serve lunch. Suddenly, from behind our house, came loud sounds of shelling. A cow shed at the back was destroyed by the shelling. Amma started to scream. My siblings and I were terrified and lay down on the floor. Abba left his prayers incomplete and lay down with us on the floor. Mr. Akhtar and his family as well as Mr. Sattar joined us on the floor. The shelling started in earnest, but from where we had no idea."

Shelly said, "The shooting had started from our side. Our youth had started it. I do not understand why they did so. They knew what had transpired the night before and in the hours that followed. They were not children. They should have understood the strength of the enemy. Before their operation, they should have cleared the entire area. There must have been at least 20,000 residents in the area. Anyway, the fighting, as I said, was started from our side. This is something I remember clearly. But the Pakistanis replied with their tanks. And I think that they also had mortars mounted on jeeps. From my window I could see that one side of Mr. Khair's double-storeyed house had been completely destroyed. I told my father, 'They are not just firing guns, they are firing cannons.' Father replied, 'All of you, hide under the beds.' All of us girls went into Amma's room. The men and boys went into Abba's room. All of us sat down on the ground. Above our heads, bullets whizzed past, striking the almirah. The wire-netting of the windows was rent; the glass panes were shattered. And the noise, it was unbelievable. This shelling continued for about half an hour or forty minutes. That is all I can remember of what happened 26 years ago ...."

"The children all started to cry. Our neighbour Mr. Akhtar's four children and the six of us. Ellie was only a year and three months;

Nellie was two years and three months. A difference of only a year. What a terrible situation! Then, suddenly, there was silence. Imagine! For 10 to 15 minutes there was not a sound. Everything was quiet. I can't recollect anything after this. There is a complete blank after this. It is still blank."

Rumana added, "The Pakistani soldiers kicked the door several times, spouting imprecations and insults. My father went to open the door. My mother held his hand, saying, 'Don't go. They might shoot you.' Father replied, 'If they do, there is nothing we can do. But we have to open the door. If we don't, there will be more trouble.' As soon as Abba opened the door, several Pakistani soldiers barged in, their faces contorted with rage. They had guns in their hands and they told us rudely to go out into the veranda. Abba told us, 'Hold your hands above your heads and come out. They are telling us again and again, "Hands up." 'Accordingly, we raised our hands above our heads in a motion of surrender, came out of the room and assembled outside. They made us stand in lines. Then they started asking Abba, Mr. Akhtar, and Mr. Sattar, 'Who fired from your houses?' Abba tried to explain that no shots had been fired from any of our houses. ' None of us have any arms. There is no question of any of us fighting. We are all businessmen, service holders. There is no *mukti juddha* here. All our children are small. And the rest of the people here are domestic help.' They replied, 'We were attacked. We had to shoot back. A great number of bullets were fired from your houses. That means that you have arms.' Abba tried to explain it was not true, but they refused to listen and hit him as well as Mr. Akhtar and Mr. Sattar on their faces with their rifle butts. As a result of the blows, Abba, Mr. Akhtar and Mr. Sattar started bleeding from their faces and lips. The soldiers frisked them and retrieved a revolver from Mr. Akhtar's waist. It was his personal revolver. They asked him, 'Why do you have arms? You are a Bihari.' It is true that Mr. Akhtar was a Bihari. After repeated questioning he replied, 'It is a licensed pistol. It is for my personal security as I am a Bihari. I live among Bangalis. That is why I acquired the pistol quite some time ago.' But they didn't believe him. They thought that he had the pistol with him in order to give us protection. After this they pushed and dragged all the men outside: Mr. Akhtar, Mr. Sattar, my father, Amin, a 22-year-old man who worked in our house, our cook Raisuddin Mia, a young brother of Mr. Akhtar's, and a young boy who worked in his house. With their rifles, they pushed and shoved these seven or eight persons outside the house. From behind we started crying loudly. We called out to them. We were afraid that Abba would not return. But the soldiers kicked them with their boots, dragged them and shoved them outside. We did not know what happened afterwards, as we could not see them after they left our compound."

Shelly said, "All I remember is that we were standing in our compound. They had made a separate line for women and girls. The small children were in this line as well. The older boys were in another line. We were terrified at their rage and their behaviour. They had hit Mr. Akhtar with the butt of their rifles before our eyes just because he had a personal pistol hidden in his waist. It was a licensed pistol. Because they found it, they killed him. Suddenly someone called me, 'Go home. Take out whatever there is.' Mother started to comply but Abba said, 'Let me go.' Amma said, 'No, I will do so as I have the keys with me.' The night before Amma had made me put away all the ornaments. Negotiations for my marriage were going on. I was too young to get married; still my parents were trying to arrange my marriage. That is why a lot of ornaments had been made. We had taken out all the ornaments from their cases and tied them up in a bundle. I remember Amma had a leather suitcase – 20/22 inches long. This suitcase was full of ornaments. It was so heavy that I told my mother to divide the ornaments into two portions. Otherwise it would be too heavy for one person to carry. Also if the person somehow got lost, all the ornaments would be lost. Amma said, 'No, nothing will happen.' Mother went inside and then… as far as I know because we didn't accompany her inside… she had hardly been inside for two minutes. We heard gunshots. But even then I didn't realise from outside that Amma had been shot. I thought that they had fired at the suitcase in order to open it. Perhaps because Amma was not giving them the keys or something like that. I do not know anything after that. From outside one of the soldiers, I think he was probably a major, cursed loudly. In their own Pushtu language. I think he did so because perhaps at that time they hadn't received orders to kill women. At this time, meaning in the very early period, 25, 26 and 27 March."

"After we heard the major curse, a soldier came outside. There must have been a difference of about two minutes between the sound of the gunshots, the major's cursing, and the soldier's emergence from inside. But Amma did not appear. I did not realise that Amma had not come out. Meanwhile, they had led the line of young boys outside the gate. There was silence after this. Then we heard one or two sounds, the sounds of gunshots. After that I stopped thinking. We continued to stand there silently. About five minutes later Mr. Akhtar's son – he was about my age and used to study in the same preparatory class with me – said to me, 'Shelly, I think there is someone's leg outside the gate.' When I heard this, I slowly went towards the gate. I realised I could see Abba's lungi. I do not know how I managed to get to him. He was lying on the ground, blood gushing forth from the lower left side of his chest. The blood was bubbling out, bubbling out. Abba was wearing a white half-sleeved shirt and a lungi. As soon as I went up to him, Abba tried to say something but only a gurgling sound emerged. He had been shot in the lungs or the heart so he survived perhaps for only five minutes. Suddenly I realised that he was saying 'Water, water.' There was a pond in front. I ran to it. I brought water and tried to give it to him. Just outside our house there was a small bridge over the road leading to the village inside. Six or seven Pakistani soldiers who were standing there saw me running to the pond, getting water from it and giving it to Abba. But they made no comments. They just stood there and watched. Then they turned around and marched out of the village, towards the main road. I continued to sit as I was. I was still sitting like that when Hiru Apa called me, 'Shelly, Phupu....' It was only when she said 'Phupu,' that I became aware that something must have happened to Amma. I said, 'Abba is no more.' Then I went inside the house. It was a terrible sight. There was blood everywhere."

"When I went inside, we found the floor splattered with blood. One bullet had pierced my mother's left hand. Another had entered her back. A third had entered her body and emerged next to the collar bone. She had been pierced by a bayonet so badly, that from the left armpit down to the waist her insides could be seen. Blood oozed profusely. Three *chunat ornas* and a sari were shoved in and the wound covered by leucoplast. We gave her Coramin."

Shelly said, "It was only around five o'clock that I told my mother that father had been killed. I said nothing before then. She kept on repeating, 'Tell your father to forgive me.' I said nothing to her, just kept quiet. But around five I told her that father was dead when I saw that she was covered with a cold sweat. I realised that she had lost a lot of blood. We tried to call our doctor, Captain Rahman in Narayanganj. He was a non-Bangali. We tried to call him. He answered the phone. He had known my mother from childhood as Dolly. Everyone in Narayanganj knew her as a famous sports woman. Hearing us, he said, 'I will try to come, though I know that I won't be able to.' This was because by this time there had been a massacre in Narayanganj. A lot of people had been killed in Narayanganj. Then we thought of taking Amma to town by stretcher from behind our house. Perhaps if we could have taken her to town, if she could have been given blood, if her wound had been stitched, she might have survived. If she could have had an operation, she might have survived. This is how the whole day passed, and the whole night. Meanwhile, I had sent my mother's aunt to town to see if she could get a doctor or do something. She never came back."

"Amma died at 8:23 pm. Before she died, she gave me all the advice that she could: 'Do this. Do that. That is in that place.' She told me whom to turn to, whom to make our guardian, whose advice to listen to. Where the bank account was."

"The night passed somehow. The next day, early in the morning, Member Mannan came, he was the village member. He was really a good man. A number of other people also came with him. They told us that Mr. Khair had sent them to take us to Lakshmipur village. They had been told to take us immediately, without delay, as there could be another army operation soon. We left our mother there, her body covered with a sheet. I locked up all the rooms. The last door was to the room where Amma was lying. After locking up the rest of the doors, we locked up the final door, the door of the room where she was lying, and left the house, with Amma's corpse inside. I had tried to bring Abba's body inside the evening before. After dark. But someone had fired a shot. I do not know from where. I moved away, but after some time I looked around and saw that soldiers were sitting on the roof of the Government Girls School. It was a four-storeyed building, I think. There were not many buildings in Masdair at the time. There was just our two-storeyed building and Mr. Khair's. I saw that they were wearing night-glasses to shoot people. I could not retrieve Abba's body. But we had a dog, a cross-breed named Tom. He sat all night guarding Abba's corpse. He sat there continuously for a day and two nights. Abba had been killed on Saturday. He and Amma were buried on Monday. These two nights and a day, Tom sat guarding him. In keeping with Amma's wish, they were buried under the tamarind tree behind the house – without any shrouds. After burying them we left, all of us siblings, for Lakshmipur. Member Sahib took us. We went part of the way by boat, part of the way on foot. People helped us a lot. We carried Elly and Nelly; we tried explaining things to Jamil."

"On the way to Lakshmipur with the messengers sent by Mr. Khair, we had to stay at our cousin's in-law in Kashipur. But this place was not secure either. So we had to leave for Lakshmipur. Everywhere the family went from village to village, sometimes on foot, sometimes by boat, we found people helpful and sympathetic. After staying in Mr. Khair's house in Lakshmipur for three days, we were taken by their younger uncle to his in-laws at Kamalaghat village in Munshiganj (Bikrampur). A few other refugee families had also gathered there. After about a month, our aunt's elder son brought them to his house on Green Road. He was also a business partner of Nilufa's father. The children lived there till October, their uncles and aunts decided to share their responsibilities by parcelling the children out and thus reducing the pressure on one relative. The separation of the members of the family obliged us to begin new lives on our own."

Separation

The separation that took place in 1971 still continues. By common consent, Nilufa and Sharmin went to their elder aunt's house at Segun Bagicha, Nasrin and Jamil went to their younger aunt's house at Missionpara in Narayanganj, the youngest one, Farzana, went to the youngest uncle's house at Narayanganj, and the third sister, Rumana, went to Punjab in November with the family of their elder aunt's second son, a major in the Pakistan army. In 1973, Rumana came back to Bangladesh from the Pakistan prison camp. She had kept a diary of her painful experiences in the prison camp.

Reunion

After three years when Rumana came back from Pakistan, the brothers and sisters decided to live together. They would live in their home, on their own. They would not live with their relatives at the cost of their self-respect. With her brother and sister, Nilufa came back to Masdair in 1974. All of them got admitted to schools and colleges. Nilufa, the eldest, had to bear all the responsibilities of looking after the family and managing their finances.

The family faced many hindrances and bitter experiences in those days. Nilufa, an unmarried girl, had to pass her days looking after her younger siblings. They had no guardian, and society frowned at their situation. But there was no one to stand by them; no one even came up with a suggestion. Nilufa had to meet the needs of the family with her father's savings and the money she got from her parent's property. Nilufa married in March 1975 and Nasrin married in May, the same year. Nasrin had to go to Dhaka after she got married. Nilufa tried to look after things from her in-laws' house in Dhaka. Sometimes she used to come over to Narayanganj. In this regard Rumana said, "The four of us had to pass lonely and difficult times in our large house in Masdair. There was no one who could take care of us. Nilufa used to visit us from time to time to shop for the whole month. She used to give us money for other expenditure. We didn't stop studying, though. We ran the family with the little sum of money Nilufa used to give us. My brother guarded the house when we were at school. He would go to the bazaar."

A few years passed this way. Looking after three sisters and a brother became difficult for Nilufa. Clothes, books, food, it became almost impossible to manage all these things with their limited funds. "But we never asked our relatives for anything. The painful situation we faced after the death of our parents is impossible to forget. Our relatives looked after us though their tongues were sharp. It was mental torture. It's not possible to translate that into language. Their behaviour made us suffer. Finally, we had to go to Dhaka." Two of the sisters went to Nasrin's house, and Nilufa kept her brother and a sister. Even this situation soon proved untenable.

For a Better Shelter

The two elder sisters, finally, couldn't continue to keep their younger siblings with them. The brother continued to stay at home as he had a disability. The three younger sisters were sent to Bharateshwari Homes School in Mirzapur. The girls became sick in their new school.

After a few days they were sent to Fayzunnesa Girls' School in Comilla. New problems arose because of the distance and the difficult commute. The girls were then sent to Narayanganj Govt. School which had a hostel.

In 1978 Rumana married of her own choice and thus ended her hostel life. But the two younger sisters passed their entire school and college lives in hostels. However, they are on their own now as they have jobs; but still they have to live in hostels. Farzana said, "Though I work, I have to live in a hostel. What a miserable life I have."

"The house at Masdair was sold in 1986. We were compelled to take this step for several reasons. It was very difficult for Nilufa to take care of the house and everything else and she was too stressed, both physically and mentally, to take such responsibilities. Further more, the neighbourhood was not congenial, our neighbours were relentless in their efforts to grab the house and property and were becoming a threat to our lives. We felt the house was ill-omened.

Vulnerability

A family should be a safe haven. Parents try their best to protect their children from all kinds of difficulty. In 1971 both the parents were killed, and as a result the children were separated. Re-union became impossible. Separation caused many troubles. Apart from financial loss and mental torture, the family also suffered socially. Farzana added: "Losing our parents, we lost everything. Society did not give us the respect it should have. We are from a good family. But society never gave us the respect we deserved. It becomes impossible to maintain one's social status if one's parents are dead. Though we have jobs, we can't rent a house because of social prejudices. We cannot go and live with our sisters because they are married; moreover it looks odd. We can't do that as we have jobs now. People do not realise, and will never realise, our sufferings. It was very difficult to make landlords understand that we two sisters wanted to rent a house and live together. They were always suspicious of our morals. How would two unmarried sisters rent a house? How would they live? Would they be able to pay the rent? How would they meet their expenditure with the little they earned?"

Rumana commented, "Our struggle hasn't ended. It's continuing. Though I have a husband, we still face problems. We continually have to hear remarks such as, 'Have they ever had parents?' People gave us food and shelter and in return they said, 'They have eaten their father and mother, they will eat whatever they get. They should have died with their parents. When will this rubbish depart?' People asked many awkward questions when marriage proposals came: 'Will they make good wives? Do they have good characters? There will be problems if our sons marry them.' We faced a lot of trouble. Two of my younger sisters are still suffering. Though they have jobs, they do not have a good place to stay. They do not get proper food. Though I am financially solvent, I cannot ask them to live with me. You can't do what you want at your in-laws."

Sharmin talked about the problems of hostel life. She commented, "Hostel life is not the only problem. We have to face problems everywhere though the blood of my father and mother was spilt like that of others for the liberation of the country. We have never got the respect we deserve. On March 26 and December 16, I remember my father and mother more than at any other time. Other people celebrate these days. We can't. And when we face problems, we think that we would perhaps not have had these problems if our parents had been alive."

Nilufa said with a heavy heart, "Jamil is getting increasingly short-tempered. He makes all sorts of demands. He misbehaves and makes scenes. Nowadays everyone avoids him. We have started a new life and want to forget our past. We have made adjustments, changed, but Jamil hasn't. He has no company, no partner. Sometimes he becomes violent. Besides, Sharmin and Farzana are unmarried. Perhaps, they will never marry. They haven't known what a family is; they haven't known how people love each other in a family. They have only seen our struggle to survive."

"In the last 25 years many political parties have formed governments. But none of them have thought about people like us, about how we are leading our lives. Even the people of Narayanganj do not bother about us. When we returned to our house in 1974, people visited us with ill motives. They found it amusing that a few young girls were living in that house all by themselves. No one even asked how we managed baby food for our younger sisters. You need feeding bottles to feed such young children. You have to change the teats every three months. Nobody asked how we bought what we needed. No one asked whether we needed five taka or ten. But they made comments about us. I hate Narayanganj. These people are supposed to be educated, but I feel we are living in a jungle, among animals. And though we are a family of martyrs, we have never asked anything from the government. We know we will never get what we have lost."

Rumana also talked about the feelings of her sister Nasrin. "She feels the most amongst all our brother and sisters as our parents are dead. She thinks that if she had a lot of money she would buy a large house for all of us so that we could live together. She would ask her married sisters to *nayor*.[4] Nasrin even thinks of asking our elder sister to *nayor*. She would cook special foods for the grooms. She wants to do what a mother does when her sons-in-law come to visit. Your daughter is taken care of if you take good care of her in-laws. Nasrin wants to play the role of a caring mother because she suffers at her in-laws. If a bride is not visited by her natal family, she faces problems at her in-laws."

Financial Loss

The members of this family suffered the loss of money and property on three occasions.

"The first occasion was when the Pakistan army robbed us of our money." Tk. 30,000 according to Nilufa, 80 *bharis* of gold jewellery according to Rumana and a 20-to-22 inch suitcase full of jewellery according to Nilufa. Some of the jewellery was made for Nilufa's marriage because marriage negotiations had been going on. Besides that, a large house, made of corrugated iron, which consisted of a guest house, a reading room and a store, was ransacked."

Nilufa said, "Secondly, the neighbours and people from the villages around Nirala looted our house three times – the first time when the dead bodies were inside the house and twice after the bodies were removed. Thus they have ruined us. They took everything they could carry: sewing machines, watches. Only the beds were left because you cannot carry them on your head. Otherwise, they might have even done that."

"Thirdly, there were some losses when the freedom fighters occupied the house and camped inside it after independence. There

[4] The custom of a married daughter visiting her parents' home after marriage. Her bridegroom also comes to visit and is entertained.

were bullet holes in the walls as they used to kill the war criminals inside the house. They broke the expensive locks of the doors. And even the doors and windows made of teak wood were broken." Nilufa remarked, "The occupation army didn't pillage to this extent. The Bangalis took away all the things with which we could have lived there afterwards. It became almost impossible to enter our own house at one period of time as the freedom fighters had occupied it. The house was recovered from the freedom fighters later with the help of a few influential persons."

Evaluating the Liberation War

When we asked the sisters who was to blame for what happened in 1971, they gave us very thought-provoking answers. They were also asked to evaluate what had happened during the course of the war and its aftermath. At first Nilufa said, "I would like to say something for the very first time if you are ready to hear something unpleasant. It won't be anything untrue, though. I would blame our freedom fighters for what happened. I won't call our sons freedom fighters; they fought the army with out-dated guns. I would say they are the reason behind all the destruction that took place. They are guilty. They should have asked the people to leave their villages prior to their operations."

Rumana added, "Whom should we blame? It's all destiny. When there is a country, there is politics. It was destined to happen. It happens everywhere."

Sharmin said, "We shouldn't blame anyone in particular because it was a question of making our motherland free. The masses had no control over anything. Only the Pakistanis are to blame; the Pakistanis who were in power then, their prime minister, their president."

Farzana said, "I don't understand who is to blame for everything that happened. If a war takes place, people die. But there should have been some sort of sympathy for children."

Nilufa's narration suggests her agony and frustration. She said, "In the last 25 years nothing has happened that should have happened in an independent country. Have we progressed in the field of education? Have we established new factories? Did anything good happen to our garments industry? What have we achieved after independence? We have been successful in increasing illiteracy and circulating black money. The people who were not supposed to have money have got a lot of money. The people who were not supposed to be armed have arms. To tell you the truth, freedom has made us undisciplined. There is no respect for elders. And the thing we have learned best is corruption; I'm sure our country will never be free from this evil. During the war, Pakistani soldiers raped women; now the rapists are the sons of this independent country, Bangladesh. Even a three-year-old child is not secure. Acid violence has increased; acid victims are living horrors. Who are more ruthless? I would like to ask the people of this country this question."

Rumana in her evaluation of 1971 said, "The pain is that no government till date has taken notice of us. No government has thought of us. On the contrary, everyone has tried to politicise things. They want to make us their activists. But this is not good. We are neutral. We don't want to be involved in politics. Many families of martyrs are passing their days in great misery. Most are unemployed and destitute. Some of them are rickshaw-pullers and beggars. There are thousands of similar instances. But neither political leaders nor governments have ever looked into these matters in the last twenty-five years. There should have been a list of martyrs' families. Yes, we have got an independent state. We are free citizens; it feels good. But sometimes when I think about it, it seems that Pakistan was better. We had a good time then. There were no terrorists. Women were not dishonoured. It was not that unsafe to move about. Necessities were cheaper. People lived in peace and happiness. At least, one morsel of rice was available. The number of beggars was not as large as it is today. The financial, political and social unrest we see today wasn't there. The country is going downhill gradually. We don't see any future for the country. We don't see any hope. All these things come to mind when I try to justify why our parents sacrificed their lives. Why have so many freedom fighters sacrificed their lives? What have we got after the War of Liberation?

"In Bangladesh, collaborators like Gholam Azam are walking about freely. They have been granted citizenship. When I see that I feel really bad. How can those who raped women, killed innocent people and freedom fighters walk about freely? I truly feel bad then. At the least the families of martyrs and *mukti juddhas* should be rehabilitated with honour. We want the collaborators of 1971 to be punished. If war criminals could be tried 50 years after the Second World War, why cannot our country try collaborators after 25 years? That is my question."

Sharmin, while evaluating the War of Liberation, said, "Lots of blood was shed for independence. But we didn't get the expected social environment in return. We hoped that people would be more loyal to the country, that the nation would progress. But this didn't happen."

Farzana said, "The war of independence gave us many things and in return we had to pay a high price. We have got an independent country. We can speak in our mother language. Personally, I've lost my parents. The most important thing is that I've lost my father and mother. Our father and mother lost their lives for our country. In return what have we got from our country? Our society never valued us. We just wanted a very little thing: honour in return for the lives for our parents. Nothing more."

Reaction

The events of 1971 have affected Nilufa psychologically. She is haunted by the horrifying experience and is afraid that it might recur, so she cannot sleep properly. Sometimes she seems to be in a trance; she avoids recalling her memories of 1971, and suffers acutely whenever she is reminded of it. She feels that she is the only one who has suffered and has lost faith in people.

In the last 25 years Nilufa hadn't talked about this traumatic incident. She hadn't given any interviews. She kept herself deliberately aloof from anything to do with the War of Liberation. She stopped reading or watching anything on this topic. She talked about her state of mind, "I found it worthless. The news and views and all the opinions are of no use. I don't want to remember. We, brother and sisters, do not talk about it when we see each other. I have forgotten many things. If anyone asks anything about the war, sometimes I can answer and sometimes I can't. I recollect events if someone reminds me. A few articles were published by my sisters; unfortunately, these were exaggerated when edited. What benefit do we gain if a newspaper sells more by publishing our stories?"

The agonising memories of 1971 haunt Rumana even today. She remarks, "I have sleepless nights and nightmares. Every week I see blood and mutilated corpses in my dreams. I dream about war, so my husband has asked me not to watch any documentary or to read any book on war. I cry in my sleep or sometimes get up from sleep and cry. These things upset my husband. This started happening after the killing took place. I can't even watch a war movie; it makes me so upset that I stop eating for two to three days."

Sharmin can't stand the Pakistanis even today because they brutally murdered her parents. She cites two incidents which are related to this. In the first incident a girl from Pakistan wanted to become friends with her after they met at a social function. But she declined as the girl was from Pakistan. In the second incident she had given an interview and been hired by a large organisation. But she refused the job when she learned that she would have to work with researchers from Pakistan.

and not mutilated corpses. In my recurrent dream about war, scenes of funeral [illegible] [illegible] with my documentary or to read any book on that [illegible] in the sleep of [illegible] get up from sleep and [illegible] [illegible]. That [illegible] happened after the [illegible] [illegible] [illegible] [illegible] [illegible] and [illegible] upset that I slept [illegible] for two to three days.

[illegible] [illegible] [illegible] [illegible] [illegible] [illegible] [illegible] [illegible] [illegible] [illegible] [illegible] [illegible] [illegible] [illegible] to [illegible] [illegible] [illegible] [illegible] [illegible] [illegible] wanted to become friends with her after [illegible] as a social [illegible] [illegible] [illegible] [illegible] [illegible] [illegible] [illegible] [illegible] [illegible] [illegible] an interview and been hired by a [illegible] organisation. But she refused the job when she learned that she would have to work with researchers from Pakistan.

Experiences of a Political Activist

Suraiya Begum

The Pakistani military committed a ruthless genocide in Bangladesh. They kidnapped many people, tortured them, and often killed them. They tortured prisoners to elicit information about freedom fighters and supporters of the liberation war. If they failed to extract any information, they killed them. On some occasions they set them free after physical and mental torture. One such person who was saved by sheer good luck is Rasheda Khanom Rina. We interviewed Rina on September 23, 1997. Rina Khan was a government employee and lived in a flat in Azimpur Colony. When we went to meet her, it was late evening. The flat was neat and tidy. There was a small sofa in the room, and two bookshelves against two walls. There was an assortment of books on the shelves, some fiction, but mostly Marxist literature. There was a large picture of her late husband on the wall. Neither her son nor her daughter were at home. Her son was at work and her daughter had gone to attend a relative's birthday party.

It was my first meeting with Rina Khan. She asked us to sit on the sofa. We had some formal conversation at first. She was very sprightly in nature. Kazi Sufia Akhter, a member of the Bangladesh Mahila Parishad, accompanied me. In fact it was she who had arranged the interview. We got down from the sofa and sat on a mat on the floor. The chat became more intimate. Rina became excited while talking about her childhood. She went on to narrate how as a student she had participated in the armed movement for the liberation of Bangladesh. Everything was crystal clear in her memory.

Rina Khan, who hails from Gopalganj, was the general secretary of Rokeya Hall in 1971. Her father, Abdur Razzak Khan, worked for

Congress during the British Raj. Later on, he became the founder general secretary of the Awami League in Gopalganj. He was distantly related to Sheikh Mujibur Rahman.

Rina stated, "My father was very broad-minded He was a *moktar* (attorney) by profession. Though Gopalganj was a very small town, it was politically and culturally rich. I grew up in the midst of politics. Both my father and my uncle, Abdus Salam Khan, were involved in politics. Abdus Salam was the general secretary of the Awami League at first and later of the Pakistan Democratic Party. Every politician, including Moulana Bhasani and Suhrawardy, who went to Gopalganj would stay or dine with us."

Even though her father was an Awami Leaguer, Rina Khan was involved with left politics. She explained how she had become interested in communism through Mukhlesur Rahman, a Communist Party worker. The Communist Party was banned during the sixties. Mukhlesur Rahman's father was in the police. But he had not been able to prevent his son being imprisoned for his leftist activities. Rina Khan said, "Because of his affiliation with the party, he went to jail. After he was released nobody gave him shelter. At that time my father sheltered him, on humanitarian grounds. Should he be shunned like this? So he live in our house. This gentleman had contributed significantly to the progressive movement in Gopalganj. When he was living in our house, he used to teach me and my siblings. Through his teaching, we acquired a progressive and rich cultural sense. I used to call Mukhlesur Rahman 'Sir.' I still do. He used to work in the greater Mymensingh region for the Communist Party. The only political party in Faridpur was the Awami League. He propagated the ideals of communism in the area. He explained the communist ideals in towns and villages, to farmers, students, ordinary people. He was a member of the Control Commission of the Communist Party. This commission would investigate and discuss the external activities of members and their organisations. This is part of the Communist Party constitution. Sir encouraged me a lot. He gave me books to read. My interest was generated by him. He influenced me greatly. That is why later I became involved in politics, Communist Party politics."

Rina Khan was admitted to the Philosophy Department at the University of Dhaka in 1967. Her cousin Zillur Rahman Mithu (who was killed in 1971) helped her to get admission. When Rina's father died in the early sixties, her mother did not want her to continue her studies thinking about the expenses involved. But Imam Uddin Ahmed, Rina's brother-in-law, discussed Rina's interest in studying with Mithu and persuaded her mother to let her go to the university. Rina had two brothers and one sister. Rina's sister was the eldest sibling. She was followed by their two brothers. Rina was the youngest. Her elder sister had studied up to class nine but the two brothers had completed their Bachelor's degree. Rina was the only one of them who went to university and completed an M.A. She was grateful to her brother-in-law and Mithu for this. In her own words: "My mother was a widow and she thought that she would marry me off in Gopalganj after my B.A. degree. I owe my present state of life to Mithu and to my brother-in-law. Today I am working and I was married to a fine person. All this would have been simply impossible if I had not studied Dhaka University or actively taken part in the Chhatra Union. That's why I remember these two persons very much."

After her admission to the University of Dhaka, Rina Khan was given a place to stay in Rokeya Hall and joined the Chhatra Union,[1] and this despite her father having been an Awami Leaguer. When asked about this, she replied that she was mainly influenced by Mukhlesur Rahman and Mithu. Mithu was involved in the Chhatra Union and secretly in the Communist Party as well. Mithu introduced Rina to senior members of the Chhatra Union, and she soon became actively involved in the party. The female leaders of the Chhatra Union at that time were Maleka Begum, the former general secretary of Bangladesh Mahila Parishad, Ayesha Khanom, Munira Akter, and others. Rina said, "Maleka Apa taught us a lot of things. Besides teaching us politics, she became friendly with us. She wanted to know about our family life. Maleka Begum had enormous influence on my political activities and social consciousness.

"Maleka Apa did not reside in the hall at that time but was attached to it. She was then the Vice President of the central committee of the Chhatra Union. Maleka Begum was very friendly and mingled freely with the activists." When she was just a first year student, Rina Khan competed for the post of Assistant Athletic Secretary. She said, "I can mix very easily with people and I won by

[1] The Chhatra Union was a left-leaning student front of the Communist Party of Bangladesh; the Chhatra League was the student front of the Awami League.

a huge margin. We women student leaders had a very good relationship with the hall Provost, the hall Super and the house tutors. They were very fond of us, and they relied on us a lot. They would discuss problems and issues related to the students with us and act on our advice. They treated the hall Union with respect. They would discuss the situation of the country as well as political issues. Among the house tutors were Roushan Ara, Meherunessa Choudhury, and Maqsuda Apa. A food manager would be appointed in Rokeya Hall. I too was appointed food manager once. It was quite a difficult job. It was not easy to arrange good food for the students. But I was able to do the work to everyone's satisfaction."

From 1967 Rina Khan became involved with the Chhatra Union. She had to go to different parts of the country to organise Chhatra Union activities. In 1970, when she was in the third year, she was elected General Secretary of the Rokeya Hall Students' Union. She later became a member of the Dhaka City Chhatra Union Committee and, in 1972, Vice-President of the Central Committee. During that time the party was actively involved in organising the Chhatra Union in girls' schools and colleges such as Badrunnesa College, Ganderia College, Moniza Rahman Girls' College, Saleha School. During the 70s the Chhatra Union was remarkably strong and well-organised. Large numbers of female students participated in its meetings and processions.

Rina Khan was able to engage freely in politics as her father was dead and her brothers did not object or stand in her way. Since Rina was a good student, her mother also did not object much though she did want her to get married and settle down. On occasions Rina stayed in the house of her elder sister, whose husband was also liberal. So she did not experience any hindrances from the family.

As the General Secretary of Rokeya Hall, Rina had considerable responsibilities. When asked about the kind of tasks she had to perform, Rina answered, "The problems related to the hall and the daily affairs of the female students had to be solved. We were able to get ration rice, sugar, oil for the students. This reduced the students' living expenses to a great extent. We got a gas connection in the hall. We raised the demand for a new hall and were successful in getting it. Today's Shamsunnahar Hall is the fruit of that movement. Through the students' committee, we arranged celebrations of important days like February 21, Pahela *Baishakh*, Begum Rokeya Day, etc. At that time the VP and GS of the various halls were taken to West Pakistan at the expense of the government. But two of us from Rokeya Hall did not go. We, the residents of the hall, had a very cordial relationship with the hall supers. We opened a school for the *ayas* who worked in the hall. We also opened a school for the elderly, and regularised the jobs of the fourth class employees. Earlier they had worked on a daily basis."

Rina was so actively involved in politics that she hardly saw her family. She did not even go home on the occasion of Eid. Her mother complained that she did not even write letters regularly.

In April 1969 Rina worked as a member of the Chhatra Union relief team to help cyclone victims and went to Demra to distribute relief goods. She went from door to door to investigate the losses people had suffered and distributed slips so that people could collect relief from the centres run by the Union. On the occasion of the terrible cyclone and tidal bore in November 1970, she and her co-workers, Mujahidul Islam Selim, Kazi Akram Hossain and Tazunnahar – the Rokeya Hall Secretary for Social Welfare – went to Char Bhata and Char Jabbar in Noakhali to distribute relief goods among the affected people.

During the election of 1970, Rina worked for the National Awami Party. The non-cooperation movement started after March 7, 1971, and committees for women were formed in every locality to carry on the struggle. Senior leaders like Rina were given the responsibility of establishing these committees. Since her sister resided at Malibagh and she often stayed there, Rina formed committees in Khilgaon, Malibagh and Rampura. Zohra Tajuddin visited these places when these committees were set up. Zohra Tajuddin worked to make the women politically conscious.

After the historic speech of Sheikh Mujibur Rahman at the Race Course on March 7, some girls left the hall. However, Rina stayed on. Later on, Ayesha Apa, a leader of the Chhatra Union and the Vice President of the hall committee, advised the students to leave the hall. At that time Rokeya Hall had three buildings – the main building, Chameli House and the Honours Building. There were apartments for house tutors behind Chameli House. The girls lived on the upper floor and the house tutors on the ground floor. Around March 20-22, the Vice President and General Secretary of the hall told the girls to leave.

The girls left the hall gradually, not only because they had been told to leave but because of the worsening situation. Though the Provost of the hall, Professor Akhter Imam, was a very strict person, she wanted to know about politics from leaders like Rina. She trusted Chhattra Union and Chhattra League. The hall administration accepted advice from people involved in student politics. The leading women leaders at Rokeya Hall were Rafia Akter Dolly, amongst others.

After the March 7 speech of Sheikh Mujibur Rahman, Chhattra Union arranged military training in the playground of Dhaka University. Every day thousands of students were trained with dummy rifles. A large number of them were women. The news of the training spread everywhere, inspiring every Bangali. On March 25 Rina was staying in her sister's house. This is what she said about that fateful night: "I couldn't understand what was happening when I heard the sound of bombing at dead of night. My brother-in-law woke us up. I saw lights like balls of fire. There was tremendous noise and I could hear the doors rattling. Curfew was imposed the next day."

At the beginning of April, Rina left her sister's place and moved to her aunt's house in Khilgaon. From there, she accompanied her cousin and his wife to the village of Baraid, where they found shelter. At that time people gave others shelter even if they were not related to them. People kept coming to the village every day. Many people huddled together in one room. At Baraid, Rina happened to meet her classmate Masuda Matin, who was also active in the Chhattra Union. Masuda happened to be from Baraid and she invited Rina to stay with her. The house where Rina had taken shelter belonged to strangers. At the beginning of the war the villagers provided shelter and food to refugees from the city. With her cousin's permission, Rina moved to Masuda's house. Masuda's family was well off. Rina's cousin and his wife returned to Dhaka from Baraid but she remained in her friend's house. For some time, Mohammad Farhad, a Communist Party leader, hid in Masuda's house in Dhanmondi. Later on Rina married Mohammad Farhad. When she was staying in the village, Rina received a letter from Mohammad Farhad through Matiur Rahman (currently editor of the Daily *Prothom Alo*) that the Communist Party and Chhattra Union members were going to Agartala in India to be trained in guerrilla warfare. She was also asked to go with them. But she could not make up her mind whether to go to Agartala or not.

Finally she decided not to go and returned to Dhaka by boat along with Matiur Rahman.

She stayed with her sister for a few days, then again returned to Masuda's house in Baraid. After a sojourn of 10-15 days there, she returned to Dhaka and then left for Gopalganj with Mithu. By then it was May. However, due to heavy bombing, they could not proceed further than Chandpur. They disembarked from the launch and took shelter in a village. After a night's stay in the village, they returned to Dhaka. After staying 10-12 days in Dhaka, they again went to Gopalganj. Conditions were very dreadful in Gopalganj at that time. The Pakistani soldiers were setting houses on fire. They also came to their home in Gopalganj on a number of occasions. Rina's mother was staying there all alone. The soldiers visited the house frequently because they knew that Rina's father had been an Awami Leaguer. But they did not mistreat her mother. They just came and went off after some inquiries. Then Rina went to Moksedpur, adjacent to her grandfather's house. Her uncles belonged to the Pakistan Democratic Party. Soldiers also went to Moksedpur, but because of her uncles' political affiliations with the PDP, nothing untoward happened. Nevertheless, Rina did not feel safe there. She moved deeper inside the village, to her maternal uncle's house and stayed there for some time. She talked about the liberation war and encouraged young people to take up arms. In June-July she came back to Dhaka. Rina could not maintain any contact with her party at that time. Mithu, who could, gave her the responsibility of collecting money, medicine and clothes and of distributing leaflets. She managed to carry out these activities among people she knew while staying in her sister's house in Dhaka.

Salam Khan, Rina Khan's uncle, belonged to the PDP. He did not want Pakistan to disintegrate, but he was also very much against the Pakistani oppression. He was a renowned politician and lived at Purana Paltan in Dhaka. Military officers visited his house quite often, considering him to be pro-Pakistani. Her uncle's second son, a student of class ten, was quite a dare-devil. No one knew that he was in contact with freedom fighters. Rina and Mithu were able to work secretly for liberation from her uncle's house.

The Situation in Dhaka at the Time of Rina Khan's Capture

From June 11, curfew was lifted in Dhaka. The freedom fighters became increasingly active from July, blowing up power stations, transformers, military check posts. The condition of the city dwellers was such at the time that if they did not hear these explosions some nights, they feared that the freedom fighters had been apprehended. "The sound of explosions reassured us somewhat that the freedom fighters were safe. Ordinary people, men as well as women, helped the freedom fighters in whatever way they could, providing them money, food, clothing, medicine. It was at this time that an increasing number of militia were being sent from Pakistan. We started to see them all over the city. On August 20, Matiur Rahman, a Bangali Air Force officer posted in Karachi, attempted to fly an Air Force plane to India but was shot down. To counter increased guerrilla activity in Dhaka, checking became stricter. In August and September, with the assistance of local collaborators, the Pakistani forces began arresting people."

"In order to show that factories and mills were working normally all over the country, strict measures were taken. It became increasingly difficult to move about in Dhaka as well as elsewhere as freedom fighters had blown up several bridges."[2]

On September 11, Rina was staying with her sister in Malibagh. Her two brothers were also in the house. There were three rooms in the house. In one room Rina was sleeping on the floor with her eldest niece. Her sister and brother-in-law were sleeping in the next room with their two younger daughters. In the other room Rina's two brothers were sleeping.

Rina Khan described that night in her own words:

"It was one or two at night. Suddenly there was a loud banging on the door. I did not hear the door opening. I saw the whole house was surrounded by soldiers. I sat up in bed, inside the mosquito curtain. My brother-in-law was baffled. Pointing at me, the soldiers asked my niece, 'Who is this?' They had an informer with them. They also asked my brother-in-law, 'Is this Rina Khan?' He answered, 'Yes, she is my sister-in-law.' Then they told me, 'Come with us.'

"I did not know at that time that my brothers had already been called out of their rooms. I do not know why, but I wasn't frightened. The military were everywhere – inside and outside the house. When I went outside, I saw that my two brothers were already seated in the jeep.

---

2 Jahanara Imam, *Of Blood and Fire*, Trans. Mustafizur Rahman, Dhaka, The University Press Limited, 1990.

"We were taken to the MP hostel by jeep. We had to ascend the stairs of a flat behind the MP hostel. It was about three o'clock at night. There were many other cars near the jeep and I saw many of my family members there as well. Mithu had been staying in his sister's house in Dhanmondi and had been caught from there. Mithu's elder brother, Mirza, lived at Khilgaon. The house of his in-laws was near the Ansar camp. Mirza was also caught. A cousin of Mithu named Halim, who was staying in that house, was also caught. I was the only woman taken into custody; all the others were men. All my family members and relations, including my two uncles who were working for the Liberation War in Dhaka, were caught that night. We were 19 in number."

"My brother, cousins and I sat on the floor of the kitchen in the flat behind the MP hostel. My brothers just stared at my face. Then a captain said to Mithu's older brother Mirza, 'Be careful. Do not let her [Rina] be separated from you by any means. If anyone wants to take her from you, vigorously resist him.' I heard this afterwards. The captain was a Pakistani. I don't remember his name.

"We were kept in the kitchen in that house. While we were sitting there, the door was repeatedly opened. People entered to look at me. I remember someone saying in Urdu, 'Is this the girl?' I was mumbling *dua Yunus*[3] then. The day dawned while we were sitting like this. Afterwards we came to understand that it was an army mess. They had occupied a private house and turned it into a mess.

"The next morning we were taken to the MP hostel on foot. There was a one-storeyed house beside the road. We were seated in the verandah. I was given a chair, but everybody else was seated on the ground. I saw a man who was also a member of the Chhattra Union. I wondered what he would say if he was asked about me for he knew me well. So I looked at him and gestured with my eyes that he should pretend that he didn't know me and that I would do the same. My older brother was beaten mercilessly in front of me. He was very mild in nature. He was beaten so badly that I felt terrible. Others were beaten too but not as much as he was.

"A major came into the room. I used to know his name but now I can't remember it. He started to interrogate us one by one. I was given a chair to sit on. I realised that they knew everything about me, so I did not deny anything. I told them that I was the General

3 A verse from the Holy Quran.

Secretary of Rokeya Hall. I did not understand Urdu very well then. So I answered in mixed English and Urdu.

"There was nobody else with the major. There was just one table and a chair in the room. I was asked about Motia Chowdhury and Bangabandhu. I admitted that I knew Motia Apa but told him that I did not work with her. I also said that everybody knew Bangabandhu. He repeatedly tried to find out if I had any contacts with the freedom fighters. I denied that I had any contact.

"At one point in the interrogation they brought my brothers one after another into the room and asked them about freedom fighters and beat them. Mithu especially was beaten badly. The army personnel told me, 'Explain to us what they are saying.' I tried to explain in a mixture of English and Urdu. At one stage they tried to intimidate me by saying, 'There is a room beside this one and we can do anything to you there if you don't tell us everything properly.' I said, 'I cannot help it if you don't understand. I can't say anything more than that.' Then they took photographs of each of us. Thus the whole day elapsed. We had not eaten anything. Neither were we offered anything to eat. Those who were interrogated in that room were all related to me."

"In the evening they told me to go with them. My brothers' faces turned pale. But they had been beaten so much that they could not protest. I was taken to the main building of the MP Hostel. I saw a few officers sitting in a big room. Colonel Hejazi was in charge of the squad. I was seated on a sofa. They had arrested my uncle's son-in-law, his clerk and his youngest son and had kept them standing against the wall. I was offered a cup of tea. Then the colonel asked me with a smiling face, 'Did you have any problem?' I did not reply. He said, 'We are letting you go. Will you go with your brothers or should we reach you home?' I realised that the main road was far from the MP hostel and, if I wanted to go with my brothers, I would have to walk. It was already dark. Besides this, if I went with my brothers, they might attack me and later claim that I had been set free. So, I told them to reach me home. The colonel told a captain or major to take me home. He also suggested that my guardians should phone them when I reached home.

"The army freed everyone they had arrested from my uncle's house. But my brothers and Mithu remained in custody. Later on they were taken to jail.

"Afterwards I came to know the reason for our arrest. My uncle Salam Khan was a leader of PDP. The son of my youngest uncle thought that Salam Khan's house would be safe. So he hid weapons inside the water tank. But we had been followed on the way to my uncle's house. Mithu and I were under suspicion because we were involved in politics. The army recovered many weapons from that house."

"When the news of our arrest reached my uncle, he approached many people for my release. The wife of my uncle's eldest son was a Punjabi and her father was a high official in the Pakistan Army. My uncle went to the MP Hostel and tried to persuade the army to release us. Afterwards I realised that we were set free because of him."

"The Colonel said to me, 'You can't go anywhere. We will keep an eye on you. Make phone calls to me every seven days and stay in the house of your present guardian.' However, I never made any phone calls to him."

"My brothers were taken to jail. There was nobody to go and meet them. So I had to risk going to them."

"My uncle was a senior PDP politician. Many Pakistanis knew him. Moreover he was the chief advocate for Bangabandhu in the Agartala Conspiracy Case. My uncle's son drove out a car on December 16 and never came back. After getting out from jail, Mithu returned to his sister's house in Dhanmondi. He left the house on December 5, but he also did not return home. Neighbours said that he was taken away in an army jeep. In fact he was seized by the Al-Badr.

"After liberation, I again became involved with the Chhattra Union. Everybody there had learned of my confinement. Afterwards I was again elected VP of the hall. In the meantime the M.A. results were published. Later I took admission in Law. I got married in 1972.

"Mohammad Farhad was a dedicated activist of the Communist Party. Even though I belonged to the Chhattra Union, I had never been introduced to him. At that time he was a very important leader in my eyes. I met him in May 1972. We were travelling in the same car, going to attend the marriage of Ayesha Khanom the present President of Mahila Parishad. Afterwards he sent a marriage proposal. I talked to him for the first time on June 13, 1972. I was not a person who talked much. We were married four months later. I met him only four times during those four months. Farhad had a friend in Goran and I met him there. He would tell me that as revolutionaries our marital life would be difficult. We returned by rickshaw from Goran. My mother did not object to my marriage to a political leader as I too was involved in politics. Before we got married, my mother met Bangabandhu (who was a distant paternal cousin of hers.) He told her, 'There is no problem. You may allow the marriage.'"

Mohammad Farhad was a full-time leader of the party. His family was not very well-off. But since his brothers were working and his sisters were married, he had few responsibilities. Their family was maintained with the scanty money they received from the party. Rina and Farhad's married life was short. Her husband was either underground or in jail most of the time. He had to go into hiding after the death of Sheikh Mujibur Rahman in 1975. Rina Khan returned to her sister's house with her son. Afterwards she had to take shelter in various places. In 1976 Rina took a job in the Family Planning Department. Then she worked in BIDS, and in 1980 she entered government service.

After August 15, 1975, Mohammad Farhad was arrested several times by the governments of General Ziaur Rahman and General Ershad. Rina accepted this as part of her life. Farhad suffered a heart attack on January 10, 1986. He was taken to Russia in 1987, where he passed away on October 9 that year.

According to Rina Khan, "My family life lasted from October 1972 to August 15, 1975. After that I no longer had my own home. From then on wherever I lived, I left something behind. This sofa set was given to me by my sister and the television set by my niece's husband. My sister gave me the bed. It can be said that after my husband's death, my domestic life attained some stability. However, I myself chose that life. So I cannot complain."

After the death of her husband, Rina renewed contacts with her party. She was also actively associated with the Bangladesh Mahila Parishad. After the death of her husband, she was not willing to take financial assistance from the Communist Party. She has a strong moral sense. She manages her family on her own earnings.

Rina Khan has a son and a daughter. When her daughter was born, Mohammad Farhad was in jail. Though their father always believed that communism would be established in this country, her children are not actively involved in politics. Rina Khan wants her children to be conscious about politics and society but she does not want to influence them. At the time of the interview, her son was doing his MA and simultaneously working in a private firm. Her daughter was a student in the Commerce Faculty at the University of Dhaka.

While reflecting on 1971, Rina Khan said, "There was no alternative to the war of 1971. But now I feel that the armed struggle was not properly organised. The Awami League also did not understand that it would turn into an armed conflict. The only power we had was the strength of the people. Everything happened very quickly after March 25. On March 7 Bangabandhu gave the call for liberation. He clearly felt that we would have to take up arms to combat the enemy. But it was only after March 26 that people actually understood what he meant."

On the participation of women in 1971 Rina Khan says, "Women mainly participated by helping freedom fighters. Some women fought with weapons but most women provided shelter to freedom fighters, took care of them or collected money, rice and clothes for them. The heroic role women played in the border areas in transporting or hiding weapons is indeed unforgettable. They did this for the country at the risk of their own lives. Many women helped me when I established the resistance committee at Malibagh. This was how we were involved."

Chittagong and Chittagong Hill Tracts

Introduction

Hasina Ahmed

The contribution of the revolutionary port city of Chittagong to the Liberation War in 1971 is, for many reasons, remarkable. Professor Anisuzzaman, who was staying in Chittagong at that time, has described those turbulent days in the following manner:

"Everyone wanted to do something for the country. Every day political parties, student organisations, trade unions, lawyers and other professionals, government employees and women were holding one or more meetings .... Resistance Committees were formed in different areas; at other areas, there were training centres. The Central Students Union of Chittagong University, in a statement on March 10, called upon the Bangali officers and members of the Armed Forces not to surrender arms under any circumstances. In the circumstances, this was an important development."[1]

In his *Ekattorer Smriti Katha (Memories of 1971)*, Brigadier Mohsinuddin Ahmed describes the situation in Chittagong at the time:

"The people of Chittagong came out on the streets when it was announced over the radio that the Parliament would not sit. The port city echoed with the noise of processions and slogans. We came to know on the afternoon of March 1 that at Wireless Colony and Pahartali, Bangalis and Biharis had clashed several times and that the fights were continuing. We came to know that Pakistani commandos were connected with those activities .... One company of soldiers in civil dress was quartered in the houses of non-Bangalis in Wireless Colony and Pahartali. I think that this was a part of the Pakistani plan. This has been confirmed now."[2]

---

[1] *Amar Ekattor* (Dhaka: Sahitya Prakash, 1997), 27.

[2] Sukumar Biswas, *Bangladesh: Geography and History of the Liberation Struggle* (Dhaka: Agamee Prokashoni, 1996), 175-76.

Journalist Jafar Wajed also provides an account of what was happening in Chittagong:

"When the Pakistan army swooped down on civilians on the night of March 25, it was Chittagong that broadcast the message of the Liberation War, marking the beginning of the war. At noon on March 26, M. A. Hannan, President of the District Awami League, read out the Declaration of Bangladesh's Independence from Swadhin Bangla Biplobi Betar Kendra. He called upon the people to embark on a war of resistance against the Pakistani aggressors. On the night of March 27, Major Ziaur Rahman read out the Declaration of Independence on behalf of Bangabandhu Sheikh Mujibur Rahman. Of course, on the night of March 25, leaflets containing the Declaration of Independence had started being circulated in the city .... The Bengal Regiment, the EPR and the Dampara Police Line rose in revolt .... On the night of March 27, shelling started from the *Swat*. The Pakistan army faced considerable resistance, but, by the first week of April, the army gained control of the town."[3] The fighting came to an end on December 16 when the joint forces of the Indian Army and the freedom fighters liberated the town and the Pakistan Army surrendered.

"During the Liberation War, the Pakistan army unleashed a reign of terror in Chittagong. They killed Bangalis in 20 killing fields in Chittagong town and its suburbs. The number of people killed in Chittagong town alone crossed 100,000. The Pakistani troops caused widespread destruction all over Chittagong. Murder and rape were rampant."[4]

---

[3] Muntasir Mamun, *Ekattorer Bijoygatha* (Dhaka: Agamee Prokashon, 1992), 46.

[4] Asaduzzaman Asad, *Ekattorer Ganahatya O Nari Nirjatan* (Dhaka: Samay Prakashan, 1992) 37.

Roksana Shaheen

A Shelter in Pakistan

Hasina Ahmed and Moushumi Rahman

Panchlaish was an aristocratic residential area of Chittagong. Mainly inhabited by professionals, the place was relatively free from political activities. There were not many shops there. It was in this peaceful locality that Major Dr. A.K.M. Amirul Islam lived with his wife and three daughters on the first floor of a three-storeyed house named *Shuktara*. On April 4 Pakistani forces arrested him from his house, along with his brother-in-law, his orderly, as well as seven or eight neighbours and later killed them. The local neighbours arranged a mass burial for them nearby without any religious ritual.

Dr. Amirul Islam's crime was that he was helping freedom fighters. His story and what happened to his family later were narrated to us by his eldest daughter, Dr. Roksana Shaheen, who had been an eyewitness. This story has been constructed mainly on the basis of her experience and memory. Some information has also been collected from books on 1971.

Roksana was born in 1958 in Karachi. At the time of the interview, she was 39 years of age. In 1971 she was thirteen years old. In 1984 she completed her medical studies from Dhaka Medical College. At the time of the interview, she was doing her Ph.D. in Medical Sociology. She got married in 1985 to a doctor chosen by her family. Her father, Dr. Islam, was 41 years at the time of his death. He was an army doctor with the rank of major. He had spent several years in different provinces of West Pakistan and had been transferred in 1968 – only two and a half years before his death – to Chittagong Cantonment. He had joined the EPR (East Pakistan Rifles)[1], on deputation. As there were no quarters suitable for him in the EPR at the time, he moved to a requisitioned house outside the cantonment,

[1] After liberation renamed "Bangladesh Rifles." In 2011 the paramilitary force was renamed as "Border Guards Bangladesh."

in Panchlaish. Roksana's mother, who was a teacher by profession, died in 1991. Roksana's sisters are living in the UK and the USA.

The following narrative is in Roksana's words.

Nine Days of the Liberation War: An Unknown Soldier

"From March preparations for resistance began in Chittagong, with everybody participating from March 26. It was only in the first week of April that the Pakistani forces were able to occupy the town. Before this they had faced considerable resistance from various quarters. My father treated many freedom fighters who were wounded in different clashes. I do not know how he got involved. But, through the orderly at our house, news would come secretly as to where he had to go. He would then go there quietly. He treated both army personnel as well as civilians who were in the resistance. He would usually be gone for a short time – none of us really knew where. I do not know where my father went between March 26 and April 4. He would go out on receiving information and come back after treating freedom fighters. My mother would sometimes say, 'Won't it be bad later on for you?' to which my father's reply was, 'No, nothing will happen to me. I am a doctor; they are asking for me and I have to go; I shall come back after attending to them. If something happens to me because of this, so be it.' Apprehension or advice of dear ones, fear of consequences or fear of death – nothing prevented my father from doing what he saw as his duty to humanity. As a result, he had to accept his cruel fate."

A Fateful Day: April 4, 1971

There are some days that transform one's life completely. April 4 was this day in Roksana's life. Only similar sufferers can feel the pain and memories of separation. "My maternal and paternal uncles went on discussing the advisability of father's joining the freedom fighters or leaving home. But, instead of paying heed to anyone, my father stuck to his decision of staying at Panchlaish. The Pakistan army somehow came to know about his helping freedom fighters. Between 11:30 and 12:00 on April 4, a group of Pakistani soldiers encircled the whole house. I do not remember how many soldiers or officers carried out this operation."

"As on so many other days, father was sitting together with my uncles and discussing the situation and what should be done. They agreed that whatever they decided, they would do it together. My mother was in the kitchen, and we were playing with our maternal cousins who were of our age. Suddenly, the soldiers hammered on the door, and, without giving anybody the chance to say anything, gestured with their guns that everyone should go downstairs. One soldier each accompanied my father and two uncles downstairs. Even my aunt, who was West Pakistani and Urdu-speaking, did not open her mouth. Others also were familiar with Urdu. But all were overwhelmed and terrified by the suddenness of what had happened. All of us were taken downstairs. My father and uncles were made to stand on one side, and we – my mother, my three sisters, two aunts and three cousins – were made to stand on the other side. One of the soldiers ordered, '*Bibi-bachchoko mar dalo*' and another ordered, '*Bibi-bachchoko chhor do.*' I do not remember if it was a hint or an order. We were told to leave. We started walking in the midst of the curfew. No sooner had we started walking, than the soldiers began to fire. We thought that my father and my uncles were killed. But, one uncle survived. As he fell unconscious, there was no scratch on him, let alone any bullet wound. He is now living in Mymensingh. It was, however, much later that we learnt he was alive."

Six Days in a Bihari Railway Colony

"After being driven out of our own house by the Pakistani soldiers, we walked down the street aimlessly under the hot noon-day sun. Someone called us inside a house. A number of people who had taken shelter in an office had seen us – eight women walking together. The family who had taken shelter inside the office had hung a lock on the door outside. I can no longer remember what questions members of that family put to us, and what answers we gave. But we were able to make them understand what had happened, and that we were in danger at that time and with no place to go. But, as they themselves were apprehensive of danger, they could not help us. As they were unable to protect us, they thought of sending us to the Railway Colony. There was only one reason why they thought of sending us there: my aunt was Urdu-speaking. They also thought that they themselves were in hiding and could not keep so many women safe. I do not remember how we finally reached the Bihari colony. But we got shelter there because of my aunt. In that colony there were two Biharis who had been employees at Dawood Jute Mills where my uncle was the Managing Director. Those two employees were very respectful towards us because of my uncle and took great care of us. It was at their house that we stayed. They were very farsighted, that's why, after the curfew was lifted on April 6 or 7, they drove us to our house to bring my aunt's certificate and mine as well as other necessary papers. My mother did not accompany us for she was very weak, both physically and mentally. On going there, we found that the place had been ransacked. As there was no time to scrutinise the papers, we brought over the whole trunk, which had not been touched, in the car. From Biharis, we came to know that some Pakistani soldiers had killed the orderly in the kitchen, as well as some 7/8 persons more in that locality. It was not possible to learn any more that day, as curfew had been lifted for a very short period of time, and as the car belonged to someone else. It was because of their co-operation that we could bring some clothes and the papers."

"In the meantime, the *Sakina-e-Arab* was preparing to leave Chittagong Port for Karachi on April 9. Many Bihari families went to Karachi in this ship. Some names were listed in the first phase, some in the second. Two Bihari employees were trying to contact our relations in Chittagong, Dhaka and Mymensingh. But they failed. Meanwhile, the Bihari families decided to go to Karachi. Our aunt also decided to go to Karachi because all her relations lived there. My mother and we three sisters would be left behind. What were we to do? The two Biharis thought a lot about this. Treating my mother as the sister of their superior officer, they gave us this advice: 'It has not been possible to contact your relations and we also are leaving. As you have some relations in Pakistan, it would be better for you to go there and save yourselves. Leave future considerations for later. If we two are not here, if we leave, you will not be able to live in this Bihari colony. Nobody will allow you to stay here. You will be finished off, killed. The people here are already saying that they have this or that relation at this or that place. If they do not find them, they will avenge themselves upon you. It is better if you also leave.' As my mother had a brother and sister in Karachi, she thought that it would be better to go to Karachi. She would think about the future later. My aunt also gave the same advice, 'Your brother is there. We also are there. Let us all go there now.' Then all of us left for Karachi."

Karachi

"We had two *mamas* (maternal uncles) and two *khalas* (maternal aunts) and their husbands in Karachi and Islamabad. One *mama* was posted in Karachi. The younger *khala* was staying in Karachi and studying at a medical college. One *khalu* was working at the Ministry of Industries, and *khala* was a teacher at a Government school. My *mejo mama*'s father-in-law came from Karachi. We had close communication with all of them. We had prior contact with many places and languages and cultures of Pakistan. I had spent several years as a child in Pakistan."

"On coming to Karachi, we started residing at the officer's mess of the *mama* who worked at the Telephone and Telegraph Department. As our *mama* was still a bachelor, he was residing in the mess. It was very difficult for all of us to stay in only one room of the mess, so *mama* applied for a house and managed to get an allocation. After staying there for six months, we went over to our *khala* in Islamabad."

"On coming to Karachi, *mami* went to her parents' place. Later on, she got a house constructed on a piece of land, which had been purchased by my uncle, with the insurance money she received. She rented out two rooms, and lived there with her daughters."

Islamabad (November 1971 – October 1972)

"A job was arranged for my mother at the Bangali-medium school in Islamabad, where her sister had been teaching for some time. *Khalu* and a Bangali gentleman in the Ministry of Education helped her greatly in getting the job. As a post was vacant and my mother had a B.A., B.Ed. degree and experience in teaching, it was relatively easy for her to get the job. We moved to Islamabad in November 1971. We were admitted to an English medium school, as we didn't know how long we had to stay there. We stayed at our *khala*'s house in Islamabad until October 1972.

"Out of fear, we had decided not to say anything to any outsider during our stay at Islamabad about our father's murder by Pakistani soldiers or about the situation which had made us go to Pakistan. The

Pakistanis were killing us, they had killed our father, yet, we went to Pakistan for shelter. We were Bangalis there. We sought no help from the military administration, though father had belonged to the army. We knew that we wouldn't be living there. We would not identify ourselves as people of that country. We would identify ourselves as Bangali. We had declared our option for going to Bangladesh."

Efforts at Homecoming

"In the meantime, we made efforts to contact people in Bangladesh. We managed to send a letter to Dhaka about two or three months after reaching Karachi. Our relatives in our maternal grandfather's house in Mymensingh were thus able to know about the tragedy that had befallen us. But it was not possible at that time to contact our paternal grandfather. We did not even know before returning to Bangladesh that the uncle who had been with us in Chittagong was alive. Our aunt's parents had been living in Chittagong. For some reason, uncle and aunt could not send news to our maternal grandfather's house in Mymensingh. We weren't able to return to Bangladesh for quite some time. First of all, we didn't have the money. Moreover, there was no direct air or other transport between Pakistan and Bangladesh at that time, nor was travel easy or safe. Everything was very cumbersome. We had found some financial stability because my mother had got a job at a government school. There was no pressure to return to Bangladesh. In spite of that, we had to come back. For, after Bangladesh became independent, the Government of Pakistan informed the Bangali employees that anyone wishing to go back to Bangladesh could do so. Jobs of those who expressed a desire to go back to Bangladesh were terminated by the Pakistan Government. My mother and our uncles and aunts were among those who opted for Bangladesh. A financial crisis started for us because they lost their jobs."

Escape from Karachi

"We had to come back to our *mama*'s house in Karachi in November 1972 as *mama* had contacted people who were helping Bangalis cross the border on payment. Many Bangalis were at that time secretly crossing the Afghan border and reaching Bangladesh through India. After finishing all the arrangements with some such party, *mama* sent information to us. As a result, all of us – *khalu*, two *khala*s, two *mama*s and the four of us – got together in Karachi, and crossed the Afghan border by truck on November 11 and 12. Apart from a few problems, mainly because of the manner of our escape, we had no major difficulties.

"On coming to Afghanistan, we had to stay in Kabul for 8 to 10 days. We contacted the Indian Embassy, which made arrangements for a special plane and food and accommodation in a hotel. I do not remember if we had to spend money for all these arrangements. But we received full cooperation from the Indian authorities. We reached Calcutta at noon the day after we left Kabul. We had to make a short stopover in Delhi in the morning. The Indian authorities did not bother about us once we reached Calcutta. From there, we would have to reach our own country at our own expense and responsibility. We had no money with us. What little we had was sufficient for only one person's plane fare. One ticket was purchased and *mama* left for Dhaka. The rest of us stayed in a hotel. After *mama* sent us tickets and money, we all came back to our homeland some time in mid-November."

Homecoming: Life in Dhaka

"We went straight to Mymensingh on coming to Dhaka. In the meantime, *mama* rented a house in Dhaka. We had to start afresh on coming to Dhaka after a short stay in Mymensingh. Everyone coming back from Pakistan had to report to the Bangladesh Government. Our *mama* who had been working in the T&T Department joined his office; *khalu* joined the Ministry of Education, *khala* and my mother took up teaching; and the others joined whatever government post they had held in the past. Mother joined Bangla Bazar School. On transfer from there, she joined Sher-e-Bangla School in 1978 and Tejgaon Boys School in 1983.

"On coming to Dhaka, we lived with *mama*. We three sisters then got admitted to Shaheed Anwar Cantonment School. When *mama* got married in 1973, my mother thought that it would no longer be wise to stay with him and that we should move away before the relationship grew strained. In the meantime, papers had been submitted to the Army for my father's pension, as we were the family of a martyr. Contact was made with the Cantonment Army Welfare

Board, informing them that we had no place to stay. We sought all kinds of help and assistance. In this matter also, *mama* helped by giving time and labour and by doing the necessary lobbying. Nothing would have been possible at that time without *mama*'s help."

Dhaka Cantonment

"A house was allotted to us in November 1973 after much persuasion, lobbying, and labour. It was a single-unit house but we had to share it with another family. That was good enough and we took possession of it. Later on, our two families divided the house into two parts according to our mutual convenience, so that there was no misunderstanding. We stayed in that house uptil 1985. When, in 1983, the DOHS (Defence Officers Housing Society) started allotting plots for army personnel, mother, as the wife of a martyr, applied for one. A two and a half katha plot was allotted to her at DOHS. Mother then took a loan from the BHBFC (Bangladesh House Building Finance Corporation), and got this one-storeyed house constructed. We then moved here. I am living in this house now. My marriage took place at that time. I then went to Bhaluka, in Netrokona district, where I had been posted. But I continue to have a close relationship with my family."

Help and Assistance

"We got retirement benefits, children's allowance, ration, medical allowance and a house allotment from my father's office. Besides this, we were able to buy land at Mohakhali. The pension corresponded to the salary my father had drawn, and, depending on the decision of the Pay Commission, it increased from time to time. As long as my mother was alive, she received it. The children's allowance continued for 21 years. At the beginning it was perhaps Tk. 100 per child. Later on, it increased to Tk. 150.

"In addition, we got the assistance of all our relations and particularly that of our maternal uncles, and that is worth special mention. Our maternal aunts also helped us in all the ways they could."

Financial Loss

"To tell the truth, we have never assessed what we lost. We did not think in terms of financial loss. We came out in the clothes we were wearing at the command of the Pakistan army. Everything was looted after we left. The furniture in the house was rented from the Army mess. Army officers generally do not make any furniture of their own, because they are transfered. We perhaps had, as ornaments, 8-10 *tola*s of gold. They looted things like watches, a refrigerator, a tape recorder, crockery and utensils, etc. – things they could carry easily. They destroyed the rest. There was not a large amount of money in the house, a few thousand takas perhaps."

"We did not get any share of our paternal grandfather's property in the village which my father and uncle should have inherited. My paternal grandfather lived in one part of the property which had been bought in Mymensingh in 1968 in the names of both my father and grandfather. Shortly before his death, grandfather gave this property to my two sisters and I."

"We managed somehow on what we had. I think our father's pension, mother's job, the assistance given by the Army Welfare and the scholarships all of us received helped us. Of course, we were not able to wear fine clothes or do what we wanted but we did not think in this way. If we had, then the problem would have been amplified. But all of us accepted life as it was. Our only expenses were on education. All of us lived on very little. Perhaps I think that I didn't suffer much because I have crossed that phase. It may just be that."

"But, though we did not suffer economic hardships, we had to face another kind of struggle. Initially it was a matter of survival, then of economic management. We depended considerably on our maternal uncles and aunts. Though our mother got a job, we stayed at our aunt's house. And, finally, there was the struggle to live independently."

Social Security

"We did not face any problems though we were four women alone. This was because we lived in the cantonment area where there was security. The area was near the market. Our neighbours were very good to us. That is how we had social security."

Who was Responsible?

"Circumstances were responsible for what happened to so dear a person as our father, so near a relation as our *mama*, and our losing everything. If I must lay the blame somewhere, I will say it was politics. Is Pakistan alone to be blamed for everything? No, I don't think so. Ordinary people do not know how the people in power played chess. Politics is responsible for what happened. No single person can be blamed. Why should I consider all Pakistanis bad? We were saved by two Biharis. I cannot say that all Biharis are bad. The troops received their orders from above. And the upper echelons are full of politics. I was friendly with some Urdu-speaking girls at the Islamabad Model School where we studied. They would ask me, 'What has happened? Why do Bangalis want to secede?' The girls of class nine or ten could not understand why Bangalis were separate. Or, why there was war between Bangladesh and Pakistan. Or, what barriers there were. They had many questions."

"We had to conceal what had happened to us. We were forbidden by our aunts from revealing under what circumstances we had gone to Pakistan. We had to keep quiet so that our aunts did not feel insecure. Our aunts were working. Our *khalu* was also working. That is why we had to live like that. We never said, 'You are Pakistanis. You have killed my father. You have killed my uncle. Even then I have come here. I am a Bangali and I am living very normally in Pakistan.' That's how it was."

Experiences of Two Indigenous Women

Chittagong Hill Tracts (CHT)

Amena Mohsin

Much confusion and controversy surrounds the role of the Hill people of Chittagong Hill Tract during the liberation war of Bangladesh in 1971. Raja Tridiv Roy, the Chakma chief, had openly sided with the Pakistan Government; this has resulted in the Hill people being branded as opposed to the Bangladesh cause. It is important to note that so far no academic work has dealt with the actual situation in the CHT in 1971. This is one of the main reasons for the above perception which again is to a certain extent responsible for their present predicament. In this context the present endeavour of Ain o Salish Kendra to explore the sufferings of the women victims of 1971 is important in two respects. First, it locates the role and struggle of the Hill people, more specifically the Hill women in 1971. Secondly, it puts into perspective the *actual* situation prevailing in the CHT in 1971.

The Chittagong Hill Tracts occupies a physical area of 5.093 sq. miles, constituting ten per cent of the total land area of Bangladesh. The region comprises of three districts: Rangamati, Khagrachari and Banderban. The districts comprise seven main valleys formed by the Feni, Karnafuli, Chengi, Myani, Kassalong, Sangu and Matamuhuri rivers and their tributaries and numerous hills, ravines and cliffs covered with dense vegetation that are in complete contrast to most other districts of Bangladesh, which consist mostly of alluvial lands. Geographically the CHT can be divided into two broad ecological zones: (a) hill valley, (b) agricultural plains. It is surrounded by the Indian states of Tripura on the north and Mizoram on the east, Myanmar on the south and east and Chittagong district on the east. There are thirteen ethnic groups in the CHT: Chakmas, Marmas, Tripuras,Tanchangyas, Riyangs, Khumis, Mros or Murangs, Lushais, Kukis, Kheyangs, Bunjogees, Pankhuas and Chaks. They are of Sino-

Tibetan descent belonging to the Mongolian groups. They closely resemble the people of northeast India, Myanmar and Thailand rather than the Bangali population of Bangladesh.

The first written accounts of the Hill people of Chittagong are found in the revenue documents of the Moghuls. British administrators of the region later provided a detailed account of these people. The Hill people do not have a documented history of their own, but rely mostly on their oral traditions. Using these three sources and the factors of social customs, language and facial characteristics, later scholars have attempted to document their history. The findings of this kind of historiography are of course often tentative. Nonetheless its importance should not be underrated for it provides the Hill people with a sense of history and continuity.

The CHT was incorporated into Pakistan much against the wishes of the local elite. Since the population was non-Muslim, it was felt that they would not have a place in Jinnah's two-nation theory. In view of the secular posture of the Congress, the Chakma elites approached the Congress leaders and pleaded for the merger of the CHT with the Indian Union. The three chiefs demanded the recognition of each of their circles as "native states" from the British, the Congress and the Muslim League. Later on they demanded a confederation with the Indian states of Tripura, Cooch Bihar and Khasia. The Marma chief by contrast suggested a union with Burma. The flag of India was hoisted in Rangamati, and that of Burma in Banderban on August 14, 1947. The Baluch regiment of Pakistan brought this rebellion down on August 17, 1947. The Hill people were never really incorporated within the mainstream of politics in Pakistan, which continued to be dominated by issues and confrontations between the Bangalis of East Pakistan and the West Pakistanis. The Awami League, the main party in East Pakistan, never attempted to bring the Hill people within the fold of its politics, nor were the problems of the CHT ever incorporated into the agenda of the Awami League. Thus the East West conflict essentially remained an issue of Bangalis and West Pakistanis for the Hill people. They could not in general identify themselves with the Bangali nationalist movement. In analysing the roles of the Chakma and Bohmong chiefs, the above facts need to be kept in perspective.

It is incorrect to assume that the Hill people in general had collaborated with the Pakistan army in 1971. It is evident from the accounts of the Liberation war,[1] that both Major Ziaur Rahman and Major Mir Shawkat Ali (two commanders of the Mukti Bahini) had initially taken refuge and carried out their military operations from the CHT. They had to withdraw and cross over to India because of raids by the Mizo activists who were helping the Pakistan army. They had earlier been trained by the Pakistan army in the CHT for operations against India. In fact it was the Hill people, as our report below will show, who had helped Major Zia to cross over to India.

It appears from the information provided by the interviewees that the situation in CHT was not much different (contrary to general beliefs) from the rest of the country. The persons we interviewed were in agreement that there was a general atmosphere of fear in the Khagrachari area, which was a subdivision at that time. The people in general did not participate in the war for they were never integrated with this movement. Nonetheless, supporters of the Awami League, members of the Chhatra League and the Sramik League had organised themselves and participated in the war. The Chakma interviewees pointed out that while Tripurans and Marmas were recruited into the Mukti Bahini, the Chakma boys were sent back. These youths initially hid themselves from the Pakistan army, which it was hunting for young people. However, later on being frustrated as they were not trusted by the Bangali freedom fighters either, some of them joined forces with the Bangali *Razakars*. In this context the interviewees pointed out that there were collaborators within the Bangalis as well, so why should they (Hill people) as a people suffer the stigma of collaboration.

Within the CHT the most intense war was fought in the Khagrachari subdivision. Rono Bikram Tripura, a local commander of the Mukti Bahini and presently a member of the Local District Council, had fought in this area. His name was even recommended for an award after the Liberation of Bangladesh but he did not receive it. He however told me that he did not fight for the award and he does not regard it as a matter of Bangali conspiracy, rather most of the awards were given to military personnel not civilians fighting the war. He told me that the Pakistan army suffered heavy casualties in this area as it was ideally suited for guerrilla warfare. The batch of the Mukti Bahini which fought in this area was composed mostly of local

---

[1] See *Bangladesh Swadhinota Judhho Dolil Patra* (Documents of the Bangladesh War of Independence) Vol. 9, Dhaka: Ministry of Cultural Affairs, Govt. of Bangladesh, 1982 pp.121-126.

Tripurans, a few Marmas, Bangalis and also a few Chakmas. They were familiar with the terrain and hence they could inflict heavy losses upon the Pakistan army.

During the course of the liberation war, the military along with the local collaborators used to hunt down supporters of the Awami League and its affiliated organisations. The local collaborators consisted of Bangalis as well as local Hill people. They also were on the look-out for Bangali Hindus. Rono Bikram Tripura pointed out that the Hindus were forcibly converted to Islam. The local people were issued identity cards (ID) by the authorities and they had to carry these all the time. Several Hill people told us that about 40-50 persons were killed by the military in the CHT and women were raped. These rapes were conducted in a very organised way. The military along with the local collaborators would usually surround a village and then a few of them would go into the village and rape them; the women were often gang raped. If they liked any of the girls, they used to pick them up and take them to the military camps where they were again raped by the soldiers. The Hill persons, however, refused to identify the villages or the women who were subjected to the above. It was their observation that the people had sent the young women to far-flung places and they used to hide themselves once rumours spread of the military's arrival. These women belonged to poor as well as middle-class families. The interviewers as also observed that nobody felt safe during that period. Villages were burnt, shops were looted. A few of them observed that they had heard that after the liberation the government had set up rehabilitation centres for the rape victims but to their knowledge very few women went there. The victims' families were unwilling to submit the names or speak out openly about because of societal taboos. But society had accepted them fully and they were never disrespected. Others observed that they were totally ignorant about the existence of any rehabilitation centres. This suggests that not enough information about those centres was available to the local people.

The respondents also observed that the Awami League was not very influential in the area. They observed that some of the educated youths were inspired by the ideals of the Awami League. There were some supporters of the Muslim League as well, but in general the Hill people remained oblivious of politics.

Methodology

Given the nature of the work, the investigation relied mainly on primary sources. Apart from the two main respondents, the family members and neighbours of the respondents were also interviewed. In order to get a view of the general situation prevailing in the area in 1971, about 10 to 12 other individuals were interviewed. Newspaper reports of the period and books relating to 1971 have also been scanned.

Limitations

The major limitation faced during the course of the work was the unwillingness of the people to talk. This became most evident while investigating rape cases. The woman and her family members were not only hesitant, but I could also sense a certain degree of hostility in their response. Due to the passage of time, many things have lapsed from their memories, so they contradicted each other while providing details of the events.

Contradictions were more pronounced in the narration by the individuals who were interviewed to assess the general situation of the CHT in 1971. Each account carried with it the baggage of the individual's political affiliation or inclination.

Location of Work

The study was undertaken in the Khagrachari district of the CHT, which is divided into the three districts of Rangamati, Khagrachari and Banderban. The Chakma chief, Raja Tridiv Roy of Rangamati, had collaborated with the Pakistan army; the Bohmong chief of Banderban, Aungshoi Pro, had also sided with the Pakistanis. It was only the Mong chief of Khagrachari, Mong Pru Chai Chowdhury, who had joined the liberation war of Bangladesh, so war was most intense in this area of the CHT.

Sanashri Tripura, Khagrapur, Rape Victim

Sanashri Tripura is an old lady of about 55-60 years today. She was about 30-35 years in 1971. She, however, looks much older than her age; poverty and her struggles with life have left her old and frail. She lives alone in a single-room mud hut. A single *chowki* (bed) is all she owns. Her only son, Surendra Lal Tripura (38), and youngest daughter, Renuka Tripura (26), live in the two huts adjacent to hers. She has four daughters and one son; all of whom are married. She has 20 grandchildren.

Rape constitutes an important and deliberate strategy in modern warfare. During war time most of the men go to the front, and it is the women who look after the family and also keep the world running for the children. In other words, women constitute the fabric of civil society during war time. By violating a woman, the enemy therefore attempts to break the sinews of civil society. More importantly, since women are looked upon as property and *objects* of honour (*ijjot*) of the society at large, so the violation of women in essence constitutes a violation of the honour of the society at large. There is, therefore, a deliberate attempt not only to shy away but to suppress these as far as possible. For the rape victim, however, such suppressions can be most traumatising for she has not only lost her most private and respected possession but is also unable to demand justice for the wrong done to her. In a way it amounts to punishing the victim herself. It is indeed a contradiction that while society glorifies and valorizes persons killed during the war as martyrs, rape victims who survive have to endure their sufferings in shame and silence.

It is this attempt to protect the *ijjot* of the society or clan or family that makes it so difficult to identify or even talk in detail to rape victims. Though I had been told that about 400-500 women were violated in the CHT, I was able to identify and talk to only one such victim, that too probably because she was a poor woman and had no guardian as such. Though I had informed Shakti Podo Tripura, the local Union Parishad Chairman, of my arrival and work much ahead of time and had requested him to talk to the victim about my work earlier so that she could be mentally prepared for it, I was told by Shakti Podo Tripura as he accompanied me to the woman's house that he could not talk to her earlier as he did not know how to place it to her. Shakti Podo Tripura looked very disturbed as well as embarrassed as we approached the village. It was apparent to me that he was reckoning with himself. He first spoke to her son and explained to him the purpose of my visit. Since they were speaking in the Tripuri language, I could not follow their conversation, but it was obvious from the expression on the son's face that he did not welcome me, and gave me quite suspicious looks. I almost felt like leaving the place. It was like intruding into the personal lives of these people which they had kept guarded for 25 years. I was more perturbed by the fact that it was their sheer poverty that had enabled me to have access to them. The son, however, consented to let me interview his mother. Then he and Shakti Prodo Tripura went over to the next hut where his mother lived. I was asked to wait in the yard of the son's house. After a while they came back and asked me to accompany them. This time the son did not come along, which explained how difficult it was for him to face the situation.

At first glance I took Sanashri to be around 70 years old, but later discovered that she was much younger. She looked visibly disturbed, and it was obvious that she did not want to talk. I sat beside her on the floor as she did not have anything to offer me to sit on. It was only then that she relaxed a bit and started narrating her story. She spoke in Tripuri which was translated to me by Shakti Podo Tripura. As she opened up, she looked very lost as if the things were deep down some where and she was speaking from her inner mind. The following is her narrative.

Sanashri used to live with her son and four daughters. Her husband used to do business in Tripura in 1971. He never came back from there after 1971. She could not remember the exact month of the incident. She said that it had happened during the month of *Ashar* or *Srabon.* They came in the morning, two or three Pathans (a term used by the Hill people to describe the Pakistan military). A number of Mizos were also with them. They had wanted to kill her son but he ran off; her three elder daughters also ran off. They also chased her niece Chandra Lakkhi Tripura who was staying with them. Sanashri therefore was left alone in the house along with her one-year-old daughter who was in her arms. The Pathans entered the house while the Mizos remained outside. The latter destroyed her banana and papaya trees. The Pathans did not hurt her child, but they assaulted her. At that point I asked her what kind of assault it was. She looked very disturbed and simply said that they had hurt her. It was obvious that she did not want to remember the pain and was wanting to finish the account as soon as possible. The Pathans also ate the food that was in the house. She did not have any material belongings, so they could not take anything. After that they left the house and never came back.

She had never talked of this incident to anyone. She pointed out that it had changed her life. Psychologically she was traumatised and still faints whenever she thinks of the incident. She also often has nightmares about it, but in her nightmares their faces become hazy. But she remembers them distinctly and sees them with her inner eyes. This suggests the struggle that is still going on within her. On the one hand there is an attempt to forget – the appearance of hazy faces is indicative of this – but, on the other hand, she has almost internalised that is why she sees them with her inner eyes. She suffers from insomnia as well. She pointed out that she does not want to think about it so she keeps herself busy with her work and her grandchildren. She never went to any one for consolation; rather she consoled herself by looking at her children. She knew that she had to lead a normal life for their sake. Her children were her source of strength.

She had never reported this incident. She was not aware of any rehabilitation centres or compensation. Sanashri does not hold anyone responsible for the incident, and believes that it was her bad fate that had led her into this situation. In order to emphasise this point, during the conversation she kept on pointing towards her forehead. But she appeared bitter about the fact that this had befallen her for no fault of hers. She said that she was in no way involved with the war. She had not supported the Mukti Bahini in any way. Rather, quite sadly, she posed the question how she could support them when she herself was struggling with poverty in her day-to-day life. She pointed out that at the societal level, she has had no problems. Nobody had ever asked her anything, rather the people in the neighbourhood were very sympathetic towards her. She refused to say if there were any direct eye witnesses of the incident; rather, in a most sombre way she said to me, "Today I have twenty grand children. What is the point now of talking about these things?" This, in other words, reflected not only her resignation to her fate, but also a complaint that, now that she is almost at the fag end of her life, there should be this interest in her story – a story that had remained within her for the last 26 years.

After the incident they fled to Gachbon, a village about seven miles from her own neighbourhood. They stayed there for a week and then came back. The military never came back. With these words she dismissed me. It was obvious that she was not ready to talk to me any more.

Then I talked to her son, Surendra Lal Tripura. In 1971 he was, a young boy of 13-14 years. Surendra did not want to talk to me. He merely said that the Mizos had destroyed their trees. He also said that since the war had started, he along with his three sisters had gone into hiding as there were reports of military atrocities. Only his mother and the youngest sister used to live in the house. They used to visit them from time to time. On the day of the incident, he along with his three sisters were in the house. He was beaten up by the military, but his sisters had run away. After narrating the above, he did not want to talk to me any further. I tried to talk to the victim's youngest daughter, Renuka Tripura, who lives in a nearby hut. But she also refused to talk on the ground that she was only a year-old then. I did not make any further attempt to talk to them for it was obvious that they wanted me to leave.

Then I talked to Bir Kishore Tripura who is a neighbour and the village *Karbari* (manager), but he too was quite reluctant to talk. He only said that he had heard about the incident and had not seen anything; nor had he ever made any attempts to ask her directly. The manner in which he said the last sentence to me appeared to me as a polite way of suggesting that if he, being such a close person, had not asked her such a sensitive question for the last 26 years, how could I being a stranger and an outsider ask her this.

I tried to talk to the villagers nearby but they were quite emphatic in informing me that they had never asked her anything. They informed me that Ramani Mohan Tripura was the only eye witness of the incident. He was Sanashri's neighbour, and through him people came to know about this incident. Ramani Mohan Tripura is dead now, so I could not gather any more information on the case.

Birangana Chakma (Mahajan Para, Khagrachari), Widow of Chittaranjan Chakma Karbari

Birangana lives today with her son Dr Sudhin Kumar Chakma, who is a Professor of Sociology at Khagrachari College. She was 50 years old in 1971. As I entered the sitting room, I saw the framed picture of a man in his mid-50s hanging on the wall. Birangana pointed at the picture and with a deep sigh told me that it was her husband who at the time of the incident was about 53 years. Though she looked quite disturbed, she was most willing to talk. She started off by saying that it had been so long that most of the things were fading from her memory. As she talked, she kept on sighing which revealed the pain still within her. The following is her account.

Chittaranjan Chakma was taken from his house on May 13, 1971 at around 7 pm. He was killed the next day at around 7 pm. The family holds Bindu Kumar Khisha, the then Union Parishad Chairman, responsible for the killing. At that time they used to live in the village Manikchari Mukh under Khagrachari subdivision. At the time of the incident, Birangana Chakma, their younger son Sudhin Kumar Chakma (26 years), his wife Konica Chakma (20 years), elder daughter Amita Chakma (24 years), son-in-law Kalachand Chakma (30 years) and youngest daughter Sanchita Chakma (15 years) were present in the house.

At around mid-day-between 12.00 to 1.00 pm. on the 13th, a farmer named Khurichoga Chakma came to their house. He asked Chittaranjan Chakma to report to the army camp. Chittaranjan was an Awami League worker, so, apprehending trouble, Birangana asked him to leave the house and go into hiding. But he refused. Chittaranjan was quite confused. He asked his son Sudhin for advice. Sudhin advised his father to stay back on the plea that he was a noted and elderly person of the neighbourhood; if he left, trouble might befall the villagers. More importantly, before that no other killing had taken place in the area, so they could not even apprehend the worst.

Chittaranjan Chakma could not go to the army camp because he had injured his foot. Besides, the Chengi river was in full spate so it was not possible for him to cross it at that time. At around 4 pm he saw Bindu Kumar Khisha, the Union Parishad Chairman. Bindu was returning from the market. Chittaranjan called him over and asked him for advice. Bindu advised him to report to the army camp. He further encouraged him by saying that the army was new in the area, and since Chittaranjan was a noted and elderly person of the area so most probably the army wanted to talk and get acquainted with him. Bindu further suggested to him to give his reference to the army in case of any problem. This, according to Birangana, suggested that Bindu had connections with the military. She further pointed out that Bindu had adopted a Bihari boy: Zakaria Khan, who had come to the area at the time of Ayub Khan's Basic Democracy. No one was aware of his whereabouts. Zakaria was involved in unsocial activities. He often got into arguments with Chittaranjan. The latter's sons had also wanted him out of the area. Zakaria was aware of it. Through Zakaria, Bindu had developed ties with the military. But at that time the family was not aware of these developments; rather it was rumoured that Zakaria was dead. Birangana pointed out that Bindu had always been envious of Chittaranjan. His was an affluent family. He was a member of the Union Parishad and people were expecting him to be the next Union Parishad Chairman. His elder son, Niru Kumar Chakma, was doing his Ph.D. in London at that time. The younger son had finished his Master's degree. Bindu often asked Chittaranjan why he was so keen on educating his sons; what was the point of it. But Chittaranjan or his family could never suspect or think that Bindu would do something as awful as this.

As pointed out earlier, Chittaranjan was an Awami League supporter. In fact he had helped Ziaur Rahman to cross over to India from the CHT. He had also helped Zia and the members of the Bangali armed forces hiding in CHT at that time in many other ways. While helping Zia cross over to India. Chittaranjan had seen quite a few dead bodies and he was told that one of them was Zakaria. Apart from this, the family was not involved in any other activity at the time, for the Mukti Bahini had not spread its activities in the area till then.

On the same day at around 7 pm a soldier came to their house. where they were offering their prayers to Lord Buddha. Chittaranjan and his son Sudhin were standing in the courtyard. Chittaranjan had his *huqqa* in his hand. The man asked for a glass of water. Konika, the daughter-in-law, was cooking in the kitchen. Sudhin brought the glass of water from her and gave it to the man. After drinking the water, he asked Chittaranjan to accompany him. This he did without any protest. The whole family was in a state of shock. Sanchita Chakma, the youngest daughter, had already hidden herself along with her brother-in-law in a nearby field of the sight of the military. They came back at around 9 pm. On hearing that her father had been taken away, she fainted. The family could not eat anything that night. They believed that the army would torture Chittaranjan and then leave him. Sudhin Kumar left the house and went into hiding. Sanchita and Konika also left and went off to a relative's house. Birangana was adamant and stayed back alone. She felt that it was her husband's house and she had to take care of it and protect it for her children.

The Chengi river was full, so the military took Chittaranjan by a boat to the nearby Maischari market. There he was beaten up, then he was taken to Mahalchari. Before being taken to Mahalchari, Chittaranjan had asked the soldiers to give him a moment as he wanted to talk to a shopkeeper. The soldier allowed him to do so. Chittaranjan went over to Minu Barua, a local shopkeeper, and told him that he was going and would not come back again. He requested Minu to go over to his house and ask his children to leave the place, else the same fate would befall them. Minu came to their house on Friday morning at around 10 or 11 am. and informed them of the incident. He also gave them Chittaranjan's message. Sanchita and Konica had come back to the house in the morning but left again for Kamaichari to live in Birangana's brother's house. On Friday morning, Bindu's eldest son, Kanak Baran Khisha, came to their house and requested Birangana to allow him to take Sanchita and Konica along with him to their house, as Chittaranjan's house was no longer safe. But Birangana avoided him tactfully and asked him to come in the evening for in the day time the military might see Sanchita and Konica leaving the house. She also said to him that other staff could also see them and report to the army. Kanak did not argue with her but he did come back again.

Chittaranjan was killed on Friday evening at around 7 pm. at Tailantangya of Mahalchari thana, Khagrachari subdivision. The news was given to Birangana by Bindu Kumar on Saturday. He came to their house in the morning and, in a very excited voice, told Birangana that the work had been finished. He sat cross-legged and narrated to her the killing. He said that Chittaranjan was shot three times. First they forced him to open his mouth and shot him in the tongue. They shouted at him, asking him why he was not talking. Then they taunted him, saying that he had hidden a lot of information in his stomach. Saying this, they shot him twice in the stomach. Bindu then warned Birangana not to disclose the news of her husband's death to anyone. He also forbade her to observe any death rituals; else he warned that the same fate would befall the rest of the family. The family never got the dead body; nor do they know where the body was buried or cremated.

Birangana remembered out that she was totally shaken. She could not eat anything for four days. She survived only on water. She had to bear it alone. Her family was away for a month, but she carried on.

Her husband was the elder of the village; he was always there to support others. Had this incident occurred in some other family, they would have supported them but with the father figure of the community gone, there was no one to support or console her. She also felt at that time that life would never become normal for her. She used to feel that there would be a repetition of the same and she would again have to go through the same pain. She was concerned about her children and was scared that all their property would be taken away. There were lots of books in the house. These belonged to her sons. She took special care of them. It was almost like an attempt on the part of a mother to protect her children who were not with her at that moment. She was scared, but she knew that she had to be there for her children so she survived.

Since then she feels that she has changed as a human being. Though she does not dream a lot, she feels that she has lost her capacity to concentrate on things. At times she finds it difficult to control her emotions. At times she suffers from insomnia as well. She also becomes agitated easily, but Birangana feels that this might also be due to her blood pressure. She does not evade her daily chores or responsibilities, but at times feels that she has no future and has nothing to look forward to. She tries to avoid thinking of the incident and searches for people to talk to and forget about it. She does not bear any guilty feeling nor does she feel ashamed or responsible for the fact that her husband was taken away in front of her. She feels that it was fated to be so. She is still suspicious of outsiders and trusts only her own family members. She consoles herself by looking at other people who had also suffered. She feels that her life has changed totally after her husband's death. She does not like staying in the city with her son. She pointed out that she has no friends there, while in the village she had her own house, garden and poultry to look after. With the loss of her husband, she feels that she has lost her guardian. Her husband was a very intelligent person and could take good care of the property. With his death, the family also lost its previous affluence and position.

Birangana holds Bindu responsible for the killing. But she feels that he is suffering for his misdeeds. She pointed out that two of Bindu's sons have died unnaturally. The elder son was killed due to a family feud; his body was put in a sack and then thrown into the river. His second son was also killed. His grandson is also missing.

Birangana still feels the anger within her and said that she could not and would not ever forgive Bindu. At times she sees him but she always avoids him. Bindu also avoids her and her family members.

Sanchita Chakma, who was a young girl of 15 or 16 at that time, confirmed her mother's narration. She pointed out that her mother had asked her father to leave as he was a supporter of the Awami League. But her father had refused. He was a religious and pious person. He used to say that he had not sinned so why should anyone kill him. She distinctly recalled the day and said that in the morning she had taken her father to the Chengi river to give him a clean bath as he had hurt his foot. She saw a few men in *khaki* uniforms roaming around. She had told her father that she was scared. In a choked voice she told me that she has lost her mental strength after her father's death. She did not see her father being taken away as she had gone into hiding in a nearby field as soon as she saw the military personnel. Before she fled she heard her mother crying out *Mago* (o, mother). She learnt about it after her return to the house at 9 pm. She could not recall who had given her the news for she had fainted as soon as she learnt about it. After regaining consciousness, she and her sister-in-law left the house again and spent the night with a neighbour. All of them went out, only her mother stayed back. The next morning she left with her sister-in-law for Kamalchari and stayed there for a month in her uncle's house. She learnt about her father's death in Kamalchari. It was the most agonising and painful period for her. She prayed to God for peace. She was worried about her mother who had to bear it all alone. She had thought that life would never become normal again. She used to dream about her father a lot, but then she prayed for the peace of his soul. Since then she does not dream much. She believes that the family was able to survive because of prayers and trust in God and not because of any moral and material support from outsiders. Sanchita holds Bindu responsible for the death of her father. She was emphatic in saying that she resents and hates Bindu and his family members. She ended by saying that she wants to ask Bindu the truth as to why he had done this to her father. As she said the last few sentences, her voice and face changed and one could clearly see the hatred and hurt still alive in her.

Konica Chakma, the daughter-in-law, was a young bride of 20 years then. She was married in February. At the time of the incident, she was cooking dinner. She saw a soldier entering their courtyard and talking to her father-in-law and husband. After a while her husband, Sudhin K. Chakma, came in and asked her for a glass of water for the man. Then she saw that her father-in-law was being taken away by the soldier. They did not have to use any force. He just walked out with him. Konica pointed out that it was a most dreadful night. The family did not eat anything. She and her sister-in-law left the house and stayed with the neighbours. The next morning they returned only to leave for Kamalchari. Her husband had also left the house the night before. He had gone to Rangamati to meet Raja Tridiv Roy to find out about his father. He got in touch with Konica at Kamalchari after a month. All through he had been in hiding and was not aware of his father's death as he had no contact with the family. Konica feels that her husband has suffered a lot. He was shattered by the death of his father and holds himself responsible for the fate of his father. But she pointed out that it was to be so and no one can be blamed for it. It was the first act of killing by the military in the area, so no one could have apprehended the worst. She feels that it was her mother-in-law's moral strength and the goodness of her father-in-law that enabled them to recover and have a normal life once more.

Sudhin K. Chakma looked very disturbed as I approached him, though he made it very clear that he wanted to talk. In a grieving tone he said that these things ought to be recorded and published. The people of Bangladesh must be made aware of the sufferings and sacrifices of the Hill people as they are being labelled today as collaborators of the Pakistan army in 1971. He said that they were always very conscious politically and were supporters of the Awami League. His father had accompanied Ziaur Rahman at Mahachari and had helped him and many others to cross over. He thinks that this was reported to the army by Bindu through Zakaria. Sudhin was standing with his father when the soldiers entered their courtyard. There were three soldiers but only one had come inside. He asked Sudhin what he did, then asked for a glass of water. Then he asked his father to accompany him. This Chittaranjan did without any question or protest. He was taken to the market by boat. Sudhin was scared, so he ran away. He did not elaborate as to where he remained in hiding, and I did not insist upon it either for his face showed or immense struggle within himself. It was clear to me that he was finding it painful to relive those days. With a lost look he said that he could never believe that his father would be killed. At worst he had anticipated that they might torture him physically for a while, but then he would be set free. After ten to twelve days in hiding, he along with one of his maternal uncles had gone to see Raja Tridiv Roy to find out about his father. Tridiv Roy offered him a cigarette. This came to him as a surprise, for elders do not normally offer cigarettes to younger persons in our society. But this scared him as well for he instinctively felt that things had gone wrong and the Raja was trying to console him. Then his worst fears were confirmed when the Raja, though promising to try the best for him, consoled him by saying that after all our parents do not always remain here with us.

Sudhin holds himself responsible for the death of his father. With much sadness he told me that his father depended on him. He had finished his Master's degree and his father looked upon him for advice since his elder brother, Niru Kumar Chakma, was in England at the time. His father had asked him in the morning as to what he should do after he was informed by Khurichoga Chakma the the army had asked him to report. It was Sudhin who had asked him to stay back. Sudhin regrets his decision today and feels guilty about it. He believes that it was this wrong advice on his part that led to his father's death.

Sudhin also feels guilty about the fact that his mother had to bear her suffering alone. He was away for six months. During this period his mother stayed alone and also took care of their household. She did not have enough money with her and was very hard up. When asked if the neighbours helped her during this period, he said that theirs was the most well-known family in the area. Had this happened to others, they would have gone forward. He like other members of his family said that there was no one to support or console his mother or the family. They bore it alone with their faith in God. The family came back after six months. Financially they were quite hard up. At that time Zakaria came to visit him once. He offered him a bundle of five- and ten-taka notes. But Sudhin refused the money and asked him who had killed his father. Zakaria evaded a direct answer and said that the pig's son who had done this would also meet the same fate. He carried a rifle with him.

Sudhin said that since 1971 he had dreamt about his father only once. He said that, according to their religious beliefs, Buddhists dream of the dead only when their souls are not at peace. Since his father had died for a noble cause, his soul must be at peace. That is why he does not dream about his father. In an emotion-choked voice, Sudhin told me that he missed his father very much and always talked about him. He regreted the fact that he could not see his dead body and perform the death rituals. He felt strongly that he had failed in his duties as a son. He also regrets that his father was not there to see the status and affluence of his sons. Sudhin believes that it was a premature death.

Sudhin dislikes Bindu K. Khisha. Sudhin also pointed out that along with his father two other persons – Gorango Mohan Dewan and Shobbochashi Mahajan Chakma – were also killed by the Pakistan army. These were the only killings in the Maischari area. Sudhin further pointed out that Bindu had his hand in the other two killings as well. After the liberation of Bangladesh, he filed a case against Bindu in the Chittagong Sub-judge Court. Bindu was found guilty and was subjected to imprisonment for the three killings. He could not recall correctly how long Bindu had been in jail. It could have been four to seven years. But he was released after the general amnesty in 1974.

After the liberation of Bangladesh, Birangana Chakma received Tk. 2000 from the government.[2] Sudhin also received Tk. 2000 each for the other two families. Sudhin pointed out that he had never wanted nor does he now want any material compensation for his family. All he wants is some kind of recognition for the people who had been martyred in 1971. In this context he pointed out that the then Awami League Secretary of the area and the DC, Mr. Sharif, had visited the Maischari High School after liberation and had promised that a Shaheed Minar (martyrs' memorial) would be built in the area to commemorate the three martyrs but it never materialised. As he spoke the final words, I could see the bitterness along with his sadness at his father's premature death – a death that has remained unrecognised so far.

In order to verify the authenticity of the incident, I then talked to a few people in Khagrachari. Notable among them was Ananta Bihari Khisha – a retired Head Master and social worker of the area. He along with the others attested that Bindu Kumar Khisha was involved

---

2 This sum was given to women victim's of the war.

in the killing of Chittaranjan Chakma. They further maintained that it was due to family rivalry that Bindu had conspired against Chittaranjan. The latter had educated his sons well, he himself was a very intelligent person and it was widely speculated that he was going to be the next Union Parishad Chairman.

Bindu Kumar Khisha, however, denied the accusations. He was quite willing to talk about this matter, as, according to him, he wanted the truth to be revealed. The following is his account. The activities of the Pakistan army had made life insecure in the Maischari Union. A woman had been raped in the Bodanala village of the same Union. He therefore was planning to call a meeting in order to discuss these matters and then go over to Rangamati to inform Raja Tridiv Roy of the developments in the area so that he could take it up with the military authorities. For this purpose he had sent Mia Ram Chakma, the Union Parishad peon, to Chittaranjan's house in the morning. Mia Ram came back with the news that Chittaranjan had hurt his foot so he could not come. Then he sent another person – he could not recall the name. He also came back with the same news. Then Bindu himself went to see Chittaranjan. He talked to him for a while, mainly about the activities of the Pakistan army. Before he left, he wished Chittaranjan an early recovery and also told him that he would have to go to Rangamati to discuss the general situation prevailing in the area with Tridiv Roy.

The same evening he went to his fields near the market place. Then he went to the market. There he came across the Pakistan military. He saw that the soldiers under the command of Captain Akbar had lined up the shopkeepers. The Hindu and Muslim shopkeepers were standing separately. Bindu had heard earlier that Captain Akbar was a very short-tempered and bad person. He harmed people wherever he went. Captain Akbar called Bindu and asked him to sit beside him. Captain Akbar was shouting at the Hindu shopkeepers. He asked them to become Muslims or face death. Afraid of their lives the Hindu shopkeepers agreed to do so. Bindu was quite scared because he was aware of Akbar's activities. The latter was not letting him go. The Muslim shopkeepers then pleaded on his behalf that he was the Union Parishad Chairman and had done much good work for the area, so he should be allowed to go. Captain Akbar then allowed him to leave.

Bindu had bad premonitions, so, while coming back, he had sent Shwalendu Bhushan Chakma to Chittaranjan's house, asking him not to stay in the house. But Shwalendu came back with the news that Chittaranjan had already been taken away by the army. On hearing this, Bindu went to Chittaranjan's house and told the other members of the family not to stay in the house for he was apprehensive that the army might come again. Bindu then decided to go to the market place where he had met the military personnel to inquire about Chittaranjan. By then it had already become very dark and other people of the area forbade him to go, so he changed his mind.

Bindu spoke with Balaram Master, Chittaranjan, brother-in-law. They had all thought that the military would release him after some physical torture. Then they had thought that they would ask people on the street to find out if they had seen where Chittaranjan had been taken. After three days of the incident, Bindu went to Balaram's house to find out about Chittaranjan. There he got the news from Balaram that Chittaranjan had been killed. Balaram learnt about it from Hemendra Lal Talukdar, who was a private tutor in Shangrachari. On inquiring about the whereabouts of the dead body, Bindu was told that the family had not asked for it as they were scared.

Bindu also pointed out that two years after the incident, while he was returning home by a small boat from Khagrachari, the boatman on recognising him had asked if some *karbari* was taken away from their area (Maischari) by the Pakistan army. Bindu got curious at his question and asked him why he was inquiring about it. Then the boatman told him that he was a sweeper in the Pakistani army camp at Mahalchari. One day he saw three Hill person whom he described. His description convinced Bindu that he was talking of Chittaranjan and the two other persons whom the army had taken along with him. The Pakistani military men were having tea and snacks. After he had finished sweeping, they asked him to give tea and biscuits to the Hill men, which he did accordingly. But the three of them were very quiet and did not touch anything. Seeing this they told them in Urdu to have the tea, but they did not respond. Then the soldiers asked the boatman to tell them in their language to have tea and speak out if they had anything to say. Still, they kept quiet. After that the boatman left and never saw or heard of them again.

According to Bindu, he was sure that the boatman was talking about Chittaranjan. He further maintained that it was Captain Akbar who was in charge of the Mahalchari camp. Since Chittaranjan had not opened his mouth, despite repeated requests by the military, he was killed. Bindu further maintained that Zakaria must have complained to the military about him for Chittaranjan often scolded him and wanted him out of the area. He must have informed the military about Chittaranjan. Bindu denied that Zakaria was his adopted son. He maintained that no one was aware of his whereabouts. He just used to call him *Baba* – a name used for any elderly person out of respect. Bindu believed that had Chittaranjan opened his mouth and talked with the army properly, his life could have been spared.

Bindu pointed out that Chittaranjan's family was jealous of him that was why they accused him. He also pointed out that he was in jail for two years as Sudhin Kumar Chakma had filed a case against him in the Chittagong Sub Judge Court, accusing him of the murder of his father. But he was found not guilty. After his release Sudhin had again wanted to appeal. But he could not do so due to some legal barriers. Bindu further maintained that he felt sad that Chittaranjan's family had misunderstood him whereas he had always wished them well.

Conclusion

Several important conclusions can be drawn from the above two cases. At the general level it is evident that women played a very crucial role in the war of 1971. They kept the fabric of civil society alive; and it was essentially the morale and support of the civil society that kept the war going for the freedom fighters. It is further evident that women suffered immeasurably during the course of the war and later as well. But so far their sufferings and sacrifices have remained unrecognised. War is generally regarded as masculine affair. Any objective and meaningful history of the liberation war has to take into cognisance this important factor. The study also revealed the contradictions and gender bias of our society. Women victims primarily fell into two categories: either the male member/s of the family had been killed/abducted or the female member herself had been physically tortured or raped. Whereas there was an eagerness and to a certain extent willingness to bring into the fore the cases of male sufferings/losses, there was a clear reluctance to reveal and even attempts to suppress the cases of female violations. This not only is a suppression of violence committed against women during war-time, but is in a way exonerating the enemy – the perpetuator – of the crime. More importantly it raises fundamental questions about the values and morés of the society that valorizes sacrifices in terms of death, but not sacrifices of women's honour, supposedly their most precious possession.

At a more specific level, it is evident that the situation in the CHT was not different from any other part of East Bengal. The people suffered and sacrificed (knowingly or unknowingly) for the cause of Bangladesh. It is important to take into account the war-time situation in the CHT for two important reasons. Firstly, it would destroy the myth that the Hill people had in general collaborated with the Pakistan army. It had been pointed out earlier that the CHT had remained alienated from the mainstream politics of Pakistan. The Awami League had never made any attempt to incorporate them within its struggle. It was essentially a Bangali nationalist movement. In this context, their sufferings acquired a more important dimension, for they were caught in a struggle, which had little significance for them in 1971. Secondly, this correction is necessary in the context of today's politics in Bangladesh. It would help to put the issues in proper perspective. This again is necessary for an objective and meaningful history of 1971.

Khulna and Satkhira

Introduction

Suraiya Begum

In 1971 Satkhira formed part of Khulna district. In Satkhira, as well as in Kolaroa, Tala, Devata, Asashuni, Kaliganj and Shyamnagar, and other towns in Khulna district, there was an active resistance during the Liberation War. Immediately after the postponement of the scheduled session of the National Assembly on March 1, 1971, a procession was brought out in protest. When the procession reached Chapra Lodge, shots were fired and a person named Abdur Razzak was killed on the spot.

As soon as the news of the killing by the Pakistani troops on the night of March 25 reached Satkhira, people started to organise themselves. A "Liberation War Committee" was formed under the leadership of the Member-elect of the National Assembly, Mr. Abdul Gafur. After this the freedom fighters continued their resistance in Satkhira, as in other areas of the country.[1] On April 21, the freedom fighters attempted to block the forward march of the Pakistan army. However, the Pakistan army shelled the area and killed a large number of civilians and occupied Satkhira. Subsequently, the Pakistan army with the help of their collaborators started a reign of terror. On August 24, the *razakars* (collaborators) conducted a raid on a team of 20-25 freedom fighters who were moving by boat in the Budh Hata area under the Ashashuni Police Station. The *razakars* killed two freedom fighters and took twelve into custody. On November 19, the Kaliganj Police Station area was liberated by the freedom fighters who forced the Pakistani soldiers, the *razakars* and members of the Peace Committee to flee. After Kaliganj was liberated, the acting Interior Minister of the Bangladesh Government, Mr. A.H.M. Kamruzzaman, visited the area.[2]

While the freedom fighters were putting up a strong fight against the Pakistani soldiers here, there was a terrible holocaust in Satkhira

---

1 Abu Md Delwar Hossain ed., *Muktijuddher Anchalik Itihash*, Dhaka: Sahitya Prakash, 170.

2 Rabindranath Tribedi, *Ekatturer Dosh Mash*, Dhaka: Kakoli Publishers, 1997, 158, 375, 507.

town. On April 20, around 2,000 people from Jessore, Khulna, and Chuknagar gathered in the Government High School in Satkhira. They had hoped to cross the border, but darkness had fallen before they could do so. They took shelter for the night in a school building, thinking that they would cross over to India the next day. But the Pakistani soldiers surrounded the school. They set up their camp on the ground floor, moving everyone to the first floor so that no one could escape. Next morning everyone, men, women and children, young and old, were lined up and shot. A large pit was dug in the school backyard and their bodies dumped into it. The Pakistani soldiers stayed in that camp up to December 7. After that they retreated.

The Bhomra border with India was only 14 kilometres away from this site. On the other side of the border was Bashirhat. During the liberation struggle, the people of this area, unable to bear the oppression of the Pakistani soldiers and in fear of their lives, had assembled there to cross the border. Freedom and life were only 14 kilometres away but the Pakistani soldiers deprived some 2,000 persons of this chance. After independence the mass grave at the back of the school was dug up and numerous human skulls and bones were found. Since then this place has turned into a ditch.[3] When we visited the place, the ditch was full of water. The reflection of the two-storeyed school building in the water was a mute witness to the happenings of 1971. The whole area during those nine months had been like a ghost town, practically devoid of any human habitation.

Similar incidents took place in Jhaudanga Market and Alipur Market nearby. People from various places used to be brought to Jhaudanga and killed. Repression and torture by the Pakistani forces lasted from March to December 1971.

This chapter includes four case studies of women who were victims of the barbarity of the Pakistani forces. Begum Rokeya Ahmed was widowed. Zulekha too was widowed, but, like Raisun and Firdousi Priyobhasini, she was also raped. Firdousi Priyobhasini's story of how she was abused took place in Khalishpur, an industrial town near Khulna city.

---

3 Interview with Kalyan Banerji, district correspondent, *Bhorer Kagoj*.

Begum Rokeya Ahmed

Endless Days of Grief

Suraiya Begum

I met Begum Rokeya Ahmed through Kalyan Banerjee, the district correspondent of the daily *Bhorer Kagoj*. I had written a letter to Kalyan Banerjee, requesting him for information about those who had been tortured by Pakistani soldiers in Satkhira district. We had written similar letters to thirty-one persons in Bangladesh. Only a few replied, one of them being Kalyan Banerjee. He replied promptly and included photographs and names of four women who had suffered during that time. On receiving his letter, I went to Satkhira in October 1997. On October 17, Kalyan Banerjee took us to Rokeya Ahmed's house. He stayed with us while we talked with her. Rokeya Ahmed was living in a two-storeyed house near the court. It was about eleven in the morning when we reached her place where some construction work was going on. We went up to the first floor where she was staying. The ground floor had been rented.

Rokeya Ahmed has three sons. The eldest is Kazi A.K.M. Rownaq, who is married. We sat and talked in the small first-floor drawing room. In a corner of the drawing room there was a large portrait of Kazi Masroor Ahmed, Rokeya Ahmed's late husband. He had been brutally murdered by the Pakistani soldiers in 1971. Although he was a lawyer by profession, he was known as 'Captain Kazi.' We introduced ourselves to Begum Rokeya Ahmed and started the conversation. She narrated her tragic experiences, often breaking down in tears. It was painful for her to continue talking. The most agonising part of the interview was that Begum Rokeya Ahmed was made to relive every painful moment, opening wounds that had healed. Whatever was possible for us to gather through this process we have reproduced here in the narratives of Rokeya Ahmed and her son Rownaq.

Rokeya Ahmed was about fifty. She spoke first and spoke slowly. Her face revealed her agony as she described what had happened in 1971. She looked completely devastated but she continued to talk about those days.

"My husband's name was Kazi Mohammad Masroor Ahmed. He was a lawyer and was known as Captain Kazi. He was an active worker of the Awami League. During the 1964 riot in India, we left Bashirhat and migrated to Satkhira. Even now most of our relatives live in Bashirhat. When the Pakistani army cracked down upon the populace on March 25, 1971, he went to India to collect arms and to organise a resistance. The Khan [Pakistani] forces entered Satkhira area on April 20. My husband had gone to India about two or three weeks before that. In India he met Mr. Ajoy Mukherjee and Mr. Jyoti Basu. Someone had taken a photograph of this meeting which somehow fell into the hands of the Khan forces. They produced this as evidence against him. We did not know about all this. He had gone to India because someone had told him that after the materials [for preparing weapons of resistance] had arrived here, he should go to India. Accordingly, he went. He came back from India and asked us to leave the place. He told me that since all the people in this area had left, I too should leave along with the children. He asked me to go to India but I refused. My parental home was in Bashirhat in India and his in Barasat. He was asking me to go to my father's home, but had no intention of making any move himself. I kept refusing to go without him but he forced me to leave the place. He was adamant about sending me away, on the plea that otherwise he would be endangered. He said that since he was a busy man and the house was full of things, he could not afford to leave it empty. When I insisted that he should leave the place, he assured me that he would follow me soon. He further cautioned me that I should follow whatever advice was given to me by a gentleman who was going to accompany us. As I could not make him change his mind, I started crying and repeated that I would not go. He argued that while he could overcome physical obstacles, by jumping over walls and the like, I would not be able to do so and that would endanger him as well. And so it was better that the children and I leave. He was politically active; even the young children of the area were very conscious about the Liberation War. I did not understand then that what my husband was doing would shatter our lives."

"I left for my father's house in Bashirhat. At that time I had three sons and a daughter. The eldest son was due to sit for the Matriculation examination, but could not. I took my children and left. My younger brother, who had come from India, was then living with me. He too was a candidate for the Matriculation examination. He stayed behind with my husband. The housemaid stayed on to look after the house."

"Sixteen or seventeen days after our departure that terrible incident took place. The Khan forces entered Satkhira on April 20. They killed my husband the next day. I heard about it from others. I cannot say how I felt when I heard what had happened to him. Even today I cannot describe it, and I do not know what to do. Even now when I hear about this, I have the same feeling, and my heart starts thumping. If any one brings up the subject, I cannot bear it. I just leave the place."

At this stage Rokeya Ahmed broke down in tears. I was feeling helpless and guilty and kept quiet, giving her time to recover. The tape recorder spun silently. When she regained control of herself, she resumed, "After I got the information, I was practically speechless for three months. My brother and my husband had both left this mortal world at the same time." She stopped again and started sobbing. It was clear that she had not recovered from her grief. At this stage her eldest son Rownaq helped her to make her narrative clearer. Rokeya Ahmed kept repeating that since she was not there at the time of the occurrence, her narration was based on whatever she had heard on her return.

"My husband, my younger brother and the housemaid were staying in this house when the Khan forces entered along the road that passes by the Registry Office. Earlier, on April 20, they had set up camp in the Government High School which is quite close to our house, about one km away. It was about 9 in the morning when the Khan forces entered the house."

Rownaq elaborated further: "I have two maternal uncles; the elder one lives in Bashirhat in India. My younger uncle was a student of class 10. As the soldiers had occupied the school on April 20, my uncle went to the school at 8 in the morning to find out where they were and what they were doing. My father was shaving. The army surrounded the house. My father noticed that the soldiers were showing a photograph to one of the neighbours, beating him and asking him whether it was that of Captain Kazi. They showed him another photograph and enquired whether he knew him. My father then came out and the soldiers asked him his name. When he told them his name, they caught hold of him and took him towards the Registry Office. At that time Major Rashid was in charge of the army operation in this area. He played the main role in all the killings. After Father was taken away, the house was shelled. We came to know about this later from people who witnessed what had happened."

"The soldiers thrust bayonets into my father's body. At that time my uncle was returning home on his cycle. While he was passing by the Registry Office, he saw the soldiers surrounding my father and holding him. My uncle jumped off his cycle and rushed to the soldiers. He fell at their feet, begging them to release my father. But they thrust him aside. My uncle then picked up the cycle and started towards the house. Then, suddenly, on second thought, he went back to the soldiers and fell at their feet again. This time the soldiers shot him. My father was next. All this happened between 9 and 9.30 in the morning. The dead bodies were lying in the Registry Office when the soldiers left. After quite some time, the local Sub-Divisional Officer and my mother's paternal cousins went to Major Rashid in the Government High School to get his permission to bury the dead bodies. Without this permission nobody dared to touch the dead bodies. Those who obtained permission to bury the bodies are no longer alive today. After this, the two dead bodies were brought to our house, which in the meantime had been demolished. Only the kitchen was left. My father and my uncle were given the ritual bath inside the room, and the local *maulvi* conducted the funeral. Nobody dared to take the dead bodies outside. All this was done inside the demolished building. After that Father and Uncle were buried in the kitchen. The situation was too dangerous for anyone to move about. Normally bamboo poles are necessary to lower bodies into the grave but it was impossible to get bamboos in that situation. Earlier the soldiers had broken the wooden beds, so the bed frames were used to make the biers on which earth was thrown."

"Most of the people of the area had fled when Satkhira was occupied by the Pakistani forces. However, one or two residents, who still remained, could see everything that took place that morning from where they were hiding. They later on described how my father and uncle had been killed. Our neighbour, Mukul's mother, was a witness to everything. She saw it from inside her house, which was next to the Registry Office. Currently I am working in KSL Company, a private security service. I have been the District-in-Charge of the company for the last ten months. A guard of this office also told me how he saw my father being killed before his eyes. He was so scared that he fell into a nearby pond. Afterwards he got up from the pond and managed to escape."

We asked Rokeya Ahmed how she had come to know about what had happened. She replied that she had learned about it that very day, that is, on April 21, at Bashirhat. She said, "My cousins and uncle were there. My uncle brought the news. As soon as I heard it, I was completely distraught. The fact that my husband and brother were no longer living and our home was destroyed caused a feeling in me which I cannot describe. For three months, I was speechless, and was hardly able to eat and sleep. I was like a mad person. My parents were alive at the time. My father did not allow me to return. Moreover, I was not in a condition to do so. For three months I was almost senseless. I was unable to go out of the house or take a bath without any help. My relatives used to prepare food for me and feed me. We stopped cooking food for nine days in our house. In our country the custom is that if anyone dies, the cooking fire is not lit and no food is cooked in that house for three days. There were two deaths in our house in one day. So our relatives used to send food for us. They did this for nine days so that we did not have to cook."

"My condition deteriorated. I could hardly speak or remember anything. My father did not send me home because of my condition. There would be no one to look after me at home. Moreover, the children too were young and needed to be looked after. When the country was liberated, my paternal cousins asked us to return home. The Bangladesh Government was giving relief then, and my children wanted to see their father's grave. Even then my father was reluctant to let me return. When my children and I returned, the children were admitted into school again. Gradually we returned to normal life."

Rownaq informed us, "The name of my young maternal uncle, who was martyred along with my father, was Sheikh Masudur Rahman. My maternal grandparents could not bear the news of his death. They were so overcome by their son's death, they did not live long after the incident. My grandmother could not see the grave of her son, as she died before she had the opportunity to do so. It was an even greater tragedy when my elder maternal uncle, on hearing about his younger brother's death, became mentally unbalanced. He has not recovered. He had come to me and asked me to narrate the incident of my uncle's death. I described it in detail. As he listened, he shuddered. After that he gradually became mad. My grandparents too could not bear this second loss. After all, they had only these two sons."

"In 1971 when these incidents were taking place, my elder uncle (who subsequently lost his mental balance) was a very well-to-do man. He owned a large tract of land. His main occupation was looking after his land. He was unmarried then and continues to be a bachelor today. My account of what had happened terrified him, and he started behaving strangely. He started confining himself in a room, with the windows and doors shut. He refused to eat, refused to come out of the room, refused to talk to anybody. He never spoke loudly but always murmured to himself. Sometimes he used to open the door, come out, talk to himself and then go back inside the room. You could say, he had gone crazy. It was as though a storm had blown over our two families, turning everything topsy-turvy."

Rownaq narrated in detail the great difficulties under which they managed. "When we returned home, Mr. Sakib, the local MP, arranged 25 maunds of paddy as grant from the Government godown. When we returned to our country, we stayed at the home of my mother's uncle, because our home had been destroyed. We sold some of the paddy that we got from the Government. With that money we bought rice and lentils. That is how we managed to survive for seven or eight months. At the same time we also tried to earn some money ourselves. We continued to study but also worked as petty contractors. We set up a ration shop which was run by my younger brother. Mr. Sakib got us a licence for the shop, which was a great help. I continued with my studies, and my younger brother looked after the ration shop. That is how we managed. We had been fairly well off before. My father was a private practitioner. So he had a good bank balance, a credit of Tk. 30,000 or 35,000. During the Liberation War the ledgers and other relevant records in the bank were destroyed. Our records too got burnt when our house was shelled and damaged. So we were unable to withdraw our money from the bank. Earlier my father had withdrawn Tk. 12,000-13,000 from the bank in the first week of March, for emergencies. This money was in bundles of 100- and 500-rupee notes. We went to India with this money but, while we were there, 100- and 500-rupee currency notes were demonetised by the Pakistan Government. So all our money became useless paper. These Pakistani notes are still in our possession."

"We had applied to the Government for help. The then MP told us that our home was going to be used as a charitable dispensary. But for whatever reason, this decision was not implemented."

"Immediately after our return from India, we stayed in the house of my mother's uncle. He has since passed away, and his sons too are no longer here. We stayed in his house for a year. My father had a life insurance policy. One of my uncles [the husband of his maternal aunt] was General Manager in that insurance company and helped us realise the insurance money. With that money we repaired some of the rooms of our house and shifted there. The house was in a dilapidated condition. Gradually we have been able to repair it, but we still need to do some more work. Now I am working in a private security company. Before this I was an information officer in the Bahar Group of Industries at Dhaka. Earlier I worked for a customs clearing agency at Khulna. That is how we managed to stand on our own feet. Our relatives also extended some help. When we took shelter in our grandparents' home at Bashirhat, they looked after us and later too continued to help. However, since they lived in a different country, they could not assist us very much.

"After returning home, my mother alone knows how she managed. We were too young to notice anything. Moreover, we concentrated more on earning money than on such matters. We did whatever was possible on our part and stayed with our mother. At times we saw her crying, but for the most part she had reconciled herself to her loss."

"After returning to Bangladesh, each victim of military violence got Tk. 2,000. I asked Mother to apply for this grant. But she refused, saying that she loathed taking this money as payment for the loss of my father. We could not even persuade Mother to see Minister Aziz who belonged to this area and was a close friend of my father. Yet my mother refused to see him."

As Rownaq was narrating this, Rokeya Ahmed covered her face and wept. Still in tears, she said, "I became a widow when I was only 35 years. I used to feel so terrible. I seemed to have lost control over myself. I hardly went anywhere or visited anyone. Nor did I feel like seeing anybody in connection with what had happened to my husband. I left everything to my sons. I always had the feeling that I was going mad. This fear troubled me a lot. If that happened and I was out on the streets, it would be a catastrophe. Who would then look after my children? Such thoughts made me concentrate on prayers and the holy Quran which I recited whenever I could. That is how I searched for mental peace. That is what I was looking for, peace and nothing else." As she said this, Rokeya Ahmed again broke down in tears.

Regarding the Silver Jubilee of Independence, Rokeya Ahmed's daughter-in-law, Salma, told us, "My mother-in-law was invited on December 16 and was given an envelope. We did not know what it contained, nor do we know if she ever opened it. All I know is that she held it in her hand and came home. We never found out what was there. We heard that these envelopes contained 100-taka or 500-taka notes. After that, she never went again, she just refused to go. She said, 'Don't press me to go. I will never go there any more.' She had gone because the Deputy Commissioner had invited her. Attending these functions pains her."

Rokeya Ahmed's son Rownaq spoke with some anger. "These days people neither remember nor recognise the martyrs. My father was the first martyred intellectual in Satkhira. This is on record. I checked again a few days ago and found Captain Kazi's name documented as the first martyred intellectual of Satkhira. But we hardly notice any recognition of him as the first martyr. In fact, many people say, 'It is not such a big thing; quite a lot of people were killed during the war.' True, we agree that many people have become martyrs. But it is a matter of pride for us that our father was a martyr. You have come here today, you have heard the facts. The only thing we want is a memorial in our father's name, nothing else. We don't want any other help. A memorial is enough. There has to be something to remember him by. We want a memorial to be built so that people will visit the place and remember him as the first martyred intellectual in Satkhira. That is all we want from our country, nothing more."

In 1971, neither Rokeya Ahmed nor Rownaq fought with weapons in their hands. Nevertheless, both of them are freedom fighters. Their fight is not yet over. After 1971, they had to struggle in order to survive. They had started their lives in comfort and happiness. 1971 completely changed their lives. The Pakistani atrocities also affected those whose families were divided by the Partition, whose members lived on both sides of the border. Even though Rokeya's parents lived in West Bengal, they too suffered the scars of 1971. Rokeya's brother had left the country of his birth, left his parents and migrated to East Pakistan with the hope of improving his family fortunes. In 1971 Pakistani forces killed that brother, snuffing out his hopes forever, destroying the family.

Zulekha

Life after 1971

Suraiya Begum

Zulekha's story was elicited from her in two separate interviews, once in 1997, and later in 2005 when I went to see her again. In her first interview Zulekha did not reveal that she had been raped by Pakistani soldiers. But in her second interview she disclosed that she was forced to pass her days in a Pakistani army camp where the conditions were terrible and life was extremely cruel. All this came to light when an organisation took the initiative of getting financial aid for her after hearing of her plight. Thus, I was able to hear the full story. On the basis of these two interviews, Zulekha's tale has been retold here.

Zulekha's house was in the Kamalnagar area of Satkhira town, three to four kilometres south west of the bus stand. When we went to Zulekha's house for the first time in 1997, Kalyan Banerjee, the staff correspondent of the daily *Bhorer Kagoj*, was our resource person and guide. He told us that the Pakistani soldiers had committed large-scale excesses in Kamalnagar. Almost at the furthest end of the locality stood Zulekha's small hut, situated along side other huts in a slum. A paddy field stood beyond the dwelling. The bamboo huts were like shed and dark inside. When we had taken our seats practically on the bare road outside, some one spread out a mat for us. As we seated ourselves more comfortably, a big crowd gathered around us. Everyone tried to speak at the same time, leaving little scope for us to speak or listen. We had to wait for quite some time for an opportunity to speak.

What we had heard earlier – even before we had come to know more – caused us great sorrow and we were at a loss to find words to console Zulekha. We learnt that her mother-in-law had breathed her last by her side in this very house the night before our visit and had been buried a short while ago. Zulekha was weeping continuously as she talked about this. We felt extremely uncomfortable and did not know how to confront her with her past grief when she was already overcome with a new sorrow that day. The crowd provided a solution. They started questioning us – who we were, where we had come from and why. That made it easy for us to bring up the topic of our experiences of the war in 1971. Gradually it became easier for us to touch upon the topics that we wanted to talk about, and for them too. Zulekha, in particular, became interested in taking part. In doing so, we felt she had found a way to ease herself of the pain that had burdened her heart for so long. All the painful memories that were stored in her heart started coming out in full force. In 1971 she had suffered in many ways. Zulekha had lost her own identity, her husband, her house and all her worldly belongings. She was homeless.

Her mother-in-law died that day without receiving medical attention and proper nutrition. This could be attributed to conditions that were created by 1971. Had 1971 not turned her life upside down, her mother-in-law might have survived longer.

It may be mentioned here that in 1997 Zulekha had narrated the suffering she had undergone. She had been unable to talk about her experience of her sexual assault. There were a few missing links in her first interview but in later meetings attempts were made to fill these in, though not with full success. Her experiences have been recast here.

"I am Zulekha Khatun. My husband Abdul Kader was a teacher in the local Jugla School in 1971. My parents' home was in Belgachhia, West Bengal, India, and my in-law's house too was in Dhankurey in India, but my grandfather-in-law lived in Bhomra region of Satkhira district in Bangladesh. It was in the border zone. While approaching this place you might have come across a concrete structure with a gate, on a piece of land about a third of an acre. That's where my house was in 1971. My husband started working for the freedom fighters in 1971. After March 25 he used to visit India regularly. My sister's house was in Bashirhat, India. My other three sisters too had their houses there. My husband used to go to my sister's house. From there he used to communicate with my other sisters. At times he used to go to Bashirhat without even telling us. Sometimes he would not even return at night, and would stay on, only to return in the small hours of the morning. Although he would not tell me what he was doing, I could guess he was working for the liberation war in the border area. He might have been involved in the movement of arms and ammunitions. He used to watch where the Khans [Pakistani soldiers] had placed barricades, and which route would be safe for the freedom fighters."

It was the seventh of *Baisakh* (the first month of the Bengali year, and possibly April 22) when the incident took place. On that day Abdul Kader was going towards the market along with their three sons. A strange feeling in Zulekha made her follow him, Abdul Kader urged her to go back home, insisting, "If the Pakistani soldiers see you, they won't spare you, but will take you away. It would be better for you to remain indoors." Zulekha ignored his caution, and continued following him up to the highway.

"The following morning, at about seven o'clock, the Pakistani soldiers came straight to our house and surrounded our place. At first eight to nine persons entered the house. As they entered, they started throwing things around and kicking right and left without asking any question. Some things were smashed and some thrown out. They all had angry looks. Then they came across something on the cot. It was long and black. I did not know exactly what it was. My husband used to talk on it all night long. It might have been a walkie-talkie. My husband seemed obliged to go out whenever he would get a call on it. I did not know where my husband had got it. The soldiers' first action was to seize it and along with it, my husband Abdul Kader.

"In those days my husband frequently communicated with Captain Kazi of this area and was very close to him. Captain Kazi was quite well known. Being a newly wed bride then, I was not allowed to go out of the house. My husband used to talk to the Captain about the liberation war. I used to understand a bit but not fully. My husband hardly discussed anything about these things with me. Often he used to go to Bashirhat to communicate with the freedom fighters. Whenever he was required to go, he made me make a large quantity of bread. He used to convince me that all this food was necessary for the freedom fighters' survival. On one occasion when I refused to make the bread, he slapped me very hard. Never before had he hit me. I was hurt and shocked, but after that he explained to me why it was necessary to prepare food for the freedom fighters."

"After asking him various questions, the soldiers held him firmly and did not release him again. After that, they started searching every corner of the house. Earlier there had been a bomb placed in a copper pot in my room. I did not know whether it was made at home or brought from any other place. I recalled, on the previous night, Captain Kazi's brother-in-law and some others had come to our house. Then some people belonging to their party came at night and took away the copper pot and a few other things as well."

"The soldiers seemed to have detected my husband's activities through the instrument known as walkie-talkie or wireless which was constantly being used for conversations: with it my husband used to communicate with various people. It was used the previous night too. Moreover, our house was used for meetings. The Khans must have known this and hence surrounded our house that fateful morning. After discovering the walkie-talkie, they held my husband's hands behind his back and pulled him towards a coconut tree nearby. Quite a few soldiers surrounded him, hurling abuse at him. We were watching in terror from within the house, unable either to speak or do anything. Some of the soldiers suggested that he be shot and killed. First they fired two shots over his head. But after that they shot him on the left side of his chest here [pointing to her chest]. My husband dropped to the ground. As soon as he fell down, the Khans stepped on his chest and pressed hard with their boots. He was bleeding profusely and I could see him panting for breath. At this sight both my eldest son and the next one, almost fainting by then, came running towards me. When I asked if he was dead or alive, the latter, without any word just kept gesturing, flailing his hands up and down. I thought he was trying to be funny, and so I slapped him. He broke down in tears saying, 'Father is dead.' Hearing this, people started running away. I started running too, with my children."

"Out of my nine children then, the eldest one, my daughter, was married and lived with her in-laws. My youngest son was in a jute cradle, and, in the frenzy, I left him behind. I placed one son on my hip and held another by the hand, and started running like crazy along with all the others who were able to run. We could not stop at any house or seek shelter. We were refused shelter because everyone was scared that their lives would be in danger as the soldiers were chasing us. We were distraught. The children were crying. We did not remember at that time that we had left our son Shahinoor in the cradle and had also left behind one daughter. My mind was not working properly then. I just ran for life with only those children who were by my side at the time of danger. With shelter refused at every place, we followed people who too were running for their lives. We made it to a place called Patkelghata."

"Sometime later, Aziz, our neighbour and a college student, kindly went back and brought my child and his feeding bottle. He was then six months old. Next morning, my sister's husband came and informed us that my husband had been buried somehow beside the pond of our house. He explained that in the morning a ditch was dug inside the house and the dead body was put into it in a hurry, lest the army take it away. After some time we came to know that a baby girl had been traced to the house of Dr. Rabbani in Patkelghata. At this news we rushed to Dr. Rabbani's house and found my missing daughter."

"My second son who had seen his father being killed so cruelly before his own eyes obviously was mentally affected. Whenever he was near me he just jumped around me with his hands raised high. There have been no signs of improvement, and even now my son behaves strangely at times."

Zulekha was at the crossroads of her life at this stage. What happened during this period was not fully revealed during the first interview, and remained obscure then. Later on, when I came to see her again, I probed further into the incidents that had taken place during this period. It was difficult for me to reopen, after so many years, the old painful topics, particularly those related to sexual assault. Nevertheless, the conversation was tactfully diverted in that direction, and gradually it centred closely around the topic. Zulekha divulged facts that were heart-rending. At a certain stage of her narration, her voice choked and she had to stop. As she was sitting by my side, I could feel how very upset she was at that moment – mentally and physically. After a brief pause and a deep sigh, she resumed, unfolding a dark chapter of her life. Her description was not well framed or consistent. So we edited and summarised it. This is given below:

"After my husband was shot dead by the Pakistani soldiers, we started running in the same direction as the villagers. We continued running that way for a number of days until I along with my children approached the village of Patkelghata. One day the Pakistani soldiers caught me near the Patkelghata bridge and eight or nine other women like me. I was quite young then. They caught us and took us to their camp. We found many other women there. During our stay there, we were not allowed to wear any clothes. All of us were put in one room, and in the same room the Pakistani soldiers assaulted the women, one by one. Each of the women was a target of assault by the soldiers, one after another, in turn."

"I was raped first by a soldier who though human in appearance was worse than an animal. He was barbaric to the extreme. While assaulting me, he caused me wounds all over my body. He bit my face so savagely with his sharp teeth that it made two visible holes on my face. These took a long time to heal. I remember the names of three soldiers. They were Aziz Miah, Ibrahim Miah and Khalil Miah. I heard these names being used repeatedly when they would call one another. That is how these names got stuck in my mind. Except for a scanty piece of cloth around their loins – an apology for an underwear – the soldiers used to be practically naked."

"After one soldier committed the monstrous deed, another would wait for his turn. That was how it kept happening to all the women. In the process I used to feel that I was dying. Once when I could bear it no longer, I cried so hard for mercy that I was spared."

"Later on, two gentlemen of the locality, Mr. Sobhan Khan and Mr. Gafur, came to my rescue. They were rich people, and were on good terms with the Khans. The Khan soldiers, while at Satkhira, used to stay in Mr. Gafur's house. These two gentlemen persuaded the Khan soldiers to release me by saying that unless they did so my children would die. The soldiers acceded to their request and released me. As I had no clothes on, Mr. Sobhan Khan and Mr. Gafur provided me with clothes and brought me out."

As she was narrating these experiences, there was a painful expression on Zulekha's face. She wore a sad look, and her body seemed to tremble ever so slightly. She constantly touched the scars on her face, which had been made by ferocious bites by her assailants. The terrible memories of 1971 flash back in her mind again and again and the trauma haunts her, especially when she gets invited by local persons to Victory Day and Independence Day celebrations.

According to Zulekha, the news of the rape did not spread at the time. Her daughter, who was married, had cautioned her mother that the matter should not be known. Otherwise, it would be impossible for her to continue to live in her husband's home. He was quite well off at that time. If he came to know what had happened to her mother, she (the daughter) would be asked to leave his house. Hence she had omitted this incident in her first interview, and restrained herself from giving all the details of what had happened. We, on our part, were careful to honour her desire for secrecy, although that may have caused many facts to remain hidden.

After her release from the army camp, Zulekha had to start her shattered life anew. She was confronted with a hard struggle in post-independent Bangladesh. There was no earning member to support her big family of nine children. Before independence Zulekha was a carefree housewife with no worry or anxiety. The 1971 war sent her from that blissful state into a cruel hard reality. She was not only a victim of rape at the hands of the Pakistani soldiers, she had also to take charge of the household, run it, and look after the children. There was no one on her side who could be of help. On the contrary, those around her took advantage of her helplessness, and uprooted her from her house. A helpless Zulekha narrated her tales of misery past and present.

"On coming back we were at a loss as to what to do and where to go. My husband was a school teacher. We had nine children. My mother-in-law wasn't fully sane. We began to pass our days with great difficulty. Our property comprised of a two-storeyed building on half an acre of land with a pond. In course of time we lost ownership of this house too.

"After our return we faced difficulties in procuring regular meals. As a married woman, I was never before allowed to go outdoors. When my husband was alive, all provisions like rice, lentils, spices, for the whole month used to be purchased by him. I just used to prepare the food for our meals. We did not know anyone and never visited anyone. After my husband's death, I faced numerous difficulties. I had to bear the burden of a large family with small children."

On being asked whether they had any relatives here who could look after them, Zulekha replied that there was nobody, because her husband had migrated to this side from India. His relatives lived in

India at Bashirhat. They were all well-to-do. Zulekha could not remember when Abdul Kader had migrated to Satkhira from India, and hence was unable to tell us the exact date. But she could at least tell us that while in Kolkata, Kader had been working as a contractor for the Kolkata Medical College, with the responsibility of mainly supplying food to the patients. When he came here, he took a teaching job in Jugla School.

After independence, when Zulekha was in financial trouble, she went to her elder brother's house at Bashirhat. On arriving there she did not find him home. He was out, along with his wife and children. On their return, even before Zulekha could step into his house, her brother and his wife asked her to go back. Deeply hurt, Zulekha had to sell a metal jug that she had carried with her to drink water during her travel, to arrange money for the journey back to Satkhira. This bitter experience had always deterred her from looking towards any relative for help.

"After the country was free, our neighbours, Tapan (pseudonym), son of Advocate Ramapada (pseudonym), and Advocate Shafiqul's (pseudonym) wife used to enquire about our needs regularly. Some sort of understanding seemed to exist between Moloi and the advocate's wife. At that time, Advocate Shafiqul's wife used to bring rice and lentils for us in a bucket in the morning. She and Tapan, continued helping us with provisions. Tapan would come to me and ask, 'Sister, what should I bring for you from the market?' I had no money, and was at a loss what to ask for! Without waiting for my reply, they went ahead with their spontaneous assistance, in the form of money, rice, cooking oil and sundries. In short, they looked after us with great care. On top of all this, they were extremely polite. There was no male member in our family to do any of these tasks. My children were too young. Two brothers and three sisters of my husband were staying on the other side of the border, in Bashirhat, West Bengal, India. They were too scared to come to this side. So my neighbours looked after us, arranging rice, giving us money to buy necessities. When Shafiqul used to come from Khulna with provisions, he used to give part of it to us. His wife used to bring these over and say that her husband had brought these for us. Thus, we used to get rice, lentils, money even before asking for anything. In this way, we got materials worth about three hundred taka from them."

"One day I was told that I owed Shafiqul Tk. 300 which was worth three *kathas* (a *katha* equals 750 sq yards) of land, and that I should transfer this amount of land in his name. I had no alternative, so I did what he suggested. I found later that he had got my signature for transfer of the entire pond too, in his name."

"The food problem continued, and I was worried about our uncertain future. On another day, Tapan came and showed a lot of sympathy about our suffering and the way I was losing control over my land and property. He then expressed great concern, asking what would happen to me if my husband's brothers came back and claimed the house. So he suggested that since my sons were minors, he would undertake the responsibility of looking after our landed property. So he got my eldest son, who was quite young then, dressed in a *dhuti* so that he might look more grown up, and took him to the court. Tapan got himself legally declared as my minor son's guardian, and got his (my son's) share of the property in his name. I was helpless since I was obligated to him for his charity. This was all done after the country had become independent."

"After the transfer was signed, you can well imagine how we lost control over our house. It became impossible to continue to live on our property. Strange things started happening that made our stay impossible. At night stones were hurled at the house. I had to take shelter with my children under the cot. In the morning we opened the door to discover night soil spread there. Also, night soil was put into packets of paper and thrown at our doors by persons we could not trace."

"It became unbearable to stay on like that so we asked for redress from the *shalish*, court of village elders, but in vain. The *shalish* never sat on the plea that someone or the other was absent. I had with me a small amount of money when I signed my property away. Unable to bear the constant anxieties and weary of passing continuous sleepless nights, we rented a small place in the house of Dr. Jamal, and shifted there, leaving behind my homestead and everything. After we shifted to Dr. Jamal's house, Advocates Shafiqul and Ramapada joined hands to demolish our homestead. My husband's grave was on my land. A wall was raised on it, on his grave, to divide the landed property. All these painful things beggar description. The concrete structure is still there. The two advocates, on the plea of helping us in our days of distress, threw us onto the streets, and are now occupying our property."

"By then my eldest son had grown up a bit. He could understood our predicament and started working as a labourer. People sympathetic to our plight used to employ him. He dug earth or carried soil for filling ditches. I used to beg for rice and water that was drained out of the boiled rice (*fyan*) from different houses. I used to collect this from a nearby hotel too. The hotel belonging to Paran Molla was a big one by the side of the road. My son used to do some odd jobs in the hotel and he used to collect the *panta bhat* (rice left over at night and mixed with water) in the morning and the *fyan* at noon along with a bit of boiled rice. The latter used to be mixed with the *fyan* for feeding my children."

"At night I had to go from house to house in search of food. In spite of the fact that once I was the owner of a house and half an acre of land, I had to struggle and beg for food now, day after day, for my children. We pressed the village members and succeeded in getting access to a tract of government land, and somehow managed to have a modest but uncertain shelter here. As the Chairman next door felt awkward about our presence, there were attempts to demolish our structure – perhaps about ten times in a month. It is a pity that we may not be able to continue to live here too. How I suffer! My mother-in-law, who was staying with me, died without medical attention. She had a big tumour which needed an operation. The much-needed surgery was not possible for want of money. She suffered long and died today."

At this point she broke down in tears. On being asked whether she had approached the local Member of Parliament or the Party leaders for assistance, medical or otherwise, she replied in a sore voice, "No one cares. I approached the local leader, Kazi Shamsur Rahman, and handed over typed papers twice to him. He assured me that when he visited us next time, he would have positive news for me, but he didn't. I was busy trying to complete all these paper formalities, but was unable to arrange the urgently needed surgical operation, and my mother died today some time ago. She was buried a short while ago."

Zulekha was sobbing with grief and kept saying, "I was unable to feed her. She could hardly take anything – only water, barely two or three spoons, during the previous one month. I tried to get coconut water for her from different people. Not long ago, l had all these in my own possession, but alas, I had to beg for these now!"

These days Zulekha's daughters live in Khulna and Narail. The eldest one was married while her father was alive and now lives in Narail. The second daughter's husband works as a mason's assistant, and the third one's husband is at home with burn injuries on his arms and legs, which is why the daughter herself has to work as a mason to run the household. "I got these two daughters married with the help of the villagers. They gave financial assistance for the wedding. My eldest son has a poultry business. He has married and lives separately with his wife."

Of Zulekha's six sons, three are rickshaw pullers, one has a poultry business, another sells *khwaja* (a kind of sweet covered with sesame seeds), and the mentally challenged one, does whatever he is capable of doing at times.

Zulekha was asked why she did not go to India like many others, when the liberation war started, in spite of the fact that there was no dearth of shelter there, with many of her in-laws living on the other side of the border. Zulekha replied that while her husband was alive, they had once travelled upto Tentultala, with the intention of crossing over to the other side. But her husband suddenly changed his mind saying, "We will rather die for the country than leave it."

When she was asked who should bear the blame for her plight resulting from the happenings of 1971, her immediate reaction was fate, and next, the Khan soldiers. She argued that had her husband not died, she would not have had to leave her home and would not have been a victim and would not have turned into a pauper. She would have spent her days well. She would not have lost possession of her house.

No improvement in Zulekha's financial condition was noticed even in 2005. She had a similar accommodation as before, with the minor difference that the low shed that she had before was now a slightly raised structure. Inside there was a cooking stove and a few cooking pots on one side. A few pieces of dried egg plant, and a few green chillies, turning red, were scattered in a cane basket. A mosquito curtain hung from one side of the bed. A *kantha* stitched from old torn saris was spread on a wooden plank bed. Zulekha live in a moderate sized hut made of bamboo. To enter the low door, she had to bend her knees and lower her head. Her son live in an adjoining room with his family. Zulekha looked more frail than before. It was apparent from her surroundings how distressed she was financially.

Zulekha was keen to show the location of the land she once possessed. "If you take the path behind my present hut and walk for five minutes, you will come across the house which once was mine. This place is 500 yards off the principal road of Satkhira town."

As I walked over to that place, I saw a two-storeyed concrete house where Advocate Shafiqul Huq lived. Advocate Shafiqul was now an influential person in this area and held an important position in the BNP (Bangladesh Nationalist Party). Ramapada sold half of the land that he had usurped, left the place and went away somewhere else. An expression of suppressed anger and despair was clearly visible on Zulekha's face, as she was showing me around the place. No words could describe the pathetic expression on her face. A distraught Zulekha had to reconcile herself to the hard fact that 1971 uprooted her from her life of comfort and security, from her home and landed property. With all these gone, she was now left helpless, with no physical support or mental peace. Everything that she valued and loved was gone forever.

This story of Zulekha's life is a typical example of the ruthlessness and barbarism of the Pakistani forces in 1971 – the atrocities that shattered and ruined the lives of many happy families in this country. It also shows to what extent numerous citizens of this land were victims of the trigger-happy Khan soldiers. It also demonstrates how determined and selfless had been the struggles of ordinary people like Kader Master, in advancing the cause of the freedom struggle and transforming it into an armed struggle for achieving independence. Both Kader Master and Zulekha equally deserve the honour of brave freedom fighters.

The damage that the Pakistani soldiers did to Zulekha has left a permanent scar on her very being. She has to continue bearing the brunt of her torture, now and into the future, till the day she dies. And it will continue into future generations. Zulekha's story is a typical history of a common housewife in Bangladesh torn apart in a struggle, which she barely understood. To her, state, power, politics, Islamic ideals, and nationalist ideals do not have much meaning, but somehow her life reflects a combination of all these ideas. Her very existence, her experiences have become mingled with this country's birth and its political history. And this is true not only of Zulekha, but also of millions of other women. Zulekha symbolises all of them.

This life experience of Zulekha illuminates the reality of 1971. Her life was affected both by the Pakistani army during the war and after the war by her neighbours. War and after war the situation is not mono-dimensional. Its multiple aspects need to be considered. Zulekha's life depicts that reality.

Rape: A Rural Woman's Experience

Suraiya Begum

It was almost three in the afternoon when we reached Kamalnagar. Kalyan Banerjee had brought us to the spot after finding out the address of a woman who had been raped by the Pakistani army. Perhaps if she were asked, she would tell us what had happened to her. Reaching Kamalnagar, we first sat down outside Zulekha's home. Zulekha came forward and told us that she would like to narrate her tragic story. Raisun was nowhere near. We therefore heard Zulekha's story.[1] By the time we finished, it was late afternoon. However, despite the lateness of the hour, we went ahead with Raisun's interview.

We interviewed Raisun in 1997. She was a small, slight, dark-complexioned woman, slightly over 40 years. She was poor, simple and unassuming. Because of straitened circumstances, her face was pale and thin. She took some time to understand what we wanted. She pondered over our questions before she replied to them in her own way. Her story has been based on the information she provided.

Raisun had been raped by Pakistani soldiers in 1971. She lived in her own house, in Zulekha's neighbourhood which she had built on a small four-*katha* plot of land she had bought. She narrated her traumatic experiences in 1971.

"In the time of the Khans [that is, Pakistan times], I used to stay in a rented place a little south of here. I had been married for about five or six years. I had a boy and a girl. The girl was just eleven days old. My husband was a mason's helper. On the day of the occurrence, he was not at home as he had gone to work. My husband is a little crazy, slightly dim-witted. My mother-in-law was at home. I do not remember exactly what month it was. But I remember the time. It was afternoon.

[1] See "Zulekha: Life after Nineteen Seventy-One."

When the Pakistani soldiers entered the village, I thought that they had come to catch the people who sold eggs in the black market. At that time a lot of things were sold in the black market here, including eggs."

"The soldiers entered about noon. I thought that the local police had come to catch people who sold eggs in the black market. Two Pakistani soldiers entered the house. One of them came inside, while the other stood at the entrance. They were well built, tall and fair, and in uniform. They entered without asking me anything. My daughter was in my lap. She was just eleven days old. They threw my daughter to the ground and dragged me into the room. My mother-in-law picked up my daughter and told them, 'You too have mothers and daughters.' They told her to shut up. My mother-in-law picked my daughter up and left the room. She did not want to see me being raped in front of her eyes."

"Taking me inside the room, the soldiers gagged me with a *gamchha*. I was terrified and, with the gag in my mouth, I was unable to make any sounds. If someone gags you with a *gamchha*, you too will be unable to utter anything. After this they did what they wanted with me. I had turned into a *kanthal* leaf with fear."

"None of the villagers had sided with the army. The soldiers had entered on foot from the other side. [Raisun gestured towards the east.] Only one of the soldiers assaulted me. After this they left. After their departure my mother-in-law helped bathe me. My insides were still raw from childbirth, and I suffered acute pain from what the soldier had done. My mother-in-law gave me some medicine to ease the pain. No doctor was called."

"The soldier had not hurt or scratched my body. I had been wearing a sari. The soldier had ripped it off. He had only opened the front of his pants."

"I do not know how long they were there."

"My husband was returning from his work. But before he reached home, he was picked up and taken away in a rickshaw. My husband has a slightly disability. He is not very intelligent. He told the soldiers, 'Why must I go by rickshaw? I want to go home. I am thirsty.' Because he was a little dumb, the soldiers let him go. On the way people told him, 'The soldiers entered your home and caught hold of your wife.' He heard everything from my mother-in-law. He didn't say anything to me. He told others, 'What was my wife to do when the soldiers caught her? After all, she didn't go with them of her own accord.' He didn't say anything much to me."

"After the soldiers left, my mother-in-law gave me a bath. My whole body was aching. Apart from this I had no other difficulty. I didn't see a doctor. My mother-in-law gave me some medicine. I had no problem having intercourse with my husband subsequently. Nor did my husband say anything about what had transpired. The people who used to work with my husband said to him, 'The soldiers raped your wife. Divorce her.' They also came to my mother-in-law and said similar things to her. My mother-in-law told them, 'I have looked after her since she was a little girl. She does not have any relations. No, I will not throw her out. And she did not go to them of her own accord."

"A lot of people were sympathetic. But there were others who gloated at my misfortune, who taunted me for what had happened. But can people really be happy at what had happened? By and large, however, people did not create any problems for me."

"I have received no help from the government for my tragedy, nor from anyone else either. At that time all my neighbours knew about what had happened. Of course, I have not asked anyone for help."

"Immediately after the incident I had to hear a lot of criticism. People would say, '*Khane laga*' or 'The Khans came to that woman.' Nowadays they don't say these things any more. The memory of those days has been superceded by other things. When they used to say those things, I would feel very bad. I would cry. At night I would have nightmares that the soldiers had caught me again. While I was doing my household work, I would be reminded of what had happened. I was troubled about it for days on end. Now I have grown old and weak. At that time I was strong and attractive. Even now I recall that incident. But what is the point of remembering?"

"We weren't able to do anything to the Pakistani soldiers. We have no one to help us, no power. What can we do? We have work enough to keep our souls and bodies together. My husband is quite unwell now. I have married off my two daughters. I had no problems getting them married. One of my sons-in-law works in a sweet producing factory and the other in a toothpaste company. This incident was not an obstacle to my daughter's marriages because her in-laws do not know. My younger daughter knows but no one else."

Saying this Raisun stopped talking. The shadows of dusk fell on her face, a blend of sorrow and helpless resignation, the resignation that has been the fate of women through the ages. Her body had been violated at gun point Her traumatic experience had left her with a sense of utter helplessness that coursed through her entire being.

Ferdousi Priyobhashini

A Hidden Chapter

Shaheen Akhtar

In 1996 after we started the Oral History Project of Ain o Shalish Kendra (ASK), we used to sit once every month or two. During this preparation period, we held detailed discussions about how we should proceed. One day the name of Ferdousi Priyobhashini came up. Since she used to live in the industrial town of Khalishpur, heavily populated by non-Bangali settlers, during the Liberation War, we thought that we might learn something about the experiences of women in that area during the war.

I became acquainted with Ferdousi Priyobhashini when she came to ASK's office. She looked quite distraught and talked incoherently. Suddenly she said that in 1971, when her husband was fighting in the war, the Pakistani soldiers came to her house. Her sister was staying with her at the time. The soldiers came to her house and surrounded it.

Although I sensed something was troubling her, I wasn't really sure whether she had been abused in 1971 or, if she had been, whether she would agree to give us an interview. However, it was decided I would go to her house and talk to her about 1971.

On December 23, 1996, I went to Ferdousi Priyobhashini's Dhanmondi residence to talk to her. On that day she related almost everything about her life to me. The cassettes I brought with me ran out and evening fell. Still she wouldn't stop. I became quite confused. She didn't resemble a victim of military violence in 1971. The Pakistani soldiers had not dragged her from her home. She had returned to her job during the war. She had been abused day after day, even though she hadn't been kept prisoner. What was the explanation for this? She discussed her family life, monetary problems, personal crisis, the attitude of society, and her problematic relationship with her male friend. It is not possible to understand Priyobhashini's experiences during 1971 without taking all these aspects into account.

The first day when I returned home and listened to the cassettes, I was unable to sort out the beginning from the end of an incident. The events were not arranged chronologically, in proper sequence. In the midst of narrating one event, she would suddenly bring in another, unrelated one. I thought to myself that next time I interviewed her, I would ask her to relate just one event at a time. However, the same thing happened the next day. Moreover, I noticed that though she related the same events that she had narrated the first day, she related them very differently. Her story the second day was quite different from that of the first. The incidents, the details, all seemed to have changed. One reason for her talking like this might be that on the second day the gap between us had reduced, making her relate many things she could not on the first day. It also occurred to me that so many things had happened in 1971 that she herself was baffled. My confusion compelled me to return to her again and again. We even talked on the phone every now and then. Once I was passing by her house and just thought of meeting her. And I did go to her place without any pen and paper, let alone any recorder. On that occasion she told me things she had not in the previous interviews. Sometimes when an interview was over and I was arranging my things to leave, she would start talking about something new, making me sit down again. Sometimes she would talk without stopping for an hour or more. She also had a strange predilection for suddenly bringing in an incident or comment while talking about something else. Whenever she saw me, she started talking about the Liberation War. Maybe it was because we had become acquainted because of 1971.

In this way I continued to meet her for four long years. Still, I felt that there were many things that I did not know or understand. Priyobhashini's '71 is just like a mine beneath the earth, endless, dark, with many complex layers in each fold.

During the interview, Priyobhashini gave me a written account of her experiences during the nine months of the war. This account is based on the interviews she gave me as well as her written version. However, I have tried to arrange her story chronologically. In other words, this is a summary of her interview. I always had to remember that this was only a chapter of a book. I have occasionally had to infer what she meant from what she said. However, whenever there is a chance of misunderstanding or confusion, I have tried to share it with readers.

At present Ferdousi Priyobhashini, a sculptor, is also recognised as a *birangana* of '71.

In 1971, when Ferdousi Priyobhashini was about 24 or 25, she used to work as a telephone operator and receptionist at Crescent Jute Mill, in Khalishpur, near Khulna, in southern Bangladesh. In 1947, this region, situated near the Bhairab river, was a veritable village. In the 1950's, factories started being set up in the area. Large numbers of *mohajirs*, non-Bangali refugees from India, were also settled in this place. As a result, the demographics of this region changed drastically almost overnight. The factory owners were also from non-Bangali communities: Ismailis, Ispahani, Bohra, Delhiites, and others. Some of the jute mills in Khalispur belonged to the Aga Khan Group of Industries, among them were Platinum Jubilee Jute Mills, People's Jute Mills, and Crescent Jute Mills, to name a few. Ferdousi Priyobhashini used to work at Crescent Jute Mills, which was owned by the Aga Khan Group of Industries.

About 60 per cent of the officers of the mill were non-Bangali. The workers too were refugees who had come from Bihar after Partition. As the Bangali nationalist movement gathered momentum, Bangali workers and employees started resenting the dominating attitude of the non-Bangalis. The conflict between the Bangalis and the non-Bangalis grew and, by the end of the 60's, the political unrest became more pronounced.

Priyobhashini came to work in Khalishpur in the mid-sixties. She was born in Khulna, which was also the home of her first husband. After the birth of three sons, she and her husband separated. Priyobhashini's mother had also had a difficult married life. After her divorce from her first husband, her mother had remarried, but her second husband had passed away by this time. She had several children from her two marriages but, unfortunately, she had no means of providing for them. Priyobhashini was the eldest, and on her fell the responsibility of looking after the dozen or so children, her own and her mother's. It was a household without men. The money that Priyobhashini earned barely sufficed to see them through the first ten days of the month. The family had to borrow or half-starve the remaining twenty days of the month.

The sixties saw the growth of Bangali nationalism, when the struggle to overthrow the Pakistani colonial rule was gathering steam. However, while people of this country were engaged in the movement against the tyrannical Pakistani rule, Priyobhashini was struggling just to make ends meet for her large family. Her marriage was also breaking up and she herself had become emotionally involved with someone else. As a result she was unconscious of the political tensions of Khalishpur and the growing enmity between Bangalis and Biharis. It is perhaps on account of this that these matters are not reflected in her narrative.

Some days before March 25, her sons were staying with their grandmother in Khulna. Priyobhashini was alone in the whole house. Even her close friend (now her husband) Ahsanullah had not visited her for several days. He was then the Administrative Officer of the Jessore Jute Mills, at a distance of about 18 miles from Khalishpur.

The following words describe the mental state of a woman left alone in a house and also the social condition of a single woman on the eve of March 25.

"There was a cemetery in front of the one-storeyed house I had rented. Beyond the cemetery was the rail crossing and beyond that was the Dhaka-Jessore main road. From the verandah one could see the busy street, the cars, the trains and the rickshaws. On that day the house was empty and my isolation seemed to suffocate my heart, making it stiff and numb. My former husband had taken my three sons to their grandmother's place. At one point I thought that since I was busy with my job all day, they would be more secure at their grandmother's. In a way this was better. I would see them at the weekend. Ahsanullah, who came every evening, had not come yet. In those days it was not easy for a man not a relating to visit a single woman in her house alone. Maybe for this reason he would not coming. The night grew darker and there was no other soul except me in my house."

"The clock struck eight. I tried to call Ahsanullah, but in vain. I couldn't contact him using any of his numbers. Where could I go at this hour of the night? Afraid as I was, even the sound of the whirring fan ruffling the papers rang a thousand times in my ears. Everything appeared frightening. I started to read a book although I could hardly concentrate. I felt as if a mountain was crushing me. The next morning I felt exhausted with sleepless, weary eyes. Probably my office was closed that day and my children were away. Ahsanullah had not come for two days. The whole world seemed meaningless."

"There was some labour unrest in Ahsanullah's mill. When he came after three days, he had a bandage on his foot. But before that my mother had come, along with my younger brothers and sisters, as trouble had started in Jessore. In the town Bangalis and Biharis had started killing each other. There was violence and destruction everywhere."

Things continued this way till March 29, 1971. When the Pakistani soldiers entered Khalishpur town and started killing indiscriminately, Priyobhashini's family, like thousands of others, fled the town leaving everything behind. Ahsanullah was with them. Priyobhashini remembers those days:

"A procession of countless people passed by my house. I joined them. As I was passing the cemetery, I stumbled over some cold dead bodies – may be two or three. I did not stop but continued till I reached the neighbouring village. Someone pointed out that the house where we had stopped belonged to someone from the Muslim League. Still, we entered. People inside offered us tomatoes, saying they were from the field nearby. It was the month of Falgun – no, it was Chaitra.[1] We spent almost an hour there and then started moving. In the group there were seven or eight families who were moving forward steadily with desperation. The Pakistani troops had encamped before the Fire Brigade office in Noornagar. They were so nervous that they would mistake a bursting rickshaw tire for a gunshot and start shooting. The asphalt road was baking hot in the blazing noon. Somehow, my mother and I, along with Ahsanullah, reached my grandfather's house in Khulna. Ahsanullah left us and went away. However, there were other relatives as well in my grandfather's house. After a few days my mother said, 'I can't bear this any more. Let's go back to Khalishpur. Let's start living there again. Who's going to kill people like us?'"

"When we returned home, we had to find food. I went to the house of a Bihari merchant named Rashid whom everybody called 'Chhoto Rashid' and said, 'I'm your neighbour. I have many small

---

1 The Bangali month of Falgun is from mid-February to mid-March. Chaitra is from mid-March to Mid-April.

children in my house. Please lend us some money. I'll return your money when the war is over.'"

"The man smiled. 'Will we meet afterwards? All right,' he said and gave me Tk. 200. They were not killer Biharis and were probably planning to leave the country. I returned home."

"Once I was hanging up the laundry in my veranda. Ahsanullah, who was crossing the main road, saw me and came running, 'Why are you here? I was going to Khulna to learn how you were. You can't stay here. They are trying to kill me. I am running from them.' By this time four or five vehicles full of soldiers stopped in front of our house. Suddenly there was the rat-a-tat of gunshots. They killed fourteen people belonging to the Munshibari. There was one cry and then silence."

"Ahsanullah said to my mother, 'Khala, we can't stay here. They'll kill me. Mohammad Ali (a Bihari) is now a *mastan* and he is looking for me. I helped the BDR to make bombs.' We didn't eat the rice that was boiling on the burner. We left it where it was. We crossed the rail line and reached Goalkhali. But after two or three days we grew tired of eating in other people's houses. Moreover, mother had her own children with her. Who was going to feed them? I had just Tk. 100 with me. I gave the money to my mother and sent her to Jessore, saying, 'Mother, leave now. Let me see what the situation is like.' They were dependent on me. Still, I made them leave, packed their things, not knowing when I'd see them again. Miserably destitute as I was at the time, I didn't even cry. I helped her get on a rickshaw. I couldn't escort her to the station since it would take money to go there and return. My younger brother, who used to work at Jessore, had left to join the Liberation War. My mother was chased three times on her way. At the time Biharis were slaughtering people on trains."

Ahsanullah and Priyobhashini took shelter in an abandoned house along with some other refugee families. An engineer also lived in the house with his wife and three-month-old baby. No one could sleep at night because of the sound of gunshots. One morning the engineer went out and never returned. Later it was heard that Biharis had slaughtered him.

"When he heard of the engineer's death, Ahsanullah said, 'He is dead. I'm not staying here any more. I am leaving.' I pleaded with him, 'Please, take me with you. Do something.' 'I'll see,' he said and left."

"But on the second day of Ahsanullah's departure, the inmates of the house got together and started planning to drive us away. The women gossiped about me as being 'characterless.' They said I was a divorcee and was carrying on with another man."

We should remember what Priyobhashini had to endure in those days. She was the breadwinner for a large family, for a brood of children, her own and her mother's. She lived alone, a divorcee, in an industrial town inhabited by rich men and jute merchants. Their greedy eyes naturally fell on the young woman. Abused repeatedly in many ways, this lone woman struggled for survival. In 1971 when everything was collapsing or was being destroyed, the open sword of society was poised even more precariously above her. Battered and shelterless, Priyobhashini finally left the house and set forth on an uncertain destiny.

"I came downstairs. I couldn't hold back my tears. I was barefoot. I had lost everything while fleeing. I didn't even have sandals on my feet. As I stood at the end of the street, my mind was obsessed with only one question: Where would I go? I didn't even know if people were crossing into India. And even if he were, which road would he take? How had I become alienated from everything? Suddenly I saw Jahangir Kerala on a motor cycle. About 25 or 26 years, he was Assistant Purchase Officer of the Crescent Jute Mills. I had known his family for a long time."

"I asked him in Urdu, 'Jahangir Bhai, where have you come from?'"

"That was the last week of April. Jahangir asked, 'Why aren't you coming to office?'"

"'Are people attending office?'"

"'Of course. Why not? Are you willing to join?'

"Helpless as I was, I told him, 'I don't have any money for food, nor any guardian. Can you help me join?'"

"That same day Jahangir Kerala, on the excuse of giving me a job, took me to an abandoned house belonging to some Aga Khanis. He said to me, 'Come inside and rest. I'll take you to the office in the afternoon.' But, once inside, he took me by force. Though I was angry at his behaviour, there was nothing I could do. I was trapped in that isolated house."

"After Jahangir Kerala went out that afternoon, I escaped from the house, convincing the guards that I would return with my belongings.

Instead, I went straight to Crescent Jute Mill. On my way I heard Bihari boys saying, 'Look, there goes the treacherous Bangali. Beat her.' They hit my rickshaw with sticks. However, the sticks didn't touch me. Some of the boys, spat on me."

In the middle of the war, she returned to her old work place.

"After I reached the mill, I saw the Aga Khani General Manager Fidai Sahib standing on the front lawn. He used to be very affectionate towards me. When he saw me, he asked in Urdu, 'Where were you? Did you join the Mukti Bahini?'"

"No, Sir, all my brothers have joined the Mukti Bahini. I am alone now."

"Really?"

"Yes, Sir. See my condition. I am helpless."

"He noticed my bare feet. 'Do you want to join?'"

"If possible, yes, Sir."

"He took out an empty cigarette packet from his pocket and scribbled a note to the Chief Accountant Nazir Ahmed, asking him to give me 300 rupees. He told me to join the next day."

"I took the money, feeling quite rich. I had some money after a long time. The faces of my young brothers and sisters and my own children floated before my eyes. When evening fell, I roamed around aimlessly on a rickshaw, unable to decide where to go. I desperately needed to find shelter before evening fell. It was then that I met Farid, an old acquaintance, who often used to come to our house to sing."

"Where are you going, Bhabi?"

"'Just today I have rejoined work. I don't know where to spend the night.'"

"'Why don't you come to our place? You can stay there,' the young man said instantly."

"I knew their family. He, his stepbrothers and sisters along with their mother stayed together. Their house was on the outskirts of the town, away from the main thoroughfare, in a village named Pabla. There was jungle around it and it was quite safe. I agreed to his proposal."

The next day she went to the office. She had worked with the Aga Khanis who owned the jute mill. After marrying the person of her own choice, she had been estranged from her family and relatives for quite a number of years. The only contact she still had was with her mother and her younger brothers and sister. For the last couple of years she had become close to Ahsanullah, who had formerly worked at the Platinum Jubilee Jute Mills. She hoped that Ahsanullah would give her the love and affection that she had never got from her former husband. They might have got married earlier if the turmoil of 1971 hadn't started. However, since the day Ahsanullah had fled out of fear of the Biharis, Priyobhashini was completely in the dark as to his whereabouts.

Priyobhashini didn't know that the Aga Khanis, who had up to that time been nothing but gentle, would set a cruel trap for her. Maybe she didn't have time to think about that. She narrated the experience she had in her office.

"After I reported for work, within ten minutes, Mr. Fidai called me to his room and said, 'Sit down. I have something to say to you. We won't let you stay outside the mill area. You must live in the mill quarters. And secondly, my family is now in Pakistan. Can you help me?' Saying this he did not delay in pouncing on me. Full of disgust and hatred, I controlled myself and left the room. I had lost all power to protest; the hyenas attacked me wherever I went. Once as I entered the telephone room, an Aga Khani officer named Sultan Punjowani also entered with me. We used to call him Pyar Ali Bhai. After he told me that the carbon had tangled in the typewriter, I started to clean the machine. Suddenly he locked the door and grabbed my breasts. I just twisted his hands with all my might, saying nothing. This again was an Aga Khani. All of them had sent away their families to Pakistan, and then they pounced on me."

"Suddenly I heard the telephone ring. It was Mr. Fidai, 'Come and have lunch with me in the afternoon.' It was about 12 o'clock. Suddenly I saw a Bangali officer coming downstairs. He was a senior officer, about fifty. 'Won't you have lunch?' he asked. I thought I could save myself if I left. He was a Bangali officer and almost my father's age. I said, 'Yes, I will.' He started to drive the car as I sat nervously beside him. I then decided that if the GM asked I would say that I had forgotten and left by mistake. We had proceeded only a short distance when the Bangali officer said, 'Look, Ferdousi, my wife is very sick. I've not been having sex for a long time. Will you help me? I can pay you if you want.'"

"Alas, half of the day was still left and I had already faced a number of propositions. What should I do? Where should I go? My mother was waiting for me. I needed to send money to my sons, to my mother. But how could I survive like this? 'No, Sir, I can't help you,' I replied. His face changed in a second and angrily he said, 'Then get down here.'"

"One day I was working in my office. A cadillac stopped under the porch. I saw an old man seated at the back. There were two Pakistani officers seated on either side, laughing: Captain Gani and Captain Aslam. Yousuf was my peon. He gave the old man some water to drink. I recognised the old man as the Jute Inspector, Mr. Fazlur Rahman. He used to reside in a small bungalow facing the building where I had my quarters on the third floor. The building was on the jetty ghat near the river bank. On March 28, the EPR[2] had taken position inside his house and killed a number of Biharis. The army officers had arrested him for the killing, saying, 'You are responsible for what happened in your house.' As I still didn't know that he was going to be killed, I asked, 'How are you, Uncle?'"

"'I'm fine.'"

"About an hour later a huge procession of Biharis emerged. He was left in their hands to be slaughtered They played *Holi* with the blood of the Jute Inspector."

Priyobhashini returned to Pabla village, to the house surrounded by trees. But she continued to face all sorts of harassment in the office every day. One day she went out to buy some medicine. Suddenly, she heard the sound of firing near the mill owner, Mr. Afiluddin's house, situated at the entrance of the village. The gunshots were followed by the sound of screaming. Just before this she had been able to make out in the dark some men, a motorcycle and the dull glow of a lit cigarette. And then brush fire. The Naxals, armed leftist groups, were active in 1971 in several areas of Bangladesh. A group of them had joined the freedom fight, attacking the Pakistani army and the collaborators. They had shot Professor Bhuiyan, ten yards from the house because he had joined the Peace Committee a few days ago.

"The day after the incident, I went to my office. The GM called me at once. As I entered, he said, "We have heard that you are involved in the murder of Professor Bhuiyan." I remained silent, sensing that

2 Renamed Border Rifles Bangladesh after the liberation of Bangladesh. Now Border Guards Bangladesh.

they were preparing a new trap for me. When I turned to leave the room, the GM said from behind, "Listen, Commander Gulzarin, the Naval Commander, is coming." I shivered where I stood, at the door. I had heard that Gulzarin, the most horrible murderer one could remember, was also well known as a rapist. No woman beautiful or ugly would ever return alive if she were sent to him. He used to rape her first and then throw her in the river. Scared to death, I fell at the feet of the GM and pleaded, "Why me, Sir?"

"The man replied slowly, with his gaze calm, "Because you are involved with the murder of Professor Bhuiyan of the Peace Committee. You were seen outside his house. We have the report."

"In the evening the middle-aged Gulzarin came in his car and took me to the Naval Headquarters. The interrogation started.

"'Tell me clearly, who murdered Professor Bhuiyan?'"

"'I don't know, Sir.'"

"'I am Commander Gulzarin. You can call me only Gulzarin. Now tell me, are you with the Naxals? You know who killed the professor.'"

"'I am not with them. Otherwise, I wouldn't have joined the office.'"

"'That's why we doubt you. You are too nice for this job. You are collecting something from here. Otherwise a woman like you wouldn't have stayed in the midst of all this danger.'"

"Then his face changed. From a roaring lion he turned into a purring cat. But this change seemed more dangerous. 'Those who come to me, never return. But what an amazing power you have in your eyes! I know you are involved with the professor's murder. You are also with the Naxals. Still, I'll let you go. But on one condition. Let us enjoy ourselves for a moment. I'm hungry for you.'"

Twenty-six years after independence Priyobhashini murmured, as if to herself, "I gave my body, cold as stone, to the worst murderer one can remember, just to stay alive.'"

Suddenly, she came back to reality and continued her narrative.

"That day the Bangalis saw me getting down from the army car. The Naval Chief himself drove the car to drop me home. As for me, I had lost all sense of past and future."

"Ahsanullah used to come and stay in Pabla. It was night when I returned home. He asked, 'Where have you been?' I couldn't tell him anything and vaguely answered that I had just gone somewhere. If I told him everything he'd start worrying. He was already half dead with fear. If he knew the truth he would leave again. Moreover, he had heard the news that his brother had been murdered on the night of March 25 near Bangabandhu's residence. He was completely shattered, unable to sleep for fear of the Pakistani army and the Biharis."

One day Ahsanullah convinced Priyobhashini that it was not safe for him there and left.

Priyobhashini thought it pointless to stay on alone in Pabla village. Until then she had stayed there, disobeying the strict order of the mill authorities for Ahsanullah's sake. She had to pay the price for her job in any case. She moved to the junior officers' colony in the jute mills a few days after Ahsanullah's departure.

Although the house was new, all the windows and doors had been broken after March 25 and had not been fixed. She moved into the broken house. Her younger sister along with her help came from Jessore to stay with her.

"My younger sister, half dead with fear, stayed with me. One day she said, 'Apa, the sound of screams "Help, 'help' come from the river bank at night. I can't stay here any more.' She started crying."

Priyobhashini was startled. She too had heard such sounds accompanied by what seemed the sound of weeping from the riverbank. Seeing the skulls of the dead bodies all around, she thought that the sounds of 'Help' came from the wind blowing through the skulls. That night she turned off the light and saw that people were being taken down from one truck after another with gags on their mouths. Their necks were thrust inside the jute-cutting machine. The machine was pressed and the heads were severed from the bodies. She moved aside from the window. The next day her younger sister left for Jessore.

One day, as Priyobhashini was preparing to leave for her office, she saw four or five militiamen near her door with a crate of hens that they had looted. First she implored them, then frightened them and finally, with the help of a Bihari neighbour, drove them away. But at her office armed hyenas were waiting to pounce. Who would drive them off?

We can continue with Priyobhashini's narrative back at the Crescent Jute Mills.

"Fazli, the Accounts Officer, was the son-in-law of Fidai Sahib. Earlier, whenever I talked to him, he used to keep his eyes down and listen. Now he had become a great *mastan*. He came to me, 'I heard that you asked 20,000 rupees from someone. Is it from some army officer?' He tried to trap me saying all those things."

"I replied, 'No, why would I need 20,000 rupees?'"

"'We were informed that you asked for money from someone. Okay, we'll see. You'll lose your job.'"

"'I don't care.'"

"'Why? Will you join the Mukti Bahini?'"

"On that day, I had taken an hour's leave to go to Khulna. I was going by car. We were passing Khulna Jute Mills. Suddenly Fazli, along with his gang, stood in front of the car. We stopped. I asked, 'Driver, what do they want?' The driver, I think it was Nuru, replied, 'He is asking you to get inside his car.'"

"'I won't go,' I said."

"'Come.' There were five or six of them including a Bangali officer. Later he started a business. He used to go to the Khulna Club and was a part of that group. I met him when I used to go there to take part in different cultural programmes. He started telling me, 'Come with us. We are going there. Join us. Look here, Sadruddin, Mahmud Bhai, we are all going there. Let's have lunch together.'"

"The Pakistani soldiers were not the only people who were after me: Bangalis, Aga Khanis all tried to take advantage of me. Suddenly Fazli started to say, 'I will give you money. Don't you go with others? Don't you go to Commander Gulzarin when he sends his car for you?'"

"And then Fazli ordered me, 'Get into the car.'"

"I got in and then said, 'I already have a car with me.'"

"'We're taking you to the naval jetty.'"

"'Why?'"

"'So, you have taken a lot of money from people?'"

"'What are you talking about? I took money? If I had I wouldn't have continued with this job of only 400 rupees. Who told you this? Tell me his name.'"

"'I won't tell you any name. Do you want money?'"

"How familiar he was being! He had started to call me *tumi*.[3] I bowed my head and kept silent. When I was on the veranda he gave me a push from behind. I entered the room. In fear I started to call them 'sir.' No language can describe what they did to me that day."

---

[3] In Bangla—as in Urdu—there are three forms of you, depending on the formality of the occasion and the relationship between the speaker and listener. "Tumi" is the familiar form.

"One day when I was working in the office, the telephone rang, 'Hello, I'm a man speaking,' someone said in broken Bangla."

"'May I help you, please?' I asked."

"'Of course, you can help me. I saw you the other day through the window. Don't mistrust me. I want to be your friend.' He said all this in English and then added, 'By the way, how are you going back this evening? I'll drive you home.'"

"'My home is inside the mill area. It takes two minutes. Our office car takes me.'"

"I feared that General Manager Fidai would come with another horrible proposal. It was better if I took advantage of the opportunity offered by this army officer. 'My office will close at five. You can drop me,' I told him. I thought, I do not know what is in my fate today."

"When I got into the car, the young officer told me that his name was Altaf Karim. Then, to please me, he started telling me how beautiful and attractive I was."

"'I am not interested in hearing these things. My life is in danger. I'm struggling for my life.'"

"'I'll help you,' the young officer said immediately."

In the course of events, one day, this young army officer did indeed save Priyobhashini's life. She was then in Jessore Cantonment. She had again been arrested on the old charge of involvement in the murder of Professor Bhuiyan.

"Late one night I just could not go to sleep. I realised that the army had surrounded the house. I knew that if they started coming upstairs, I wouldn't be spared. So, I stuck out my head from the balcony and asked, 'Who is it?' I saw five or six cars below."

"'Come down. We have a warrant in your name,' they roared from below."

"'I won't go in the middle of the night. Go and bring the GM.'

"'We have come with the consent of the GM.'"

"Suddenly I saw before me Fazli, the son-in-law of the GM. I pleaded, 'Won't I get protection, brother? Please call the GM.'"

"'*Main kya janta*? *Agar aap klin hain to darti kyun*? (What do I know? If you are innocent then why are you afraid?) Go with them. The GM has given the written order.'"

"I got in the car without saying anything.

"In the car were Capt. Sultan and Lt. Korban, both dead drunk. They had been invited to the GM's house last night and that's why there were so many cars. They pounced on me in the car. Dawn was about to break. I don't remember anything afterwards."

"The car stopped at the Jessore Cantonment. One of the officers got out of the car and ordered, 'Take her to the Officer's Club.' I was taken to a room that had a billiard table. As I sat there, I started to doze off. I became aware that a number of army officers were standing before me. As I straightened up, one of them said, 'I am Col. Khatak and he is Major Abed. We have some questions. Be easy.' And then they started questioning me."

"'What do you know about the Mukti Bahini? What is your opinion about independence?'"

"'I can tell you just one thing. I've been separated from my relatives and am spending my time in absolute insecurity,' I said as I shook myself awake. 'I don't have any idea about my own country or about any foreign country. All I know is that I am alive. Besides, I have a question – what have I done so wrong that the soldiers broke into my house at five and brought me here with them?'"

"'Is that so? This is not right.'"

"'May I offer you a cigarette? Do you smoke?' asked Lt. Col. Abed as he offered me a packet of cigarettes."

"'No, Sir, thank you.'"

"'Look, we have a report that you killed Professor Bhuiyan. You help Mukti Bahini boys.' He lit his cigarette with style."

"Suddenly I felt a void in my heart. My younger brother used to come late at night to see my mother and would leave while it was still dark. Did they know that? However, I said, 'I've been living in the jute mill quarters for the last four or five months. All my movements are monitored. Now you decide, can I do something like this?'"

"'Stop being so clever. Gulzarin was unable to extract any information from you. That's why he has sent you to us. Tell us the truth. Otherwise you will be in big trouble.'"

"'I have been punished though I haven't done anything wrong. Do what you think right. I am not guilty.' I started to cry."

"'Don't cry. Speak.' I heard someone's voice."

"'I want to go home, I beg of you.' I kept sobbing. Suddenly I saw a look of lust on their faces, a look that I had got used to by now. I scuffled and protested vehemently, and both of them left the room."

"That evening, I saw two officers playing billiards. One of them raised his hand in greeting. I could hardly distinguish between uniformed officers. In the room where I was sitting, there was a small bed and three low sofas. It was almost evening. I had returned my lunch uneaten. I thought that my relatives must have come to know that I was in the cantonment and they must hate me. But nobody knew my real situation."

"Two persons again came in the evening. They told me, 'Lt. Khatak has asked these questions. We'll let you go tomorrow or even this very moment if you tell us the truth.' They tried to grab my hands and touch my hair as they spoke."

"Later that evening an officer entered the room, 'How are you, madam?'"

"'Fine.' I kept my head down. I knew that if I looked into his eyes, I would see the lust in them."

"'I'm Major Altaf Karim. Do you recognise me?'"

"Oh, Allah! He is the one I'm looking for, I thought to myself. He was the one who promised to save me."

"'You didn't enquire about my condition.'"

"'I salamed you when I came to play billiards in the evening. I didn't talk because you hadn't recognised me.'"

"Altaf told me many things. 'Today they were discussing that they will send you to a cell tomorrow.' I didn't even know what a cell was. He had been given the responsibility to show me the cell that night. He would write the final report after interrogating me. He had asked for the job. 'Let's go. I'll show you the cell first. However, don't let anyone know that you know me.'"

"As I accompanied Major Altaf down the corridor where the cells were located, I started. There was the sound of crying all around me. Some of the prisoners looked depressed. Some naked prisoners were crying, while some looked quite normal. I felt scared and returned to my room. The next day Altaf came with another officer. I stood up immediately seeing them."

"'Major Ekram will take you. Go to the office with him, sign a letter and then leave,' said Altaf."

"Major Ekram took me to Brigadier Hayat who gave me a release order and said, 'The interrogation is not over yet. So don't go anywhere else, but stay where you are. We must find you when we call.'"

"I didn't go back to Jessore after leaving the Cantonment. My whole body was bruised, my fingers swollen with their cruel touches.

"I came home and went to sleep. When I woke up it was 3 o'clock in the morning. Then I went back to sleep again. The next day when I reached the office, the GM phoned."

"'Come up, you have a call.' It was Major Altaf. Then he spoke to the GM and asked him to arrange stronger protection for me. How could the soldiers take me away from my house when I was working for him, in his presence, etc.? This made the GM quite angry and although he stopped pestering me, he started to misbehave."

"Suddenly one day there was a phone call from the Martial Law Office."

"'What's the matter?' I asked."

"'Farid, a young man of the house where you stay, has been caught at the Gallamadi Radio Station. His younger brother betrayed him out of jealousy. He said that he has a sister-in-law who worked in the Crescent Jute Mills and that she alone can save him. Can you save him?'"

"'It's not a question of whether or not I can save him,' I replied."

"'He's asked you to go to Jessore. They've strung him up all night long. They'll kill him,' the man on the phone said."

"I thought that I had taken shelter in their house. Now their son was in danger. Besides I was then so annoyed with Ahsanullah, who had left me, that I didn't fear for my own life. I took leave and went there. They'd sent him to Jessore for trial. There was a Major Banuri in charge there, a very cruel man."

"'Why are you here?' Major Banury asked."

"'I have a ....' I tried to say."

"'No, no, it's impossible. Why did you come? Are you also Mukti Bahini?'"

"'I have my identity card. I work in Crescent. I know Commander Gulzarin,' I told him."

"'It's all right. I'll set him free. Come in tomorrow morning. I'll do something for him.'"

"Now he'll get hold of me, I thought. I know he won't do it. Everybody knows about him."

"'How do you know Naval Commander Gulzarin?' he asked."

"'Our office is just beside his office. He comes to our office. That is how I know him,' I said."

"I managed to meet Brigadier Hayat. I told him that they wanted to shoot the boy. He would die. It was my obligation to save him because I had stayed at their house. He told me not to worry about it."

"Then I went to meet Major Ekram who treated me with kindness."

"Why have you come?"

"'I used to live with a certain family. One of their relatives has been caught.'"

"He was a bit better in his behaviour than the other soldiers and didn't try to take advantage of me."

"'All right,' he said to me."

"I went to the cantonment with him. 'Will you go to the cantonment with me?' he had asked. So I went there with him to save the boy. Many Bangalis who saw me go to the cantonment later called me a collaborator. They saw me with him, but they did not know why I had gone. When we reached the cantonment, we found they had just hung him upside down. Ekram ordered, 'Let him go.' And they let him go immediately. Lt. Korban was torturing him – I can clearly remember the names. He was torturing him in such a way that his tongue was sticking out. The way they were rotating him, I thought he would die. I saw the scene for a while and then couldn't bear to watch any more. Farid was released within an hour and I came back with him. It felt good that somehow I could pay back my debt. The Brigadier handed me a certificate, 'He is innocent. Somebody had caught him out of enmity.' He signed the letter and gave it to me."

Once Priyobhashini was returning from Khalishpur by bus. In Rupadiya a *razakar* wearing a *kabuli* outfit boarded the bus. Priyobhashini had faced all kinds of tyrants in the last six or seven months of the war, but she hadn't seen a *razakar* before. Now a *razakar* joined the list of those who abused and assaulted her. She described what happened that day.

"The man, who had shoulder length black hair, got on the bus with a heavy thump. He had pistols of all sizes in his pocket. I was the only female passenger in the bus. I thought that he was a *mastan* of some sort. The man walked up and down the bus. He suddenly stopped before me and asked, 'Hey, what do you do? Where are you going?'

"'I'm going home.' The man repelled me and I didn't want to talk to him."

"'Where's your home?' the man poked me with his pistol."

"'I won't answer so many questions.'"

"As I said this the man retorted, 'Wait. Why am I talking? This bus will stop at Abhoynagar Thana. You'll see if I can show you any law and order there. A girl like Shanti has been shot.'"

"Shanti used to work with the Naxals of that area."

"'Can't we do that to you? Come down.' He continued to hit me with the pistol and then forced the driver to drive up to Abhoynagar Thana. I was sure that I was going to die. His rifle was close to my body and he could pull the trigger at any time."

"'I won't get down.' I was defiant."

"'What? You won't come down?' He started to drag me down from the bus. The conductor of the bus fell at his feet and pleaded, 'I beg of you on her behalf. Please forgive her. Don't drag her like that.'

"'She won't learn anything unless raped by a hyena.' The *razakar* pointed his finger at me. The passengers of the bus were dumbfounded. Suddenly a young man shouted from the back, 'Why are you talking like this to a lady?' But the others stopped him. 'Please stop, she'll get into more trouble because of you.' Then all the passengers on my behalf apologised to the *razakar*. The bus started again after he got down. I learnt from the passengers that the man was Commander Sadullah. He had burned village after village. Every day he had killed three or four persons. He dragged out any woman he saw on a bus. Later, after independence, I saw the horrible death of this man. The freedom fighters pinned one leg down and pulled the other till they ripped him apart. What a horrible sight that was!"

"From October my troubles gradually lessened. The militia didn't disturb me for fear of Major Altaf, and the cruel claws of the army officers slackened considerably. Then Altaf proposed marriage. He said he would take all the responsibility for my children. In this way he tried to win my heart."

That was the first time that Priyobhashini was able to think a little about herself.

"It was quite natural for Altaf to think about marriage," said Priyobhashini. "I too had started to feel grateful to him for my survival. I was indebted to him, grateful for his kindness towards me. However, I couldn't marry a Pakistani, even though he had saved my life. I couldn't go to Pakistan. That would have been betraying my country."

The thought of marriage didn't last long. The war was coming to an end. Altaf's duties increased. Often he would come and say, "The country will become independent, probably you're getting your freedom very soon." By then the Aga Khanis were about to flee and would often move back and forth between Khalishpur and Dhaka."

Priyobhashini went to Jessore after learning about her mother's illness. There she met her younger brother Shibli, a freedom fighter. "He told me that Jessore would be freed first and the flag of Bangladesh would fly there."

It was December. Some of the Aga Khanis came to office while others didn't. One day the Bangali officer who had assumed charge of the Managing Director's post said, "Stay in the office till late evening. There might be some important phone calls and you might have to take messages." Night fell. At one point the Bihari driver Rashid came and said, "Baji, you're working very late. Let me drive you home."

For two years Rashid had been driving Priyobhashini. He had seemed very polite. Priyobhashini shut the telephone board and said, "Let's go." As she got in, the driver pulled the car onto the road. His mouth smelt of liquor. "Let's drive around for some time," he said in a lustful voice. From where she was sitting at the back, Priyobhashini pulled at his collar and then opened the door and jumped out of the moving car. She cut her left hand in doing so. By that time, however, the Biharis of the locality had surrounded the car. 'She tried to seduce me and started to scream as I turned the car. They should be devoured by dogs,' Rashid tried to say. The Biharis, if they could, might have pushed her back into the car. In the commotion, Rashid suddenly pushed her, "Go, walk." She ran for some time and then boarded a rickshaw.

At last December 4 arrived. Priyobhashini received a call from Major Altaf, who informed her that Jessore had fallen and he was coming to see her. Two days later, Ahsanullah called, "Come quickly. I'm waiting for you."

Priyobhashini once thought she wouldn't go anywhere. One day she had come to this mill for shelter and food. If anything happened, it would happen here. Ahsanullah called again, requesting her to come back. When he finally told her that if she stayed in the mill any longer, she might be killed, she realised that she was only endangering herself. The armed non-Bangalis were guarding the mill, locking its gates. They were not letting any Bangali leave the mill. Priyobhashini came out, telling them she needed to buy some medicine. After some time a Bangali clerk, whom she knew, was murdered by them inside the mill.

Priyobhashini told us about the incident.

"I had already left the mill. Anwar Bhai, who was a clerk, was murdered that day. He used to live on a floor of the house where I lived. The Biharis had locked all the three gates of the mill. It was probably 2:30 in the afternoon. I saw a rickshaw and boarded it as I had no energy left to walk to the gate. The savage faces of the Biharis were all around me and amidst that a militia told me, 'Leave quickly. They'll kill Anwar Bhai right now.' I had met Anwar Bhai earlier. He had told me, 'Things are not all right in the mill. It's getting late. You go where you can. I'll take care of your duties.' The Biharis killed him as soon as he entered my room. I didn't have time to feel sorry for anyone nor was I in any condition to do so."

Ahsanullah was staying in Rajghat, some distance away from Jessore. He had contacted Priyobhashini from there about a month earlier, but it was on that day that he started entreating her to join him. She stood on the crossroads of life. Death was behind her, and in front uncertainty. She did not know what to do. "As I stood there, I was uncertain whether to go right or left, to Rajghat or to Khulna, where?"

Finally she went back to Ahsanullah.

The country was liberated. Priyobhashini went back to her office and found Bangali officers and staff. As she sat down in her usual seat, the labour leader came running to her, "You can't join. You are a Pakistani collaborator!"

"He started to abuse me. I called the administration and found the Personnel Manager whom I had known from before. He used to be the Labour Adviser of the mill. He had been promoted. He hadn't joined the office during the nine months of the Liberation War but had remained in hiding for fear of the non-Bangalis. During that period he had come for help to me once or twice. I had requested General Manager Fidai for his salary once and sent it to his home. I phoned him and asked him to help me."

"'Sir, you know whether I was a collaborator or not. Please explain to them.'"

"'People are not going to listen. They are saying that you are a collaborator. What can I do?' he replied. I lost my job. One day the police came to arrest me."

It was a new country with a new government. The country had been liberated after a gory war. Priyobhashini had been raped because of this war. But she said: "Even the people who raped me and abused me for nine months didn't snatch my food from my mouth. Now, in a free country, I felt the ground give way under my feet. I left the mill with a heavy heart and didn't try to get back my job."

To her relatives, she was a violated woman, which was as painful as being a collaborator. On her head hung two swords, one of rape and the other of collaboration. Ahsanullah stood by her during all the adversities she faced after the war. In March 1972 they got married, ignoring the vehement opposition of Ahsanullah's family. After her marriage, when Priyobhashini went to Ahsanullah's workplace in Jessore, she found that people there somehow knew about the incidents of '71. Gossip spread in the air like wisps of cotton. Her husband had a transferable job, and she thought that they would be more comfortable if they started a new life somewhere else. Ahsanullah was posted to the hilly region of Sylhet, surrounded by jungles. They spent some untroubled days there. However, there were a few people from Jessore there and through them everybody came to know about what had happened to Priyobhashini.

Priyobhashini had had enough of human beings and decided to erase their existence from her world. She would see whether she could live without human beings. I don't know to what extent she has been able to do that. But now she thinks that she has found another sanctuary in her world of art.

References

1 Sheikh Gaus Mia, *Mahangari Khulna: Itihasher Aloke* (The City of Khulna: A Historical Perspective), Khulna: Kakoli Press, 2002.

2 Kazi Anwarul Islam, *Amar Ekattar* (My 1971), Dhaka: Abashar Prakashan, 1998.

Kushtia and Natore

Introduction

Suraiya Begum

As part of "Operation Searchlight," on March 25, 1971, a company of the 27 Baluch Regiment moved from Jessore Cantonment to Kushtia and imposed a thirty-hour curfew. The commander of the company was Major Shoaib. The leader of the liberation forces in the greater Kushtia area (comprising Kushtia, Meherpur and Chuadanga) was Major Abu Osman Choudhury. The people of Kushtia had erected barricades on all the roads. Near a one-storeyed building in front of the present Civil Surgeon's office, Ronny Rahman, a member of the Rangpur Chhatra Union, was killed while attempting to throw a hand grenade. He was Kushtia's first martyr.[1] In response, the Pakistani forces retaliated, killing seven people. This only made the resistance stronger. On March 30, the freedom fighters launched an attack under Abu Osman Choudhury. The Pakistani forces had entrenched themselves in three places: Kushtia Zila School, the Police Lines, and the Wireless Station. The freedom fighters attacked all three places simultaneously, and the fighting continued till the next day. The Pakistani forces retreated towards Damurhuda, Alamdanga and Jhenaidah.[2] In this fight, along with Major Shoaib, 200 Pakistani soldiers were killed. Three junior officers, including Lieutenant Ataullah, surrendered to the freedom fighters. In the fight, the *Mukti Bahini* captured a large amount of Pakistani arms and ammunition.

On April 16 the Pakistani forces re-entered Kushtia and unleashed a reign of terror. From April 16 to April 30, the Pakistani forces killed about 2,000 people. Biharis were released from jails and recruited as *razakars*. Several people were also killed in Kumarkhali. On May 28, a representative of the World Bank visited Kushtia and gave the following statement: "The town resembles the scene of German towns bombed by the Allies during the Second World War."[3]

---

[1] Fatema Zohra and Abu Mohammad Dilwar Hossain eds., *Muktijuddher Anchalik Itihash* Volume I (Dhaka: Sahitya Prakash, 1994), 213.

[2] Rabindranath Trivedi, *Ekattorer Dash Mash* (Dhaka: Kakoli Prakashani, 1997), 92.

[3] *Muktijuddher Anchalik Itihash*, 217.

After liberation, many mass graves were discovered in Kushtia, perhaps the most heart-rending being the discovery of the mass graves in the police barracks. In 1971, Kopotaksha and Gorai rivers bore away innumerable bodies. On April 17, when the Pakistani forces were unleashing a reign of terror in Kushtia, the Bangladesh Government-in-exile was set up in Baidyanathtola, in the liberated area of Meherpur. Sporadic fighting continued between the Pakistani forces and the freedom fighters. On August 4, at Paltigram, *razakars* killed two freedom fighters and captured two. Khelafat Ali, Chairman of the Peace Committee, and Shahidul Islam, his son, killed six more freedom fighters. There was extensive fighting in Kushtia during the entire month of November. On November 28, Jibannagar was liberated. Darsana, Meherpur, Chuadanga followed. By December 11, all of Kushtia was liberated. The *Mukti Bahini* had liberated 800 square kilometres of this region, enabling the people of Bangladesh to breathe the air of freedom. However, this freedom was won after intense fighting and at great cost. The Pakistani forces did not limit their retaliation to killings, lootings and destruction but carried out countless rapes of innocent women. Sexual brutality was used systematically to humiliate and subjugate the Bangali nation.

In 1971, Pakistani occupation forces terrorised the entire country. There was no peace or security in either town or village. No lives were safe, no houses. Women dwelt in constant fear of being raped. The fear of being killed, of losing one's home, of being raped led countless people to leave their homes in search of a safe haven. They wandered from one end of Bangladesh to another. Many of these experiences have been narrated; they are stories of people who, in retelling their stories, again relive the horrors of that period. They describe their feelings of insecurity in voices quivering with emotion. Four accounts of women from Kushtia are being retold here to illustrate their painful experiences in 1971.

Two other case studies of women who tragically lost their husbands have also been included in this chapter. One of them is Begum Hosne Ara, the other is Fatema Kalam. In 1971, Latafat Hussain Joarder, Begum Hosne Ara's husband, was Principal of Darshana College in Kushtia. In July, he was taken to the army camp and did not return. Golam Kibria, the husband of Fatema Kalam, was working in Gopalpur Sugar Mill, in Natore. On May 5, the Pakistani forces attacked Gopalpur Sugar Mill killing over 300 person. One of the persons killed that day was Golam Kibria.

Masuda, Elijan, Duljan, Momena

Rape as a Weapon of War

Suraiya Begum

In the month of Ashwin (mid September-mid October), a hundred or so Pakistani soldiers took shelter in Hashimpur Bazar and in a school at Kumarkhali. They were assisted by a number of *razakars* including one named Mozam (SP). Mozam showed the Pakistani soldiers the homes of persons who were either related to or associated with freedom fighters and who supported the Liberation War. With the support of the *razakars*, the Pakistani army launched a reign of terror on all they suspected of being in league with the freedom fighters. They killed suspects, they pillaged and burned homes, they ravished women. Almost all of Bangladesh underwent a similar shattering experience. There is no place in Bangladesh where the Pakistani army did not perpetrate sexual atrocities. By the time this research started, 25 years had elapsed since independence. During this time women who had suffered sexual abuse were subjected to insults and indignity by their community and rejected by some families. As a result women were not willing to talk about their experiences. Therefore, it was difficult to collect accurate information.

We heard of four women who had been sexually abused by the Pakistani military in the Kumarkhali, Hashimpur, Dayarampur and Mathmalir areas of Kushtia district. In 1992 Masuda Khatun, Elijan Nessa and Duljan Nessa went to Dhaka to give testimony at the Ghatak Dalal Nirmul Committee Gana Adalat[1] organised by Jahanara Imam. Because of the attack on the gathering, the scheduled programme could not continue. Therefore, despite being present that day, these three women were unable to say anything. The next day, however, two papers published their photographs. How and why

[1] People's Tribunal for Trial of the Collaborators.

these three went to Dhaka and what happened to them subsequently is narrated in the following pages.

When we went to Kumarkhali, the conditions for interviewing the women were not favourable. The women were financially hard-up and emotionally distraught. They were angry at those who had taken them to Dhaka and given them various promises but had let them down. In these circumstances it was not very easy for us to conduct our interviews. It was like entering the cannon's mouth. I took the interview in October 1997. With me were Zubaida Nasreen and Akmal Hussain, the local *Sangbad* representatives, and our liaison persons. In 1998, Prime Minister Sheikh Hasina gave each of these women a cheque for Taka 50,000. The following account only covers the interviews that we conducted in 1997.

Masuda Khatun

Hashimpur is a village in Kumarkhali Thana in Kushtia. One has to take a bus from Kushtia and cross the Gorai river by boat in order to reach the place. On the other side of the river, tempos[2] and twelve-seater motorised rickshaws are available. One can also take a van cart – a modified version of a rickshaw with a flat board on top to seat four to eight passengers with their legs dangling. We had to get down from the vehicle and walk along the footpath to enter the village. It is a small, not very well-to-do village, with a mosque and an NGO office.

We first went to the home of Masuda Khatun, accompanied by Selim, who was from the village, and Akmal Hussain, the *Sangbad* correspondent. By the time we reached Masuda Khatun's home, it was about 11.00 am. There was no one around, but, within a few minutes, a crowd gathered. Masuda Khatun's husband, Sheikh Mofizuddin, who was present in the house, spread a mat for us in the courtyard. Before we could meet Masuda Khatun, Sheikh Mofizuddin asked us many questions. Where had we come from, what were our intentions, what did we want to do, and what could we do for them? We had to answer all these questions. We got a detailed narration of the incident from him. After this we were ushered inside to meet Masuda Khatun who was indisposed.

The room revealed the impoverished condition of the couple. When we entered, Masuda Khatun got up from bed. We sat on her

2 Three-wheeler motorised vehicle (small shuttle) common in rural Bangladesh.

bed and talked. Masuda Khatun spoke very slowly and in a faint voice. The following narrative has been pieced together from her account of the day.

"My name is Masuda Khatun. This house where I am staying is my paternal home. My parents had only three children, all of them girls. That is why, even after my marriage, I continued to stay at my parental home. My father had died, so my mother made my husband a *ghar jamai*.[3] I was the eldest. My younger sister has a defective leg and is unmarried. She works next door in the teacher's house. My youngest sister is married and lives near us."

"When I got married, our circumstances were fairly good. My husband worked all day in the fields, ploughing, weeding, looking after the crops. We did not have much land so my husband had to work as a share cropper in other people's fields. My mother was staying with us. We were fairly well off. In 1971, I was the mother of three children, two boys and one girl. My eldest child was a girl, the next two were boys. My youngest son was just a baby of three months."

"During the war I knew that my husband supplied information to the freedom fighters secretly. Also that he would help them in various ways. I used to fight with him over this. I would say, 'I stay alone at home with the children. You are out the whole time.' Occasionally there would be rumours that the military had entered the village. But the day that the army actually entered, we were taken unawares. All the villagers were more or less at home that day. No one had really fled or gone to India. The days we heard that a military attack was imminent, I would dress my son and go somewhere else. On other days, with my child in my arms, I would flee across muddy streams. Everyone would flee hearing the alarm: 'The soldiers have entered the bazaar.' But the day the soldiers actually came, we thought that no one would not come. That day there was no rice in the house, and I was pounding rice in the *dheki*. It was about ten or eleven in the morning. I had not had my breakfast, thinking that after spreading the rice in the courtyard, I would go and eat. One of the neighbouring women was pounding the rice, and my mother was sitting beside her, occasionally helping by adding handfuls of paddy to be husked. I had my son in my arms and was just about to go inside the house, when the soldiers entered. We hadn't seen them coming. We weren't

[3] Custom of husband living with the wife's family.

staying here but elsewhere at the time. It was a big house, with a *charchala*[4] tin roof. There was a separate cookhouse as well as a room for the *dheki*.[5] The place was neatly fenced."

"We were pounding the paddy in the *dheki* room when the soldiers were suddenly upon us. The soldiers said upon entering, 'Are there any eggs, eggs?' I trembled with fear upon seeing them. I had put my youngest son down to sleep. My mother too was startled upon seeing them. The soldiers were wearing the type of uniform policemen wear. That is all I can remember. I was not in my senses at that time. My mother was also terrified. I was trembling with fear. Suddenly they caught hold of my right leg. I continued to tremble, but still they held on to my leg. Two soldiers had entered. The others remained outside. My mother was crying and trying to come to my aid. But one of the soldiers prevented her. The other soldier caught hold of my right hand and dragged me inside the room. My youngest son was sleeping on the bed. They flung the boy down. I started to cry loudly. By that time all the villagers had fled. My mother was crying loudly. I was crying, my son was crying. By this time they had forced me inside the room. After this I lost consciousness. They did not beat me. But once when I attempted to escape, they threatened to shoot me with their guns. Both my mother and I. My mother clung to their feet and said, 'My sons, I beg of you, let my daughter go.' They replied, 'If you talk, we will shoot you.'"

"I do not remember what they did after they brought me inside. I was not in my senses. They didn't call me names, but they held the muzzles of their guns to my face. I couldn't say a word. I was just not in my senses."

"In 1971 I was about 18 or 19 years. I was quite pretty at the time. My mother had married me off at the age of 10 years. My first child was born when I was 12."

"When I came to my senses, I found my husband weeping beside me. He was bemoaning his fate. He said, 'Alas, alas. They have ruined me. Alas, I have been ruined.' He kept on saying, 'My honour is gone. Alas, what have they done to me?' Like a mad man he caught hold of whatever he could and started hitting me with it. Everyone tried to hold him down. After this he would not stay at home. And whenever he was at home, he would curse his fate. He would wander

---

4 Tin roof slanted on four sides.

5 Manually operated local tool, made of wood, used for paddy husking.

about in a dishevelled state all over the village. He wouldn't even come home for meals. He wouldn't take a glass of water from me. He would not eat what I cooked. The elders of the village had to forcibly get him to eat something. He had become like a mad man. His eyes would be red all the time and he had turned into an old man, though he was still fairly young. He used to be nice-looking. He was light-skinned and had a fine figure. After what happened to me, he wandered about for about a month. He would not eat or dress properly. At the beginning he was displeased with me and would rebuke me. He didn't want to take me back. He didn't want me to be his wife any more. He refused to eat what I cooked. Afterwards, the elders of the village persuaded him that I had not been at fault. 'Your wife has done nothing wrong,' they said. 'She did not do this thing willingly.' They also said a lot of other things to him. After a lot of coaxing on their part, he accepted me once again."

"After he took me back, my husband did not insult or scold me further. He said whatever he had to immediately after the event. After he accepted me, he did not refer to the incident again, but carried on as if nothing had happened. He didn't even refer to it when we were together. But I suffered afterwards. It affected our conjugal life. Intercourse was painful. Even now I have problems. During my periods, I bleed profusely. I feel unwell and weak."

"Because of what the Pakistani soldiers did to me, people insult me. My son is referred to as 'the military brat.' My son, whom the soldiers flung to the ground, is called the soldiers' son. My children are social outcasts. They have to listen to insults and snide remarks. Even my son says to me, 'You should have drowned yourself in the Padma. Because of you we cannot show our faces in society.' As a result of what happened to me, my daughter has problems getting married. My oldest daughter I have been able to marry off. I do not know whether her in-laws know of the incident. She has never come and told me that she has been insulted because of what happened to me. Everyone blames me, but my daughter doesn't."

"This incident had been more or less forgotten till people came and persuaded me to go to the *gono adalat*. That is when a lot of people came to know about what had taken place. People started insulting us. The villagers ridicule me now, saying, 'You listen to whatever outsiders tell you, but you have gained no benefits from this. You have besmirched your honour, but have gained no material benefits or recompense.'"

"The soldiers did not hit or scratch me. But my sexual organs and my lower portion were hurt. Afterwards I had to go to a doctor. Sometimes I bleed. I get sharp pains in my abdomen. And when I have my periods, I bleed as profusely as if I am urinating. I was taken to a doctor immediately after the incident."

"I do not remember how many soldiers assaulted me. But I do remember that two entered. I wasn't wearing a blouse. The soldiers had taken off my sari. I was just in a petticoat."

"After the soldiers left, my mother dressed me. She attended to me."

Masuda wept and said, "Sister, sometimes I want to commit suicide. I am ashamed to show my face to my own children. They say, 'You go to whoever calls you. You go and sing your song for them. Why didn't you poison us?' All four of my sons are jobless. Because of me they do not get jobs. Our family knows want and suffering. My eldest son was a daily labourer, but after my history became known people stopped hiring him. I had arranged my son's marriage, but, because he cannot earn anything here, he left for Dhaka. There he pulls rickshaws. Because I gave evidence at the *gono adalat,* this is what has happened to us. My children did not know what had happened because they were small at the time. But after I spoke at the *gono adalat,* what happened to me has become common knowledge. My youngest son has managed to study with great difficulty. There are several NGOs here. None of them has ever helped. Everyone makes promises, but no one keeps them. I am now in very straitened circumstances. I used to be fairly well off. Now I have nothing. I have been ill for four months, but I am too poor to get medical assistance."

"I feel sad about what happened to me. I suffer for it. Then I think that Sheikh Mujibur Rahman also suffered a lot but he too was killed. Allah, if we had been killed along with him my shame would have been no more. I would not suffer like this."

"I did not become pregnant as a result of the rape as my son was just three months old at the time. I wasn't having my periods. Later I had two more sons and another daughter."

"It was after that incident that my health suffered. From that day I have not been keeping well. My spirits are also low. I often think of what happened that day. I have not forgotten. I have nightmares. When I am lying in bed, I think that I am about to die. I realise that my honour is gone. My entire body seems to break out weeping.

People do not say things to my face, but they talk behind my back. When I hear what they say, I ask Allah for justice. It is my fate to hear these insults. I do not go anywhere. I stay in bed with this suffering body of mine. I do not even go to the homes of relations. I have been to Dhaka only three times. That too because Naseem Bhai took me. There has been a lot written about us in the papers but nothing came of it. I would like to see the Prime Minister and say a few things to her. She too has suffered as I have. I would like to tell her about my inner suffering. Once my husband went to see the Prime Minister (Sheikh Hasina), leaving no food for us at home. He spent Taka 300 and went from door to door but had to return home without seeing her. When he returned, I scolded him. 'You left no food for the children and me, but went to Dhaka and spent the money without achieving anything.' Whenever anyone says anything to my husband about the possibility of meeting the Prime Minister, he jumps up and goes to Dhaka. He hopes that he will be able to meet the Prime Minister. I also hope I can meet her." Masuda Khatun wept and said, "When I meet the Prime Minister I will tell her my story."

Masuda Khatun first went to Dhaka to give evidence at the *gono adalat*. At that time she had stayed in the home of Jahanara Imam. Masuda told us that her slippers were torn and Jahanara Imam had given her her own slippers to wear. Masuda said, "When we stayed with her in Dhaka, she looked after us very well."

When she came to Dhaka subsequently, her time was spent moving from one office to another. She went to the ADAB office where she met Khushi Kabir. "At the time, there was a conference of grassroot level organisations," Masuda said, "but I was unable to go because I was not well."

Masuda's husband, Mofizuddin, told us that in 1971 he used to work on the farm and was able to provide intelligence to the freedom fighters from time to time. Among the freedom fighters were Osman, Kalu, Mofiz Jallad. Mofiz Jallad supported the Liberation War and harassed people who worked against it. That is why he was known as Mofiz Jallad, Mofiz the Executioner.

Mofizuddin narrated his experiences during 1971. He said, "During the liberation war there used to be a freedom fighters' camp in Kalyanpur. They used to stay there. They used to come at night and say to us, 'It will not do to sleep like this. Won't you fight for the independence of your country?' I said to them, 'I have small children.

I have worked for independence endangering them. If all of us take up arms who will look after the country, do what things need to be done? It is necessary to keep the country going. For example, you all have come here. You have come because I am here. You carry rifles, but even though we haven't taken up arms we are also working for independence.' After I said this, the freedom fighters left. It was because I helped the freedom fighters that my house was attacked."

"One day the *razakars* tortured some people from our village. I do not know whether they said anything about rifles, but when I was cutting the grass in the field behind, some *razakars* caught hold of me and said, 'You rascal of a freedom fighter, get into the pond.' They were *razakars* and Biharis. They forced me to search for weapons inside the pond. The water in the pond was about five to six feet deep. 'Put your head beneath the water and see if there are any rifles there,' they said to me. As I groped under the water, suddenly I felt a rifle. But I thought that if I brought the rifle up I would be killed. So instead, I thrust the rifle even deeper into the mud. When I came up empty-handed, they hit me with my sickle. 'You rascal, we asked you to bring up the weapons. Why have you failed?' They said, 'He is a rascal. He is a *malaon*, a Hindu.' Then they started beating me. Then they forced another man to descend into the muddy waters of the pond. The other man brought up the rifle. At that time I was standing on the eastern side of the pond where there was a jute field. I managed to run into the field. The *razakars* tried to catch me but I managed to elude them."

"One day the *razakars* announced, 'None of you must leave your homes. No one will be hurt. No one will come here. And there is no fighting going on.' I was working in the fields when suddenly a cry arose that *razakars* and Pakistani soldiers had entered the village. The soldiers had surrounded our home. It was the Bangla month of *Ashwin*. Hearing that the soldiers had surrounded our hut, I ran home as fast as I could but I could not enter. Afterwards I heard what had happened. Two soldiers had entered along with a *razakar*. There was a lot of stuff in the house. They took away whatever they could when they left."

"I got the news immediately but I thought that I was unarmed and alone. When they entered my hut, there were no villagers at home. They had all left. How could I do anything alone? I would be killed."

"The soldiers left after some time. They did not burn the house down, but they did take whatever they could. At that time we were quite well off. We had a plough, and I was able to work. We managed quite well. The soldiers took away my wife's gold earrings as well as some money and two bullocks, which we used to pull the plough."

"After the soldiers left, I returned home to find my mother crying with my son in her arms. She [Masuda] was lying unconscious. I took her to a doctor for treatment. After several years, she developed heart trouble. She also suffers from ulcer and gastritis."

After independence they had not sought assistance from the government. They somehow managed to survive on his daily wages of Taka three. They ate ground *khesari dal* and rice costing taka twelve per kilo, but they did not raise their hands in supplication to anyone. Their youngest son had gone to the relief camp. He had waited the whole day for a piece of bread, but he had not appealed to anyone for special favours. In Mofizuddin's words, "We have given our honour for the nation, why should we go begging to people?"

On March 26, 1992, the Kumarkhali Muktijoddha Sangsad arranged Masuda's trip to Dhaka to give evidence at the *gono adalat*. Naseem, who came from Kushtia and belonged to the Kumarkhali Muktijoddha Sangsad, took them to Dhaka. They were helped by Baby Maudood and Ahad Choudhury as well.

Naseem was the District Commander of the Muktijoddha Sangsad. He came and told them about going to Dhaka. However, he did not explain at the beginning what their purpose was in doing so. Afterwards, when they received a letter, Mofiz went to Hasan, the local Muktijoddha commander. Hasan advised them to go. "It is all right. You should go. Jahanara Imam is an MBBS doctor.[6] Your wife is continually ailing. She will get medical attention there."

When they went to Dhaka, they were taken immediately to the stage. "They did not tell us earlier that we would have to narrate our traumatic experiences. Still, we agreed. Before this, there was a meeting at Kushtia where demands had been raised for Golam Azam to be hanged. We had been taken there as well. It was there that they slowly disclosed what was expected of us. After this we were taken to Dhaka, where people spoke of our independence. After this some gentleman came and taped my wife's account of her experience. He touched my son's head and said, 'You will either be given a job in this

[6] Jahanara Imam was not a doctor. The man was giving Mofiz false hopes. Jahanara Imam lost a son in the Liberation War. She also wrote an account of her agony as wife and mother in 1971 titled "*Ekattore Dinguli*." In 1992, she started a movement for the trial of war crimes and headed the People's Tribunal to try war criminals.

country or you will be sent abroad.' Promising this the gentleman left. We never saw him again. Everyone makes fun of my son. 'What happened to your job? Aren't you going abroad?' My son was finally so disgusted that he left home and is now a rickshaw puller in Dhaka. My other two sons and my daughters and sons-in-law stay in our village. They are the butt of jokes and sneers. In the past, I managed to do a little farming. But now I get no more work."

"I spoke to Mr. Naseem. He said he was powerless to do anything. But now that Sheikh Hasina, Bangabandhu's daughter, is Prime Minister, I am going to try once again. I will try to meet the Prime Minister. I will tell her about our problems. I had approached several people requesting a meeting with the Prime Minister, but no one helped us. I had also written several letters to her, but received no reply. I had approached Moslehuddin Swapan Bhai who works in an NGO called Roots. I have also tried to get the help of Muktijoddha Chetana Parishad, but no one has helped me to get an interview with the Prime Minister."

"After we gave evidence at the *gono adalat*, many powerful persons who were opposed to the liberation war threatened us. They say they will ostracise us. This is how we are eking out our existence these days."

Masuda Begum's mother, Ranijan, witnessed the Pakistani soldiers raping her daughter. Ranijan narrated the incidents of the day.

"We were at home at the time. My daughter was pounding rice in the *dheki* room. I was helping her. That was when they came. My daughter had her baby in her lap. They flung the baby to the ground. Then they caught hold of her. They had guns in their hands. What was I to do? There was no one to help us. What could I do? I appealed to them; I cried aloud. They dragged my daughter away. My daughter started to cry. They shut the door behind them. They opened the door after about an hour. Then they left. They beat my daughter inside the room."

Ranijan told us that she had stayed outside because when she tried to go to her daughter's aid, they had aimed their guns at her. When the soldiers left, they smashed up whatever utensils they could find and looted their things. The girl came out of the room and started to cry. Ranijan didn't know what to do.

She said, "My daughter was crying. What could I do? I was alone. But I did what I could. Her condition was pitiful. There were scratch marks on her breast. I tried to console my daughter. I told her to stop crying. No one came to our assistance, no one came. My son-in-law was not at home at the time. He came afterwards and rebuked us angrily. 'Couldn't you die? Couldn't you manage to escape?'"

"After the soldiers left, I bathed my daughter and washed her clothes. Afterwards, many people came to our place. They said all sorts of things. 'The soldiers came and put their seals on your daughter.' You know, don't you, what mouths villagers have? They say all sorts of things. People taunt the children when they go to school, saying they are the soldiers' brats."

"Afterwards, my daughter would not go anywhere. She fell ill. She couldn't work properly. Brooding over her experience, my daughter grew ill. Even now, she cannot forget what happened to her. She just lies on that wooden bed all day. People continue to say all sorts of things to her. You all have come. After you leave, they will again say all sorts of things. They will say, we are going around giving pictures to people, we are going to meetings. This is how we manage to survive."

Elijan Nessa

Elijan Nessa, who came from Hashimpur village, was raped as well. In fact, she was raped the same day as Masuda Khatun. In 1992 she too went to Dhaka to give testimony at the *gono adalat*. She suffers the same social ostracism as Masuda Khatun.

When asked to speak of her experiences in 1971, Elijan exclaimed, "My life is over. I have told the story over and over again till I can repeat it no more. I can bear this no longer. Why don't you shoot and kill me? We do not want to live any more. We are reviled by everyone."

It took a long time for Elijan Nessa to calm down. Then, slowly, she started to narrate the events of the day. "We had heard that the soldiers would be coming at that time. I was just married, and I was so young that I did not know anything. I was so innocent that I would wear just a blouse and petticoat. After our marriage, my husband left me with my mother-in-law. I hadn't been married very long. Perhaps just for about five months."

"The day of the incident I was at home, lying in bed. My mother-in-law entered my room and said, 'Daughter in law, don't you see that the soldiers have entered the village? Get up, get up and go wherever you can.' My mother-in-law had a small baby. She said to me, 'Take the child and run away.' I took the baby in my arms and went next door to the house of an artisan who made brassware. The man told me, 'Don't come here. They will burn down my house.' I had gone to his place with some brass and bell metal utensils. I was young, I was married, but still they turned me away. I returned home and kept the utensils and ran towards another house. The place was full of people. Terrified for my life, I hid with them. The soldiers soon came. They entered the house and made us all come out one by one. There were about 20 or 25 of them. All of them were in uniform. After making everyone leave the house, they caught hold of me. They held my hand and threw me to the ground. By that time the rest of the soldiers had left, leaving only two behind. There was no one else with them. They first went to the market and then entered the village."

"They flung me on to a wooden cot. I was crying and screaming. They threatened to shoot me with their rifles. I was wearing a sari and a blouse at the time. Throwing me onto the cot, they started doing all those things to me."

At this point Elijan started to weep. Then she continued with her story. "After one of them had finished, another one who was waiting outside entered, and he too did the same thing. Then they left. When they assaulted me they did not tear my clothes. They could see that I was very young. I didn't even have breasts. But before this I had had relations with my husband."

"After the soldiers left, my mother-in-law took me to the pond and gave me a bath. She changed my clothes and took me to her sister's house. I stayed there for two days. After staying there for two days, I returned home."

"My husband heard of the incident and returned home. He too was young. The neighbours told him, 'This is what they did to your wife, this is what happened, etc.' He was very upset, but he did not beat me. I am a poor man's daughter. I have suffered all my life. But this suffering will never go away. After this when I conceived my eldest daughter, people went around saying, 'She is not that man's daughter, she is the soldiers' bastard.' I pretended not to hear. It was in my fate, it was written in my destiny, that is why this happened to me."

"After staying at my uncle's, I returned to my in-laws' place. After I returned to my in-laws' place, no one said anything to me."

"But my parents-in-law did not say anything to me. They did not say, 'We will no longer accept you as our daughter-in-law.' My father was dead. My mother heard what had happened. But what could she do? The person who had arranged my marriage – he was a sort of maternal uncle – came and took me to his place. He told my father-in-law, 'If the girl had stayed at my place, perhaps no harm would have come to her. You took her to your place and allowed this to happen to her.' Then my uncle brought me to his place. When I was at my uncle's, I was unable to eat. Perhaps because I was terrified. I became like a skeleton. I am still that skeleton today. I used to weep all day. What did I do for this to happen to me?"

Elijan also described similar events that had taken place in her village that day. "The soldiers did the same thing to other women in our village that day. Masuda Khatun had just had a baby; her insides were still sore from her pregnancy. How they assaulted her! And I was just a child. The way they assaulted me, can that be forgiven? It would have been better if they had killed me. Then I would not have this pain inside me. My story would not have been published in the papers, and I would not have been shamed in the eyes of the people of my country. At present no one respects me. People look down on me. People do not look down at shoes as much as they look down on us. No one invites us on social occasions. I work at home. I wind thread on to bobbins. I do not visit anyone. Perhaps they will talk about what happened. That is why I don't go to people's homes. Especially after going to Dhaka and saying all those things, I have no face left in society."

"I have two daughters. I have sent one daughter to Dhaka to get food and clothes. I cannot feed her."

At this point Elijan broke down. After some time she continued. "Why did I have to send her to Dhaka? I used to work and feed myself. I was quite all right. People tempted me and said that I would be better off. My husband can no longer work. People do not give him work. No proposals come for my daughter. They talk of money. Where will I get money?"

"They took me to the *Gono Adalat*. I do not understand why they took me there. Before taking me, they had said, 'Come with us to Dhaka. You will get houses and all sorts of material benefits.' They had said, 'You will speak about what happened in 1971. You will narrate what happened to each of you.' That is what we narrated. After we told everything, they stood us in the dock and made us give our testimony. My husband had appendicitis. The people who took us to Dhaka helped him get an operation and also gave me two or three thousand taka. We have no hesitation in speaking about what we received. But after the *gono adalat*, our sufferings increased."

"People ridicule us for having gone to Dhaka and talking about all those things. People laugh at us and say we went to Dhaka for money. We have to listen to all sorts of things. What are we to do? We are poor. What should we do? Should we commit suicide? My children did not know. Now my son-in-law tells my daughter, 'What happened to my mother-in-law? She goes here and there. She goes to Dhaka. What is the matter?' Everyone now knows what had happened."

We also talked with Elijan Nessa's husband, Akbar Sheikh. He narrated the events of the day.

"In 1971, I used to catch fish. I had a boat of my own and would catch fish in the Padma. The *mukti joddha* often used my boat to go back and forth. On several occasions they came and stayed at our place. Next door to me lived a schoolmaster, Munshi Abul Hussain, who was associated with the Awami League. We were friendly. When the trouble started, *razakars* and Biharis started killing Hindus. They killed the Halders who lived next door to us as well as Hindus from the villages of Dayarampur and Hashimpur. Many people from the Sardar area were killed. Three of the Halders were killed: Nil Halder, Siddheswar Halder and another person whose name I cannot recall. A net covered with coal tar was flung upon them and they were burnt alive. Seeing all this, I fled, leaving behind my paternal grandmother, my mother, and my wife. After some time, I fetched them and kept them in a place a mile or two away from our home. When the trouble subsided, we returned home. At that time I used to catch fish on the Padma. After about three months I heard that the soldiers had entered. Consequently, people from Dhaka and Pabna were crossing the Padma and trying to flee to India via Kumarkhali."

"The soldiers did not enter our village first. The *razakars* and Biharis were the first to do so. One night the army entered Kushtia. When they entered Kumarkhali, I fled once more, to my sister's home about two or three miles away. A month or so later, I returned to my fishing. One day I saw that the army was moving out of Kumarkhali towards Shilaidaha. From the river, I could see the village burning. I used to sell fish at Kumarkhali; the *mukti joddha* used my boat to move to and fro. Several times they stayed on my boat. One night when they were staying on my boat, I had gone for some work to

Kumarkhali. I was cooking at the time. It was then that the soldiers entered the village. I saw that in the direction of Pabna, that is on the other side of the Padma, the military had set fire to the village. There were gunshots. Fires blazed. The place resounded with the noise of gunshots. We were on this side. Suddenly, a cousin of mine, accompanied by the schoolmaster's brother, came running and boarded my boat. They were followed by Tunu, my youngest uncle's son. I released the boat. We reached Karimpur, and they got down and went to the home of Razzaq, a freedom fighter. Then they all returned to the boat and told me to cross the river quickly. Accordingly, I manoeuvred the boat across the river as quickly as I could. I saw that lots of people were fleeing in that direction, that is, towards India. Two of the youths who were in my boat said, 'Uncle, row quickly.' We reached the other side. We had no idea of what was happening on this side. We did not know about the atrocities committed by the soldiers or that they had raped women. We were on the other side. I was alone with the three of them. They asked me if I had any rice. I told them that I had rice, oil, chillies, everything. Fish was cheap across the river. I bought fish and cooked a meal. We ate together. Meanwhile, the soldiers had committed their atrocities on the other side and left. I ferried the three youths back to this side, and they departed for their homes."

"In the evening I was cooking dinner. Two of the youths were to return and eat. I would eat and then catch fish at night. Just then my cousin returned and said, 'Brother, I have something to tell you. Bhabi has been assaulted by the soldiers. People have been killed.' On hearing those words, I left the pot of rice cooking on the stove in my boat and rushed back to the village. When I reached home, I learned that my family had taken shelter next door. There were about 50 to 60 people there. My wife had also fled there out of fear. That was where the soldiers had caught hold of her. She was my new bride. We had had no children as yet. When I returned home, my wife started crying and weeping. What was I to do? She did not do anything willingly. She had been forced into submitting to them. They could easily have killed her. Had I been at home, I too might have been killed. The soldiers entered once more. That time too I fled. After this the country was liberated."

"Abul Hussain Master was my next-door neighbour. After the liberation of the country, he called me. He said, 'I will write about the incident, about how your wife was assaulted.' I replied, 'What are you saying, Bhaijan? What is the point of writing all this?' He said, 'If I write this then you will get a monthly allowance. When you have children, they will get medical treatment. You will get clothes, etc.' I said, 'If that is so, then write.' Accordingly, he wrote. I heard nothing for some time after this. About four or five months later, we were called to Kumarkhali. There we were given one small pot and three aluminium plates. About three months later, I was called to Kumarkhali by Mr. Hannan, a freedom fighter. There were also four journalists there. I was given 54 seers of rice. I will tell you only the truth. Subsequently, I received 15 seers of rice and three *paus*[7] of *moog dal* from Jonodpur Union. Before this we had received a card because we had been affected by the war. They kept the card. They said, 'Leave the card with us. We will call you every month and give you rice and *dal*.' We gave the card to them in all innocence. After this we never saw the card again, nor did we get any more rice and *dal*. We had given the card to Mizan, the thana commander. The card was in Elijan's name. I do not know what was written on the card."

"Much later, about four or five years ago, Hannan Bhai escorted three *biranganas* from here. He said, 'I will take photographs of you.' I said, 'What is the point of taking photos?' The ruler at the time was Khaleda Zia. He said, 'We will give it to Khaleda Zia. You will receive a house from the government. There will be a fish farm on the large lake on the other side of Methorpara, where the three roads meet. The place will be in the name of the three women who were assaulted. All the profit will be given to you.' Saying this, he took photographs of all four women. He promised us all sorts of things. But we haven't received anything as yet."

Duljan Nessa

Duljan Nessa was raped the same day as Masuda Khatun and Elijan Nessa. On this day, the Pakistan army along with their cohorts, the *razakars*, attacked each and every village of Kumarkhali.

Duljan Nessa lives in the village of Dayagram. Her husband is Teshar Ali Mondal. They have two sons and three daughters. She has married off her eldest daughter. Her husband is a day labourer. We visited Duljan's home with Akmal Hossain, the local correspondent of the daily *Sangbad*. Duljan was far more reluctant than Masuda

7 Three quarter of a seer.

Khatun and Elijan Nessa to grant us an interview. She was just not willing to talk to us. She had suffered as a result of participating in the *gono adalat,* and, because of this, she was unwilling to say anything about her experiences. Finally, of course, she did agree, but, before granting us an interview, she asked where I had come from and who I was. I had to write everything down for her. I had to win over her confidence. After this she spoke about the sad experience of her life."

As she spoke, she was overcome by emotion.

"When the country became independent many people suffered, so did I. We had hoped that there would be peace in the country. That is what we had striven for. During our liberation struggle we had been inspired by Sheikh Mujibur Rahman. We did not leave Bangladesh; we did not run away to India. We remained in our homes. My house is on the junction of three roads. That is why it was always dangerous."

"For some time we had known that the Pakistani military had entered the bazaar. And for some time we had also heard that the military would enter the villages. It was the month of *Ashwin,* in 1971. I do not remember the day or the date. My eldest daughter was a baby. I was still nursing her. The army surrounded us on three sides the day they captured us. There was no road by which we could escape. We could not escape from the back because there was a big ditch there."

"My mother-in-law hesitated, unsure of what to do. We were four of us at home that day: the three of us married to three brothers and our mother-in-law. My husband and my two brothers-in-law were outside at the time. I was fairly young, and had been married for a couple of years. I was fairly nice-looking. My eldest daughter was about three or four months old. My sisters-in-law were also fairly young. The three of us were thinking about fleeing. My younger brother-in-law had caught some fish, *tengra* fish. We had just cut and cleaned the fish and were debating which way to flee when the soldiers entered and surrounded us. *Razakar* Mozam had shown them our house. I was standing in the courtyard, with my sisters-in-law clutching me. The soldiers said, 'How many children do you have?' The soldiers had asked us in their language and we had not understood what they said. Afterwards we managed to understand what they were asking. I told my elder sister-in-law, 'They are asking about our children. They will not harm us.' But I was terrified inside. I then said, 'I have eight children.' The soldiers aimed their rifles at my eyes and were about to shoot when my elder sister-in-law quickly corrected me. 'No, sir, I have one daughter, she has one daughter, and she (meaning my youngest sister-in-law) doesn't have any children yet.' The soldiers grabbed hold of my sister-in-law, who started crying and screaming. I continued to stand where I was. I did not have the courage to flee. At this time my mother-in-law started screaming. The bastards turned to see what the matter was, and my sisters-in-law took advantage of their distraction to run behind the house. I also tried to run, but I was holding my baby. Before I could escape, one of the soldiers caught hold of me. Two of the soldiers had entered our house. The others were standing outside, on the road. The soldiers threw me to the ground. I somehow managed to sit up. My sisters-in-law had meanwhile fled. But my mother-in-law remained standing in the courtyard, because I had been caught."

Duljan Nessa kept quiet for quite some time. Then, in a tearful voice, she continued her story.

"After being caught, I pleaded with them to let me go. I said, 'I beg you, do not do this to me. Kill me, but do not dishonour me.' At this point, she could no longer suppress her tears. She started sobbing, covering her face with her sari. After calming down somewhat, she continued her story. "They poked me here (pointing to her left breast) with their bayonets. I do not remember how many slaps I received. I cried a lot. I was wearing a petticoat and sari. I wasn't wearing any blouse. Women did not wear blouses in those days, and, anyway, I was a mother. I continued to cry. I pleaded with them to let me go. My mother-in-law walked up and down in the courtyard. I pleaded with the soldiers, I begged Allah to save me. But all my pleas were in vain. At this moment my husband returned home. They caught hold of him and were about to throw him to the ground. He asked for some water. They let him go saying, 'Go, drink water.' He went inside the house and my mother-in-law hid him underneath a quilt. I managed to flee and enter the house. Where else could I go? Except run inside the house."

"When I ran into the house, the Pakistani soldiers started beating my mother-in-law. Finally, my mother-in-law pleaded with them to let her go. 'Don't beat me any more. I will go and get my son and daughter-in-law for you.' The old woman shouted and cried. Inside the house I was trembling with fear. I pleaded with Allah and asked Him what I was to do. I was afraid of losing my honour. Finally I told my mother-in-law to quickly bring my husband out. I understood that we were in danger of losing our lives. My daughter was wearing a piece of torn *gamchha*. My mother-in-law took it in her hand and said, 'If I bring him out just like this they will kill him. Tie up some rice in this rag so that he can pretend that he had gone to get some rice. If he says anything else they will kill him; they will accuse him of being a *mukti fouj*.'"

"When my husband came out, someone said, 'This man has contacts with the *mukti fouj*. 'The moment the soldiers heard this, they started to beat my husband. They beat him so brutally that they broke his bones. He started bleeding. Along with their beating, they started to curse him."

"My mother-in-law started wailing. 'What have I done? We have lost our honour and now I am going to lose my son.' At one point she struck me on the head, 'You shameless wretch. They came for you and now they are beating up my son. Get out of here.'"

"I knew that there was no one but Allah to save me. 'Help me, Allah,' I pleaded. 'There is no one who can help me but you.' I left the room." Duljan started weeping at this point. "I approached the soldiers, begging them to let my husband go. I touched their feet and asked for mercy. But they just kicked me aside. I was young at the time. I thought that I would kill them or die myself. I would not give up my honour. But they caught hold of me and took me towards the door. They didn't release my husband, but started beating him even more.

"One of the soldiers stood by the door, while the other did it. They threatened to kill me. I said, 'Go ahead, kill me. The three of us will line up together. Kill me. But do not dishonour me. Don't you have mothers and sisters of your own?'"

"There was a Bangali with them, but he was not from our village. They were wearing uniforms and carrying weapons. They were wearing boots. There were a lot of them but four entered the house, then two went out again."

"The two soldiers held me firmly. What could I do? I did not have any strength to throw them off. Right there, in front of the door, they dishonoured me. They could not carry me inside. My mother-in-law was standing there. But what could she do? She kept on wailing and pleading. She had been beaten. My husband too was inside the house."

Duljan Nessa didn't tell us, but we learnt that her husband had been tied up in the courtyard and the soldiers had raped her in front of him. Two of the soldiers had raped her, one after another.

Duljan said that the soldiers had struck her left breast with their bayonets. "No, there was no bleeding, but there was a wound. I was never able to give that breast to my babies. My daughter had been in my lap at the time. They put my baby down next to me and did that work. They besmirched me. They held me down with their feet and opened their trousers and did their work. They forced me. I had pleaded with them. Does any woman willingly give up her honour? Does anyone? I was willing to give up my life, but not my honour. 'Won't I have to lie in a grave? Don't we all have to die?' How I pleaded with them not to do this sinful thing, but I was unable to save my honour."

"They left after doing what they did. I was almost half-dead. I suffered a lot afterwards. There was a sharp, sudden pain in my intestines. I could not do hard work. My chest would hurt. Even now, I hurt on the left side of my chest. This is how I continue to live."

"After the soldiers left, my mother-in-law attended to me. I also sought medical advice from Dr. Dhiren because of medical problems."

"My husband abused me after that incident. He could not accept what had happened to me. And it had been to save my husband that I had emerged from inside the room. Even now my husband calls me all sorts of names. Even now he says that it would be better for him if I were to leave him. My neighbours do not know how he abuses me. But where will I go? I do not have a mother; I do not have a father. I have just one brother who pulls a rickshaw van. Where can I go?" Tears rolled down her cheeks. "I had inherited a small bit of land from my father. I sold that to build this house. We just manage to get by. Masuda Khatun of the next village lives in her mother's house. Her husband abandoned her. Mine has not left me. But he is not able to look after me properly. Look at me. I am not wearing a nose pin. My husband has not made me one. Even now if we quarrel, he brings up that incident to humiliate me. 'Get lost, you whore.' I have no one but Allah."

"I got no sympathy from my neighbours for what happened to me. People say all sorts of things to me. I want this shame to be wiped out. People shun us. Do you understand?

"We gained nothing through independence, but we lost our honour for our country. The country gained independence. We had not thought about what material benefits we would get from independence. We did not sacrifice our honour for material gains. We sacrificed our honour for our country. But this – baring our shame for all to see again and again – what does the country gain by it, what do *we* gain?"

Duljan had not wanted her experience to be exposed to the public eye. She had not willingly publicised it. She had been the victim of circumstances. She made it very clear that she felt that it was her ignorance that resulted in her experiences being made common knowledge.

Regarding her giving evidence at the *gono adalat,* she said, "One day I was in the courtyard sunning the clothes and quilts. Hannan Mian of Kumarkhali and Hira Mian came to me and gave me a pan and two plates. That year the crops had been damaged by severe hail storms. There was scarcity in the country. It was at this time that the two came and said, 'Keep these.' I asked them, 'Brothers, why are you giving me these things?' They said because of the hailstorms. They didn't say anything further. They had brought a camera with them. They photographed him [my husband], and also suddenly, before I could understand what they were doing, they had taken my photograph. They then said that after a few days there would be wheat in the godowns and I should go and get it. We wanted to know what the wheat was for. They said, 'You are a *birangana,* a war heroine. You helped liberate the country during the time of war. That is why you are being given this wheat.' When I heard those words I felt ashamed. Just then the *chowkidar* came and said, 'Go and fetch the wheat.' Finally I did go and get the wheat."

"The commander of Kumarkhali sent word to me to go and meet him. I went. He gave me some papers and said that I had to go to Dhaka. He also said it would be good for me to go to Dhaka. I asked him what he meant by 'it would be good for me.' He said that I would be given some work. I said, 'I am illiterate. I don't know how to read and write. What work can I do?' He said that if I could just sign my name I would be able to work. I could get a job as an ayah or a peon. I replied, 'No, I do not want a job. I have a daughter. Give her a job. Help her to get a job. I need to find a groom for my daughter and marry her off.' After I said this, they photographed my daughter and told me that she needed a certificate that she had passed class eight. I had to deposit the papers at their office. I did so.

I also gave them a photograph of mine. After a few days they informed me that I had to go to Dhaka. I asked, 'Why do I have to go to Dhaka?' My husband did not understand my objections. He said, 'Go. They are going. Why don't you want to go? He is a commander. He is taking you to help your daughter get a job. And perhaps he will also give you something. This is why he is taking you.'"

"After hearing this I went to Dhaka. I was lodged in someone's house. My words were taped. The next day I was taken to another place. There were a lot of people in that place, giving their stories. The man who had taken us had told us, 'We will give you everything. We will give you a house, we will give your children jobs, we will give you money.'"

"When we returned to the village, people insulted us, treated us like outcasts. I regretted what I had done. A few days later three more people came. One of them was a man named Moslem. His nickname was Swapan, and he worked in an NGO named Roots. He gave the three of us five thousand taka each. I bought tin sheets with that money and sold them to buy essentials. That same year, the ADAB conference was held. We were told to go there as well. One day, Shyamal Ghosh, who worked for ADAB, came and said, 'You have been invited to go to Dhaka.' 'Has the Prime Minister invited us?' Shyamal replied, 'It doesn't matter who has invited you. You should go.' 'Why should we go? The last time we went we were made fools. We received no benefits. Instead we were covered in shame. We will not go again.' Shyamal then said, 'Bhabi, you don't understand. Someone from your village has told me to take you. Master has told me to take you. He said to me, Shyamal you take them.' The place where the meeting was to be held was quite nice. And then we would also be able to meet the Prime Minister. We would have to stay for three days. Finally we agreed to go."

"We travelled to Dhaka by bus. I was not used to travelling by bus, so I was very sick along the way. I thought I would die on the journey. Dhaka was very noisy. I did not feel like staying any longer. I told the man who was with us, 'Uncle, I am not feeling well. Please help me to go back home.' The man gave us our return fare and we returned home. ADAB had given us a form and told us to fill in the condition of our homes. 'Write about the hopes you had, about how you worked to liberate the country.' I do not know how to read and write. My daughter has studied up to class six. She filled up the form and posted it. But I have still received no reply."

"After I returned from Dhaka, everyone knew about how I had been raped. We were ostracised. We were criticised for having gone to Dhaka and revealed what had happened to us. Our stories had been printed in the newspapers, people said. All this has brought disgrace to the community. They said that they would not give us Eid *shinni*, they would not come to our homes and we could not visit them in theirs. We could not show our faces to anyone. Our children had not known any of these things. Now they knew everything. I had got my daughter married. After I went to Dhaka the first time, the family learned what had happened to me, and she was sent back. I married her off again. This time as well, her mother-in-law insulted her. My daughter had been married for 18 days. For all 18 days, she had been abused and beaten. Finally I brought both her and her husband to stay with me. Now my son-in-law pulls a rickshaw."

There is a lot of anger in Duljan's voice. She sacrificed her *izzat*, her honour, for the sake of the country. What is happening now is wrong. She feels that women should not have been exposed publicly. They were not even aware that they would be exposed in that manner. Nor were the promises kept that had been made to them before they went to Dhaka. That is why they have become suspicious of people like us who come from outside and ask them personal questions. Nevertheless, their poverty has weakened them, doesn't permit them to refuse to narrate their stories. There is also a faint hope that perhaps they will get some recompense. And at the same time, the fire of anger and hatred burns again in their breasts – anger against those Pakistanis who violated them, blackened their lives. That black shame has affected not only them but also their children.

Momena Khatun

On the same day in 1971, Momena Khatun, another young woman from Kumarkhali in Kushtia, was raped by Pakistani soldiers. At the time we met her, Momena Khatun was about 35 years old.

Momena Khatun's house was located some distance away, at a place called Mathmali Hat. Her husband's name was Abdur Kader. When we went to their house, a huge crowd had gathered there. It was not possible to talk in front of them. It should be mentioned here that though everyone knew that Momena Khatun had been sexually assaulted by Pakistani soldiers, she had not gone to give a statement at the *gono adalat*. That is why she did not experience the social ostracism suffered by Masuda, Elijan and Duljan. The neighbouring women banded together to pretend that nothing had happened to Momena. According to them, her husband did not know that she had been raped. It was difficult to believe that her husband was unaware of what had happened to her. We were going to her place because of what had happened to her. If we outsiders could know about her, how could her husband be in the dark? This was not something we could believe. But because we were told this, we had to converse with Momena in low voices, in a secluded corner of the house.

Evening was descending by the time we reached. The room was becoming dark. It was in these circumstances that we talked with Momena. It was a very short interview. We are including her story because it occurred in the same place and in similar fashion as the others. This is Momena Khatun's story as she told us.

"My parental home was in the village of Kalyanpur. My younger brother died while the war was going on. Accordingly, I returned to my father's place. I went to see my dead brother's face. I stayed on there. Three days after my brother's death, the soldiers entered the village. I was standing with my parents under a tree behind our house. Suddenly the soldiers came and caught hold of me. They pulled my hand and forced me inside the house. Lots of soldiers had entered the village, but only two entered our house. They were all in uniform, in trousers and boots. They were carrying long rifles. It must have been about ten or eleven in the morning."

"I was very young at the time, 13 or 14 years only. I had just been married. When the soldiers were pulling me inside the house, I started begging and pleading with them. But they did not listen. They forced themselves on me. Both of them. One after the other. While one of them raped me, the other stood by. I was wearing a sari, petticoat and blouse. They cut the string of my petticoat with the knife in front of their guns. Then they opened the zippers of their pants and did it. I was very young. I could hardly breathe. I was badly hurt. My stomach swelled afterwards. A lot of the soldiers had entered the village, and two or three of them entered every hut. Apart from raping women, they also looted the place and set fire to houses."

"After the soldiers left, my mother entered the room. While the soldiers were raping me, my parents had been standing outside, in the courtyard. When the soldiers caught hold of me, my father held me by the hand. He tried to prevent the soldiers. They struck my father repeatedly. My father's name is Iju Sheikh. Our home is in Kalyanpur."

"After the departure of the soldiers, my mother gave me a bath. My parents did not tell my husband anything of what had happened. All he was told was that the soldiers had held my hand. I used to be very frightened after this incident. I would stairs now and then. The moulvi sahib was called to exorcise me. My stomach had swelled in pain. Afterwards, the swelling slowly subsided. I was terrified by that incident. For several nights, I would wake up suddenly, with a start. I couldn't eat properly. My mother tried to console me."

"We are five sisters. My younger sister was in the house at the time, but the soldiers had not been able to do anything to her because she had escaped earlier. Our house was in mourning because of my brother's death. And then this incident took place. I fell ill. We were too poor to seek medical help. That is why my mother called the *moulvi sahib* to cure me. If I had been rich, money would have been spent on doctors' fees and on medicine. But we are poor people, for me the prayers of the *moulvi sahib* were sufficient. My mother did not tell the doctor the truth. She told him that the appearance of the soldiers had frightened me. The prayers of the *moulvi sahib* would cure me. Afterwards, I did take some medicine."

"Learning that the soldiers had come to Kalyanpur, my husband came to my parents' place. But I couldn't tell him the truth. I just told him, 'The soldiers grabbed my hand.' But the news spread somehow."

Momena rejoined her husband about 15 or 20 days after the incident. She had no problems because of the rape.[8] Momena stayed with her mother-in-law those few days. Momena's husband, Kader, had two wives; Momena was the second wife. Kader's first wife dwelt with them. At present Momena has two children. Her first child was born five or six years after the war. Her son was about 18 or 19 years and her daughter was 16-17 years during the time of the interview."

"I still get upset when I think about 1971. I wonder why this happened to me. It is unthinkable that any strange man should even

8 She was referring to the fact that she was able to resume her marital relationship without any difficulty.

touch me, but the soldiers robbed me of my honour. I cannot tell you in words what this feels like."

"At first I did not tell my husband what had happened. But he got to learn about it from Hannan of Kumarkhali. My eldest brother-in-law had told Hannan about it, and Hannan had taken a photograph of mine and disclosed what had happened. But we had no help whatsoever. Even after independence we have got no recompense from the government. After father died there was no one to look after me. After that incident, my parents grieved for me. My father brooded over what had happened to me so much that he died within three years of the incident."

"Several years afterwards my husband learned the truth, but he didn't say anything. What could he say? After all, I didn't go with them willingly. They forced it on me. My husband has another wife. That is why I have been able to stay in this family. I have tried to keep the incident a secret but others have not. Lots of people know about what happened to me. It's like being raped twice. It is only fitting that I should get some justice from the government."

Momena holds on to the hope that she will get some justice for the sexual abuse she suffered during the war. When she met us she expected that we would do something for her. Like Masuda, Elijan, Duljan, and Momena, many other women have undergone untold sufferings for the sake of our independence. They continue to suffer in manifold ways today.

Begum Roushan Ara

A Husband's Death: Hidden Suffering

Suraiya Begum

The Department of Women's Affairs under the Ministry of Women and Children is responsible for implementing various projects for women's development, such as job creation and providing legal and other support. It was established in 1984, by merging the Women's Rehabilitation and Welfare Foundation, which was founded in 1972, with the Women's Affairs Cell and a National Women's Organisation. The Women's Rehabilitation and Welfare Foundation was set up to rehabilitate the war-affected women through skill training, job creation and other forms of support. The Foundation offered employment to women who had lost their earning members or their homes or who had been sexually abused by the Pakistan army. Begum Roushan Ara (pseudonym) was a Deputy Director in the Women's Affairs Department.

I heard of Begum Roushan Ara from Taherunnessa Abdullah, who had actively worked at the Women's Rehabilitation Centre after independence to help women who had been affected by the war. With the help of Taherunnessa Abdullah, I contacted Begum Roushan Ara. She agreed to talk with me in her office. We talked about her husband, Latafat Hossain, who had been captured by the Pakistan army in 1971, and was still missing.

Begum Hosne Ara talked at considerable length about her husband, their marriage, their life after marriage, how he was captured and about her life after 1971. She related how the memories of 1971 remained deep in her heart.

"I met Latafat Hossain when I was a student at the University of Dhaka. I was studying in the Bangla Department and he was studying English. He was two years senior to me. We fell in love and got married. That was in 1967. One month after our marriage, Latafat joined the Australasia Bank. He went to Lahore after a year on a training programme. I did not go as I was studying in the Master's final year. There was no question of abandoning my studies to go with my husband. Besides, my daughter was only two months old. She was often sick. She was unwell at that time also. I had a hard time coping with my studies on one hand and my baby and Latafat's absence on the other. So I came to my father's place. My husband was in Lahore for six months. On his return to Dhaka, he was transferred to Narshingdi as a Branch Manager. Again I could not go with him because of my studies. After four months I joined him and stayed for two months. Then after a few days Latafat was transferred to Brahmanbaria. My Master's examination was drawing close, so I filled the examination form and went to Brahmanbaria."

"Results were announced in July 1970. I got a second class. After my results, my husband and I started to apply for jobs in response to vacancy announcements in the newspapers, especially for lecturers in both Bangla and English. Latafat used to type the applications and I would mail them. We got responses from a number of places. We joined Barisal Kalaskathi College on August 26, 1970, I as a lecture in Bangla and Latafat as the Principal."

"In February 1971, we joined Kushtia Darshana College. My in-laws' house was in Jhenaidah. We chose to go to Darshana because it was near Jhenaidah and we could both work. Latafat became the Principal and I was appointed a lecturer. We were at Darshana in March 1971. I had two children by then – a girl and a boy. My daughter was two years old and my son was only one. At Darshana we had no idea of the atrocities committed on March 25 in Dhaka. A couple of days later we heard sounds of bombing and shooting. Later from news broadcasts we learned what was happening in the country."

"On April 11, my father-in-law came to take us to Jhenaidah as the situation was deteriorating. My children and I went to Jhenaidah by rickshaw. It took us two days to get there. My husband stayed back at Darshana since we could not leave the house completely empty. Besides, as Principal he had some responsibilities. Even if the college was closed, the unusual situation that prevailed in the country might lead to anything. So he had to stay. I did not know then that he was actively involved with the Awami League and helping the *Mukti Bahini* in secret. He had been involved in politics as a student, and had been the Vice-President of Chhatra League at Jhenaidah K. C. College. It is discussed in detail in *Jhenaidah Itihash*. When Latafat started his career he was no longer actively involved in politics. That is why I didn't understand the situation.

"I was never involved in politics. Not even as a student. That is why I didn't realise that I should have tried harder to persuade him to leave. No, I never realised that, never. Even though I worked, I was really a simple housewife. I had two children to look after and a job. When my father-in-law came, I asked Latafat to come with us. He refused, saying, 'I can't leave my boys alone.' His boys were his students. I thought his responsibilities as Principal were holding him back. I did not understand he was hinting at something else, about his involvement with the Awami League. Later I found out that his students who had joined the Liberation War kept in close touch with him. That is why he did not want to leave Darshana.

"About ten days after I went to Jhenaidah, Latafat came to visit. He told me a lot of things. In the meantime many of our neighbours were leaving for India. I told him, 'Let's go to India.' He replied, 'I can't go. I have responsibilities.' He along with some other teachers had formed something like a Freedom Fighters' Council. I do not recall the exact name after 25 years. Latafat requested me not to say anything about it to my father-in-law. So we kept quiet. Latafat's college was closed but as far as I know there was a camp in the college where Biharis were imprisoned.

"Latafat used to come to Jhenaidah once a week. He would stay for a day. At night he used to tell me what he was up to, but in whispers, so that no one in the house overheard. I had mixed feelings. I realised that he was taking part in a noble cause. But my children were small. I could not tell my in-laws what Latafat was doing. We could not go to India. He was in one place and I was in another. This was also bothering me. I was very upset. His journeys between Darshana and Jhenaidah used to worry me, as the situation in the country was turbulent. We used to hear about what was happening from Swadhin Bangla Betar Kendra. But there was nothing to be done. He would not go to India."

"Meanwhile the war was intensifying. The freedom fighters were crossing and re-crossing the border frequently. The Bangladesh government-in-exile was formed at Meherpur, that is, in Mujibnagar. The original name of the place was Meherpur. Afterwards it was renamed Mujibnagar The committee at Latafat's college provided information to the freedom fighters. Gradually Latafat became more actively involved in providing food and medicine to the freedom fighters. He became so engrossed that his visits to us became infrequent. The situation in the village was also getting worse. We often used to hear that the Pakistan army was on the march. We used to run from one village to another with our children in our arms. I was not at all used to village life since I had been brought up in a town. I had to run through the fields carrying my baby. Our house was beside a road that the Pakistan army used. On many occasions we had to hide in the jute fields. We never slept at home. My in-laws were very well off. Theirs was the only brick house in the village. My father-in-law had been the Chairman of the Union Council for 26 years and was well known. So we used to leave the house at night to sleep in other people's houses. A different place every night. Most of the time we stayed in poor people's houses."

"May and June passed like this. I was upset as I had not been to Dhaka for quite some time to meet my parents. We are from Comilla, but my parents are settled in Dhaka. I was brought up there. I had my younger brothers and sisters there. I told my husband that I wanted to go to Dhaka. I was so persistent that he could not say no. He said, 'Let me find out about the road situation. I don't think you'll be able to go. But let me see if I can manage a way.' He asked me not to mention this to my in-laws as they were elderly. There was no way they would allow me to go. My younger brother, Alamgir, used to stay with me at Darshana. He was in class eight then."

"July 31, 1971 was a Saturday. Latafat returned to Darshana that day. He had rice for breakfast. I do not remember all the dishes but I remember there was *koi* fish and *laushaker bharta,* his favourites. After breakfast he played with the children for a while. He told me that he was arranging my visit to Dhaka. Then, touching his mother's feet in farewell, he left for Darshana, taking my brother with him. If the situation at Darshana was all right, Latafat would send my brother with a message so that my father-in-law would let me go to Darshana. From there I would go to Dhaka with my brother. The road journey was terrible. They had to go by rickshaw, on foot, then by bus, then by boat and then again by bus. They reached Darshana around 1 pm."

"At 2 pm. when they were having lunch, a boy asked to see Latafat. He said a major from the nearby army camp was looking for the Principal. I was, of course, not present there. I heard about it later. Apart from my brother, there were two other teachers with Latafat: Rafiqul Islam, a Bangla Professor, and Fazlul Haq, an Economics Professor. The boy who came to fetch the teachers was from Latafat's college. At first they decided that they would not go because they had no connection with the soldiers. Moreover, all those who had been asked to go had some relationship with the freedom fighters. Going might be risky. But they also realised that if they didn't comply, the army would pick them up in any case. Therefore, they would not be safe if they did not go. They had been sent for by name; that meant the army had some information about them. If they did not go, everyone would be rounded up. That is why it would be better if they went. All this happened in front of my younger brother. And it was from him that I heard all this."

"Having decided to go, they came out of the house and found a jeep waiting for them. So they did not have any option but to go. Those who came to call on them were fully prepared. They took the three of them in the jeep. They were not taken in a disrespectful way, they were not handcuffed. They were told that they would be freed within a few hours. But they did not come back. The rest of the teachers waited until it was dark. At that time there was curfew every evening. Once they were taken away, there was no further news of them."

"Next morning, the other teachers sent back my younger brother to Jhenaidah with some money. They had already realised that there was no possibility that the people who had been taken away would return. My younger brother did not have any money. The teachers gave him some money and said, 'Go back to Jhenaidah as soon as possible and inform the Principal's father. He will take necessary steps.' Then the teachers dispersed in different directions. I did not know where they went. At that time everyone was worried about his or her own life. My younger brother tried to inquire about my husband in the morning. But he was too young for such work, so he actually could not do anything. He returned to Jhenaidah in the afternoon. We learned about what had happened from him. I did not believe anything bad could happen to my husband. I had the feeling that no one would dare to kill the respected principal of a college. It seemed impossible. Actually I did not have a clear idea of the war. Though I had heard Swadhin Bangla Betar by that time and had also heard that innocent people were being killed, I did not believe he could be killed. I have not told you, but my husband was a very handsome man. Wouldn't they feel sorry if they killed such a handsome person? I thought they would just keep him locked up. My father-in-law inquired about him from various sources. One day he learnt that my husband was locked up at Jessore cantonment. Another day he heard that he had been taken to Rajshahi. He told me, 'I hear that Lata has been taken to Dhaka.' Actually we were not getting accurate information. My father-in-law tried to get news from whatever sources he could."

"I did not have a clear understanding of what was happening around me at that time. Still, I remember that I sent an application to the President of the country. I sent it to my father because he lived in Dhaka. I told him everything and asked him to get whatever information he could. Father was also trying his level best but there was no accurate information. Nor did we get his dead body."

"The army camp was inside the Carew Company in Darshana. Carew Company was the biggest sugar mill in the country. The place was not so densely inhabited because people were leaving the place to cross into India. When we were trying to get information about my husband and the other missing teachers, nobody told me that they had been killed. So I believed that he was still alive. We did not hear of any other persons getting arrested from here before my husband. Maybe the Pakistan army had information that my husband was helping the freedom fighters. Probably that information was given by some students of his own college. The boy who brought the message from the major was also a student. I do not know whether he was later identified or not because I never went to Darshana again. I remained with my in-laws until the country was liberated. My brother and other teachers were eyewitnesses of that incident. However, I could not go to meet those teachers because my own health was delicate at the time. I was pregnant. I had been brought up in town and did not have any experience of living in a village for such a long time. There was no one to take care of me during my pregnancy. There was no doctor or hospital in the village. During my previous pregnancies, I had had regular checkups. But this time my whole pregnancy passed without a checkup. It was not possible for me to go to Jhenaidah for a checkup or to bring a doctor to the village."

"We had to flee from this village to another because of the army. I did not know what to do. I had small children, my health was poor. On top of it all, my mother-in-law used to cry every day for her eldest son. For all these reasons I could not go to Darshana at that time. My father-in-law continued to search for my husband. In the meantime cholera broke out in our village. Seven people died within nine days in our house. It was the month of September-October. I was in an advanced stage at the time. After seeing so many people dying, I became both emotionally and physically ill. I did not have the ability or the power to search for my husband at that time."

"One night I dreamt that my husband had come back and was telling me, 'I took two hours' leave to see you.' I offered him some food. But he did not eat it. He said, 'No, I'm here for only two hours. So I do not have time to eat.' After having that dream, I grew more confident that he was alive."

"When we are in some trouble, we become weak. We want to believe others no matter what they say. Even though I was an educated working woman, I have done whatever people said to learn the whereabouts of my husband. When the villagers came and told me, 'You can get information about your husband if you apply holy oil on your nails,' I did that. My mother-in-law also tried holy oil, holy water and things like that. I did these things because I was mentally weak. But we didn't get any news about my husband. Nine months passed like this. The country gained independence. On January 10, my father came to Jhenaidah from Dhaka and took me back to Dhaka with him. On January 25, my youngest son was born at the Azimpur Maternity Centre. I had only 180 taka with me at the time. That was all I had with me, nothing else. After coming to Dhaka I needed a job. I still had the job at Darshana College but I decided not to go back there."

"Even after coming to Dhaka, I used to expect that he was alive, that he would return some day. I could not believe that he was dead. When I was in Jhenaidah, I thought they had locked him up at Dhaka. During that time many people told me things like that but no one had any proof. That's why at the end I stopped checking rumours. But deep down in my heart I believed that he had been kept in Dhaka. I was not getting accurate information because of the turbulent situation. But when there was no news of him even after I came to Dhaka, I thought that he had been taken to Karachi with the other prisoners. Though I had heard that millions of people had been killed, I did not think they would kill my husband."

"The Bangalis started returning from West Pakistan but he was not among them. Even then I hoped that he was alive. Nobody ever told me that he had been killed. I believed for many years that he was alive. When I moved about in Dhaka by bus or rickshaw or on foot, I thought I would meet him all of a sudden. You might feel like laughing, but I had this weird thought that he had been caught but somehow had managed to escape from the cantonment and gone to India. Perhaps he had forgotten us after going to India. But he was alive. I had this hope in my mind. But now I do not think in that way any more. He has not come back in these 25 years. Now I do not expect he will return at all. But my daughter still thinks that her father will return one day."

"In 1971, my daughter was only two years old. At present that little girl has passed her M.Sc and is working. She loves her father and misses his presence and love. That's why she wrote about him in Panna Kaiser's book *Hridoye Ekattor*. She wrote what she could about her father from what she had heard about him. I felt that someone should write about him. But to be honest with you, I have struggled a lot in my life; my whole life is a story of struggle. The country became independent after nine months of bloodshed and violence. However, my real struggle for survival started after this. A long, painful struggle. It began on July 31, 1971 and has not yet finished. Can you tell me how much blood a person can shed from her heart? That's why I could not write about him even though I wanted to."

"My father brought me to Dhaka where I lived with my stepmother and eleven siblings. I was the eldest child. And now I added my two children to this large family. My father gave me shelter and mental strength in all the ways he could. My children often asked, 'Where is our father?' My father always noticed it and tried to make up for their loss. He used to take them in his arms and take them away from me. He knew that I would not be able to answer their questions."

"I stayed at father's place for some time. He retired from his job in 1973 and moved back to our village in Comilla. He had his own house in Dhaka; nevertheless, he preferred to spend the rest of his days in Comilla. I had to look after my family. My youngest son was born on January 25, 1972. I had to look for a job leaving my seven-day-old son at home because I did not want to depend on anyone. I didn't want to be obliged to people. When people gave me something, it seemed to me that they were showing me pity. Even when my father bought clothes for my children and me on Eid, I felt the same. It seemed to me that he was doing it because my children did not have a father. Of course, I should not have thought so as my father had given his grandchildren and me clothes before. But that year it seemed as if he was pitying me. I had become very sensitive.

"Another incident will reveal how much I had changed psychologically. It's a very personal matter. On January 25, 1972, the day my son was born, I had been having pains since morning. I realised that they were delivery pains. Yet I chose not to tell anyone. Father wanted to take me to the clinic. But I did not want to spend his money. My husband was not there, but why should I take help from my father? For the confinement of my older children, I had gone to good clinics because my husband had borne the expense. We felt that they were our children, children we had desired. So we had to do whatever we could for them. But in 1972 I had a different feeling. I decided not to allow my father to pay my expenses. When the pains started, I did not tell anyone anything. My father understood from my movements that I was in labour and told mother that I needed a doctor. I said to my father, 'Don't worry. Go to office. I will go to the doctor by myself.' Then at around 9-10 am, I went to a free clinic, Azimpur Maternity Centre, with my brother. I took neither mother, nor anyone else with me. I had decided that I would not take anyone's help. I had to manage on my own."

"Later, when I started looking for a job, I needed to go to different places by rickshaw and it cost me two or three taka every day. I did not even feel like taking this little money from my father. When he realised this, he gave me five taka and told me, 'Take it dear, you will need it.' I took the money reluctantly. I went to many places, looking for a suitable job. I went to different colleges, but could not get a job. During that time Mumtazuddin Ahmed was the Director of Public Instraction, Department of Education. He told me, 'Keep contacting different colleges. I will increase the government aid of the college that appoints you.' Even after that, unfortunately, I could not get a job. Then I became so desperate that I went to meet Bangabandhu."

"It was the month of February 1972. First I went to Bangabandhu's Dhanmondi residence. As I was quite ignorant, I was not sure where to go. I walked all the way to his house. There the security guards informed me that I could not meet him there. They told me that he met people in the afternoon. They gave me an address where I should go."

"I did not tell anybody at home that I was doing all this. I did everything on my own. At that time Bangabandhu met people in the evening. I went again that day, alone. I found many women waiting there. All of them were looking distressed. All of them had lost someone in the war, either a husband or some family member. Everyone was narrating her own sufferings to Bangabandhu. When my name was announced, I stood in front of him. I still remember that meeting. He was such a tall person that I had to look up at him. As far as I can remember he was fair. He was good-looking and handsome. I cannot compare him with anyone else. It seemed to me that he was a very fine-looking person. I *salaamed* him. I was so spellbound that I could not tell him much about my suffering. How could I tell such a dignified person about my trifling agonies? Though my agonies were very significant to me and I was in a desperate situation, at that moment I chose not to tell him anything about it. I only told him that my husband was the principal of a college, Pakistani soldiers had taken him away, and he was still missing. What was I supposed to do? As far as I can remember, he told me in his deep voice, 'Will you work?' I answered, 'Yes.' It seemed to me that I had already got the job. His one sentence made me feel secure. His principal secretary, Rob Choudhury, was with him. I did not know him then, I heard his name later. Bangabandhu told him, 'Put her somewhere.' Mr. Choudhury said to me, 'Please come with me.' He took me to the next room, gave me his card and told me to meet him three days later. I came back home. I did not tell anyone at home about it. I felt a certain amount of anger growing inside me; I still cannot figure out against whom. Perhaps I was angry at my own fate. I thought why should this happen to me? I had enjoyed married life for only three and a quarter years. The time seemed like a happy dream to me, a dream that had been shattered even before I could realise it fully. Maybe I was angry with myself, with life, with fate or perhaps with my Creator."

"I met Bangabandhu Sheikh Mujib because I felt that the war had taken place because of him. I had lost my husband because of him. He would solve all my problems. Yes, he had to. After three days I met Mr. Choudhury. He asked me what kind of a job I was looking for. I told him that I was a college teacher. He said, 'We cannot put you in a college right at this moment. We have established a rehabilitation centre for women who were affected in the war, especially those who were raped. Doctors from foreign countries will come and treat them. We need an interpreter to communicate between those doctors and the women. Can you do the job of an interpreter?' I did not know whether I would be able to do it or not. Nevertheless, I needed a job. So I replied, 'Yes, I can do it. But I'm not so good at English.' He asked, 'Then how will you do the job of an interpreter?' I said, 'I don't know, but I have to have the job.'"

"Mr. Choudhury sent a slip to Mr. Awal to appoint me as an interpreter. Mr. Awal was a retired secretary and the director of the rehabilitation centre at that time. I met him and was given the job of interpreter to the doctors. I did not have much problem doing the work. Though I'm an M.A. in Bangla, I had studied English at the Intermediate level. Moreover, my husband was an M.A. in English. So I had some practice. I could manage to do the job with my knowledge of English. I could translate the questions the doctors asked and the answers the women gave."

"The rehabilitation centre was situated in Dhanmondi, at Road No. 3. Basically, it was a clinic. The average number of patients who received treatment here was around 20 at any given time. Most of the girls who came for treatment were pregnant. They gave birth to their children here. Many of the pregnancies were aborted, though a few were delivered full term. Some of the girls went through abortions, some had a wash. That was a tough time for me and I encountered many shocking experiences during that period.

"When I got the job my salary was 500 taka. Though it was not a bad amount, I had a whole lot of expenses. I had three children; the little one was an infant and I had to appoint a nursemaid. I was still living at my father's place. Father gave me a room for myself and my children. I continued eating with my parents even after getting the job. Nonetheless, I had to spend a lot for my children. I needed to buy milk for them. Gradually I discovered that 500 taka was not enough to meet all my needs. Some problems arose in my father's family also. We were particularly bothered about taking care of my little son. That's why I sent my three-month-old son to my younger sister. My sister took care of him for three months. When she got pregnant, I brought my son back and he stayed with me for four months. When my son was ten-months-old, my brother-in-law came to Dhaka. I bought plane tickets and sent this little child to his grandmother with my brother-in-law. It was not possible for me to look after him. I didn't have any other option. My office hours were from 10 am-5 pm. So I used to be outside the house all day and moreover I could not find any suitable person to look after my son. You can realise the suffering of a mother who has sent her child away. The suffering is unbearable. I still feel that pain."

"I had five siblings and six more step-brothers and sisters. So we had different kinds of problems. That's why I sent my son to my mother-in-law. I did not even ask her whether she could keep him. I just sent the child with my brother-in-law. My son lived with his grandmother for ten years. I brought him back to me when he was eleven years old. During those ten years I regularly visited my in-laws. I took my two children with me every year. My in-laws also used to visit us. My father-in-law died in 1973. Then my brother-in-law used to pay us visits. He still does."

"My little son, who spent ten years apart from me, is now a student at Delhi University. He is studying honours in English. He is very good-natured, though he was the one whom I neglected the most. I sent him away from me and could not give him the love he needed as a child. Yet he never complained about anything."

"The girls who came to the Women's Rehabilitation Centre willingly went through abortions if they were one to three months pregnant. Most of those girls were between thirteen to 25 years old. Educated girls also came to the clinic. Their parents brought them to the clinic. I still remember the face of one of those girls'; she was a graduate. and came from Tangail. I witnessed her suffering with my own eyes. She went through excruciating pain at the time of delivery but I did not see her making a single sound. She had such extreme hatred inside her that she remained silent all the time. She tolerated the agonising pain. It seemed to me that her main concern was to get rid of the unwanted child, no matter how painful it was. Many girls did not even want to see their babies. None of them wanted to keep their babies. No one ever said, 'I want to take my baby with me.' People from Mother Teresa's Home took away the children who were born. Some of them were later adopted by childless couples. The children were adopted by Bangalis as well as foreigners. As far as I can remember, those children were born healthy."

"The girls who got admitted to the clinic used to reside there until their babies were born. They did not volunteer any information about themselves willingly. Then we started to take interviews of them on behalf of the Women's Rehabilitation Board. Each girl's case history was recorded. We were appointed specially to take the interviews. We noted down all the details with their addresses, the date when they were captured by the Pakistan army, where they were taken, whether the soldiers took them to the cantonment or whether they were raped in their own homes, how they were tortured and who tortured them. We also asked them where and how they had passed their days subsequently. Everything was recorded. Sheikh Mujib established this Rehabilitation Board on February 18, 1972, and I joined it on February 28."

"The girls at the rehabilitation centre never talked freely about anything. They neither chatted with each other nor did they talk with us. They only answered what they were asked by the doctors. Life had become meaningless for them, and they had started to hate it. They did not even eat properly. They ate only as much as they needed to survive. I noticed another thing: the guardians of these girls never enquired about them after they were admitted here. When the guardians were informed after the delivery or abortion, they would come one day and take the girls home. Meanwhile, none of the guardians would come to see the girls or enquire about their condition. People seemed to think that it was a great shame to be seen visiting this clinic regularly. Everybody had this feeling working inside his or her mind. People started to call it the *Birangana* office and that meant whoever came to this office was a raped woman. This type of assumption started to spread. So we decided to stop calling them *birangana*."

"At that time the *birangana* issue aroused a lot of controversy. Girls could not be called *birangana*; the office could not be called *Birangana* Office, etc. Then we tore the addresses from the case history book and burned them. At that time Justice K. M. Sobhan was the chairman of this Board. Some of the other members of the Board of Directors were Begum Rafia Aktar Dolly, Begum Sajeda Chowdhury, Begum Lily Chowdhury, Mrs. Basanti Guhathakurta, and Dr. Nilima Ibrahim. They took a collective decision that the identity of these girls should be kept confidential. If they could be part of society again, let them. That's why we destroyed the addresses. So the case histories were anonymous. The records were kept in that office for a long time. Later on, in 1975, the Bangla Academy took the records to write the history of the Liberation War. We were told that the Bangla Academy was writing the history of the war and the case histories of these girls were needed. We gave them all those records because at that time we did not think they were important. Our office was not exactly a research centre. So we did not keep any copies of those files. We did not even inquire later what they had done with the files. That's how we lost all the case histories. Personally I feel that these files were very important for us and they should have been kept properly. The loss of these documents is a great loss. Perhaps one day these histories will be needed."

"Actually, at that time my personal struggle was more important to me. I had to maintain a family with 500 taka. I had to think about feeding my three children and giving them a proper education. Moreover, I was under continual mental stress. I was only 23 years old. Girls of this age are not even married nowadays. However, at this age, I had three children and I had to rearrange my traumatic life again with them in mind."

"At first my parents tried to marry me off. My relatives used to say that I should not live like this. I was still very young and I should think of marrying again. Initially I felt that I would never let these people come to my house. I had taken part in radio and television dramas when I was a student. After liberation I contacted the radio and television and took part in some programmes. But, wherever I went, when people learned that I had lost my husband, their tone changed radically. Or their point of view changed drastically. I cannot tell their names now but I encountered many situations like this. I've seen so many difficulties in life. I knew the good and bad sides of life at that young age. After my father's retirement, I had to take all the responsibilities because I did not have any elder brother. So I had to accept harsh reality. I needed protection. Maybe not from the financial point of view, but, from the social point of view, I needed some sort of protection. So I got married again in 1975. Everyone told me that it was good for me. I also felt that I had done the right thing. After all, we live in a patriarchal society. Here it's important to be under the protection of a man. It does not matter whether the marriage is perfect or not. What is important is being under a man's protection."

"I will not say that my second marriage was not good for me. It was good enough. But it would be a lie if I said I was truly happy. The memory of my first husband will always remain in my mind, even though I do not talk about Latafat in my house. Naturally my present husband does not like it. I cannot upset my present husband by bringing up the topic of my dead husband. That's why I do not bring up this topic in my house."

"My children have grown up very differently from other children. They did not hear much discussion about their father in the house. Whatever they have heard was quietly, privately, sometimes from me or from their relatives. My daughter realised it first and I also became conscious about it through her. She titled her reminiscences, 'Not Memory but Hearsay,' to indicate that she had not experienced the story directly but had learnt from others. There she has expressed her feelings, the pain and grief of not having a father. She contrasts herself with those who are blessed with the love of their fathers. For example, when they see their cousins playing with their father, or going for a walk holding their father's hand, or sometimes when their father brings biscuits, oranges, bananas or some gift for them or plays some kind of hide-and-seek game with them. My children have never experienced such pleasures. These are very trivial things, but life is after all the recollection of such trifling memories. Their desire for such a life was not fulfilled in the past and it will not be fulfilled in the future. These are not material needs. It's not like I could not feed them well. In fact, I never let them feel the want of anything. They have a different kind of need, the need for love and affection. Unlike children whose fathers have died, my children carry a different kind of throbbing in their heart because of my second marriage. They are not allowed to talk about their father openly; that is another painful situation for them. They have two pains: the grief and sorrow of not having a father and the sorrow of not being able to express the need for a father. I also have similar feelings. If I want to share with my children any memory of their father, I cannot do that whenever I want to. I need to find a convenient time when we are alone and that makes the sorrow greater."

"One incident will make my meaning clear. I had kept one photograph of Latafat in my room. But my present husband did not like it; he did not want me to keep any memory or photograph. So the photo was removed, not only from my room but from the house itself. I sent the photo to one of my relatives, and gradually it was damaged. I had very few photographs of my first husband with me. When my daughter grew up, one day I found one of our photographs in her album. She kept it secretly so that my present husband would not see it. Also there was a black-and-white passport size photograph of him. My youngest son enlarged it and had it framed in India. My daughter put that framed photograph in her cupboard instead of hanging it on the wall. She can look at it whenever she opens the cupboard. Though she wanted to gaze at her father's photo openly, she could not hang it on the wall. They have to hide their feelings just like she hid the photo. This feeling cannot be expressed properly. I cannot blame my present husband fully for this situation, but I do not forgive him completely. I don't know how to explain things. I cannot even figure out whom I should blame. Myself?"

"My present husband married me knowing my past history. He saw my children, and he agreed that they would live with us. It still makes me laugh when I remember that he even agreed with me at that point that my photograph with my previous husband would hang on the wall of our bedroom. Later on when the promise was not kept and some problems related to my children and other trivial issues started to arise, I asked him why he was acting in this way. He had agreed to everything earlier. His reply was also logical and I had to accept it. He said, 'Why have I changed my position? Yes, I had agreed earlier. I thought that I would be able to handle everything easily. But I'm not able to do it now. What do you want me to do?' After all this is life. What am I supposed to do? Live apart? That is not something I can do. Moreover, we have a son together. If I leave him to please my first husband's children, I would be putting my youngest son in the same miserable situation. So I have to compromise though it causes me great mental distress."

"It is I who have to deal with everything. This fine-tuning is a hard thing to do. For example, I tell good things about my present husband to my children and vice versa. After all I have to preserve my family. I need to hide their faults from each other. Again it is I who have to maintain the equilibrium. I will not say that I had to starve because of the war. I was not directly affected by the war, but all this is also a kind of torture, suffering. I'm trying my level best, but the struggle is not over yet. My children are yet to be established, my daughter is not married yet. Can you tell me when my struggle will come to an end?"

"Panna Kaiser[1] requested me to write for her book *Hridoye Ekattor*, but I avoided doing so. Perhaps I would become emotional while writing about my first husband, perhaps I would express some feelings about him as well as some words of love and affection. And it would not be possible for me to keep the book away from my present husband when it was published. When he read the book he might feel that I had been hiding these feelings about my first husband from him, that I still harboured secret feelings for him. That might create discord between us. I didn't want that to happen. So I told my daughter, 'You write about your father. You have the right to express your feelings about your father. Even if your Bapi[2] comes to know about it, he won't protest. You have the full right to write about your father and he cannot prevent you from doing so.' I live in the conflict between the past and the present."

"Some problems arose with the passage of time. Nevertheless, some of the problems have been solved. I visited my first in-laws' house with my children at Jhenaidah regularly up to 1990. My present husband did not mind our going there. Moreover, I took him there twice and my in-laws were such warm people that they almost loved him like their own son. Perhaps I showed too much boldness because many people told me that I did not need to do that. But it seemed to me that if we took everything in our stride, we would face fewer problems. My present husband accepted this at the beginning. But slowly a sense of competition arose deep inside him. It did not grow intentionally or all of a sudden. It developed gradually."

"Earlier I had had regular links with Jhenaidah; my brother-in-law and sisters-in-law also came to visit me. Later on I found that my husband disliked it. Once he said to me, 'Let the children visit their grandparents' place, but why do you need to go there?' Sometimes

---

1 Widow of the journalist and writer Shahidullah Kaiser, who was taken away by the Al-Badr and killed.

2 Meaning father, referring to her second husband.

he asked me not to go there. At first he endured it. But at the end he started to create all sorts of difficulties whenever I wanted to go to Jhenaidah. It became difficult for me to go there. He did not forbid me directly but he used to create a situation that would make it impossible for me to go. So I stopped going there after 1990. I did not want to create another problem."

"These days I have another reason for sorrow. Earlier I did not have this pain. All these years I had thought that I could be father as well as mother to my children. I never let them feel the want of anything. I tried my best to protect them, to make up the absence of their father. But the absence of a father can never be made up."

"My daughter is now 27 years old. She is working after finishing her Master's. I have been thinking about her marriage for the last two years. Though people tried to persuade me that it was high time for her to marry, I did not think of marrying her off earlier because I know what life is all about. If I had not been educated, I would not have been able to come this far in life. My education enabled me to become financially independent. I was able to keep my children with me even after my second marriage only because I had a job. This is not an insignificant thing. I know very well what is the value of education in life and that's why I had decided not to marry my daughter off before her Master's. Many proposals have been coming for her. In some cases the match was almost fixed. But when it was revealed that her real father was not alive, the groom's side broke off marriage negotiations. Two of them said that they didn't want to take my daughter because she doesn't have her real father. I was stunned to see that young men and their guardians still have such an attitude in our society."

"However, as an educated girl and as the daughter of a freedom fighter, she deserves a very good marriage. It's not that the girl is not beautiful or not well educated; the only objection is that her father is not alive. But life and death are not in our hands. My present husband is a Deputy Secretary. For the last 20 years he has been the guardian of my children. He has been like their father, but society does not recognise him as such."

"Nowadays if any proposal comes, at first I make it clear that my daughter's real father died in the Liberation War. Then I married again and her stepfather brought her up. If you accept all these facts then we can talk further, otherwise we should stop the conversation at this point. The surprising thing is that after hearing this some of them say that it's a matter of honour that her father was a freedom fighter. And nobody should back away from the marriage because her father is dead and that this negative attitude is very bad. After saying all these words, they go away and never come back again."

"This is a new suffering for me. Actually we do not respect our Liberation War from the bottom of our hearts, no matter what good things we say about it. If we really honoured it, I would not have to face this situation in my life. On radio and television all the time we speak about the spirit of the Liberation War, but in real life we do not show that spirit. Rather, we see the reverse in our daily life."

"I have always protected my children from the harshness of the outside world. But how can I guard them from this rejection? I cannot change the mentality of people all alone. The same thing happened to the daughter of one of my colleagues. I know that it is happening to many other families. Particularly the widows of freedom fighters who got married again and have marriageable daughters are facing this problem. What will happen to these girls? Are these girls never to get married? I have to face this mental agony."

"Maybe I did not fight physically on the battle field, but since then I've been fighting for the last 25 years, with myself, with society, with my husband, with my family. This fight has neither battle lines, nor an end."

"When I came back to my father's place from that of my in-laws, my relatives came and sympathised that I had been widowed so early. I found this sympathy unbearable. I was only 23 years old at the time. I could not tolerate such pity. That's why I did not go to their houses. I liked to be alone and did not attend any marriage ceremony or party. I abhorred wearing make-up. Before my second marriage, I did not attend marriage ceremonies. However, I was not really becoming abnormal. I used to wear a white sari with a red border because I liked it, not because I was a widow. I used to like this dress even when I was a student. After starting to work, I wore white saris. My colleagues still remind me that I used to wear white saris."

Reference

Panna Kaiser, ed. *Hridoye Ekattor*. Dhaka: Agami Prakashani, 1993.

Fatema Kalam

A Lonely Struggle

Suraiya Begum

Fatema Kalam works in a government office which she had joined immediately after independence. Hosne Ara Kasem, who works in the same office, helped me contact Fatema. My first meeting with Fatema was in her office in 1997. When I told her that I was doing a study on the Liberation War and that I wanted to talk to her about it, her reaction was unforgettable. She was visibly annoyed. She did not say anything; she did not even offer me a seat. After a prolonged silence, she said, "What's the use of such talk? I don't want to say anything about it." It took me some time to convince her that she and others like her are an integral part of history.

"Unless people like you who have taken part in the Liberation War in different ways – have fought, have suffered, have lost husbands, children, parents, brothers and sisters – unless you cooperate with us in compiling the history of the Liberation War, what legacy do we leave to our future generations? This work should have been done a long time ago but it has not yet been done. It is high time that we make a beginning now. And if women like you continue to keep quiet, then the history of the Bangladesh Liberation War will remain completely silent about the role that our women played during the war. The war affected people in different ways. Unless we talk about the war and record people's different roles and experiences, we will forget our past forever. We will lose the significance of our independence."

My words seemed to have an effect on her, and she started talking. As she spoke, the long-harboured pain and suffering stored deep in her heart seemed to find an outlet. She started by saying that it was the first time that anyone had taken a real interest in her and her experiences and had approached her for details relating to 1971 and to the war. She had, therefore, never spoken about her experiences before. She had an unspoken anger that no one had spoken to her earlier.

The following is her account.

"My ancestral home is in Noakhali but I studied in Comilla. I met my husband, Gholam Kibria, while he was studying at Comilla Victoria College. He was from Companyganj, Noakhali. In 1971, my husband was a final year student in the Department of Political Science at Rajshahi University. He wanted to study and work, so he took a migration certificate to continue his studies at Rajshahi University. He also worked part-time as a Personal Assistant in a Japanese firm, as a rice expert. Later on he joined the North Bengal Sugar Mills in Gopalpur, Rajshahi."

"I graduated from Comilla Women's College in 1969. I was active in student politics and was associated with the Students' Union. I was the General Secretary of the Women's College Students' Union in 1968-69. It was at this time that I came to know Gholam Kibria. We developed a liking for each other and got married in December 1969 in Comilla. At that time Kibria had joined the North Bengal Sugar Mills. As I had yet to complete my B.A., we delayed the social function."

"Kibria's MA examination was scheduled to start on March 3, 1971. However, on that day the Pakistan military laid siege to Rajshahi University. Not being involved much in politics, my husband left his hall of residence and went back to work. My examination was over. Kibria suggested that I visit Gopalpur, not to set up house but just to spend some time there. He would arrange temporary accommodation for the two of us. As I intended to continue my education and get admission in the Master's course at Rajshahi University, I thought it was a good idea. We both moved to Gopalpur."

"We got accommodation on the premises of the North Bengal Sugar Mills. After March 25, Kibria avoided staying home at a stretch. In May, he gave up attending office. On May 5, hearing that the army had entered the mill premises, he came home, probably to tell me something. That was when the Pakistani soldiers caught him."

"It was about 9 in the morning. There was a knock on the door. I opened it and saw Kibria standing outside. He asked me if I was afraid. I felt rather shy but replied, 'No, not at all!' and added jokingly, 'Have you absconded?' No sooner had I finished saying this than I noticed the soldiers behind. The soldiers had been following him. He had not even entered the house. I could not understand anything. I screamed loudly when I saw Pakistani soldiers standing behind him. Eight soldiers had followed him in. They were all Pakistani soldiers."

"The army had a camp at Ishwardi. They had come to Gopalpur on an operation. About 300 persons were killed in that operation. The soldiers lined up the Bangalis in a row and shot them down. My husband was possibly coming to warn me about this, but he was not able to say anything to me."

As I was 3-4 months pregnant at the time and quite sick, we were unable to move to any safer place and continued to live on the mill premises. After the Non-Cooperation Movement started, Kibria used to stay away from home at times, in nearby safe places, returning only at night. The night that preceded his arrest he had stayed at home but had left early in the morning. Why he returned again at nine, I cannot say. He might have wanted to tell me something, possibly warn me about the army entering the mill premises, and about the operations in the offing."

"The soldiers brought him to the verandah, checked his pockets, took off his wristwatch, took away his pen, made him open his wallet, take out his handkerchief. They made him do all these things himself. They took all these things. I fell at their feet, begging for mercy, but they kicked me hard and flung me aside. When my husband saw this, he tried to come to my aid. But the soldiers hit him with the butts of their guns. They beat him up mercilessly in front of me. One of them said something, perhaps asked my husband to lie down. They made him lie face down. One of the soldiers stood on my husband's back and trampled on him with his boots. They then asked my husband to turn and lie face up. I cried out again and fell at their feet begging for mercy, but they again brushed me aside, hitting me with the butt of their guns. I fell against the door. The soldiers grabbed my blouse and pulled me up, tearing my blouse in the process. After that four soldiers took away my husband. They spoke among themselves in a language that I did not understand, but their gestures seemed to mean that the place would be full of blood if he were killed there. So, four of them, two on either side, took him outside. Four others stayed on in the room."

"While my husband was being taken away, he did not say anything. He could not say anything. But at other times he used to advise me, 'If ever there is an army raid, you must run away and hide yourself from them.' Later on I used to wonder sadly why he used to give me that advice. What would happen if I came face to face with the soldiers?"

"Four of the soldiers stayed with me. They held me and brought me inside. When the soldiers had come to the house, the neighbours had all shut their doors tightly. The whole place was empty, not even a bird could be seen. The soldiers took me inside the bedroom and, while still holding me, broke open the wardrobe and our suitcase. Being newly married, I was wearing gold ornaments, and there was jewellery in the briefcase and in the attaché case. While two of them held me, two others broke the locks and took the gold ornaments and something from the top of the showcase, possibly a radio. Somehow, I wriggled out of their grip, I do not know how, and ran towards an eight-foot ladder leaning against a wall in the courtyard behind the house. It had been brought the day before for some electrical work and left there."

"There were four soldiers inside the house and four guarding the main gate. So, fleeing that way was out of question. I ran out through the door leading to the courtyard and climbed up the ladder, all the time looking behind to see if they were following me. I jumped down from the eight-foot-high wall. I had the feeling that they would not spare me and kept looking back over my shoulders even as I was jumping down. I jumped into the premises where the fourth class employees had their quarters. I discovered they were Biharis. While I was looking back to see if the soldiers were still chasing me, the Biharis caught me and started saying things like, 'You're looking charming with your ornaments. You better take them off, otherwise you will be taken away by them.'"

"I had been involved in politics during my student days. Had I been a simple housewife, I might not have been able to run like that. As soon as they were about to reach for my ornaments, a chain and a locket, weighing a *tola* and a half, and a pair of bangles, I started taking them off very slowly. Something revolted within me. I was not going to hand my ornaments over to Biharis. I looked at the people who were surrounding me. I saw this unshaven person, whom I thought I had seen earlier, but I was not sure whether he was a Bangali, a Hindu, a Muslim, or what. I put all my ornaments together, and, with my back to the Biharis, I offered them to him. 'Take my ornaments.' Hoping that he was a Bangali, I said, 'If you can return my ornaments to me, please do. But if you can't, I will not hold it against you. I give up my claim over them. These people are not going to let me out of their clutches.' I discovered later that he was indeed a Bangali, and a few days later he delivered the ornaments to my village home."

"Many who had run for their lives then had taken refuge in Bihari houses. That gentleman was also one of them. At that time Biharis occupied that locality. After divesting myself of my ornaments, I took shelter in a Bihari house. One or two Bangalis were there too. I saw a few Shanti Bahini [pro-army] people, with white bands wrapped round their heads, loot my household articles, my sewing machine, my saris, my electric iron, all my furniture, and stack them in front of me. And I was wearing only a sari, petticoat and torn blouse."

"When night fell, some six or seven of us left that place and started walking aimlessly. We had no idea where we were heading. I did not know the place. I had been in Gopalpur for only about seven or eight months so I did not know the roads well. The army had left the area after promulgating Section 144, which restricted our movement. We started walking towards the countryside, through the paddy fields, over the stubbles, and on the raised strips of land that separated the fields."

"At that time it did not occur to us to worry about the fate of those who had been taken away by the soldiers. Perhaps there was a vague hope in our minds that they would return some day. It was not possible to approach anyone for their release, because the army had massacred countless people in the area. They had bundled together as many as they could at a time and shot them by the side of a lake known as Gopal Sagar. That day was a working day and a meeting was scheduled to be held in the office, but no one had turned up. In their bid to create an impression that everything was normal in East Pakistan, the army made the head of the office call the managers to a meeting. My husband had guessed that it was all an eye-wash, and that they actually had ill intentions. He used to say that the army would come and arrange a meeting to create an impression that the mill was functioning properly and that everything was normal in East Pakistan. But what they actually did was take all these people who had come for the meeting to the banks of the Gopal Sagar and shoot them dead there."

"In our urgency to reach the countryside, we would walk the whole day and, at nightfall, we used to look for shelter. If we were refused at one place, we used to look for another place. By then our number had swollen to about 20 or 30. We did not think of crossing over to India because there was no one to guide us there."

When she was asked whether she had thought of going to her village home in Noakhali, Fatema replied, "Yes, I did. In fact I would have been safe if I could have gone to my village. But how could I go? Who would take me there? Where would I stay? What would I eat? I was quite young then. I was at a loss, I did not know where to go. With my husband taken away from me in front of my eyes, my mind just did not work. I could not say anything. I have forgotten a lot of what has happened. But again I perhaps remember a lot of the painful experiences of those days."

"I always used to move with the group. Many people refused to give me shelter because they were afraid that this might invite an army raid on their houses. Sometimes we had to stay in a cowshed, sometimes in a barn, and sometimes on a verandah. In this way we used to pass our nights, only to resume our uncertain journey at break of dawn. Our experience with the poor and the lower middle class, people who live from hand to mouth, was usually good. They proved to be more generous than those who were better off. It was from them that we got the most, in terms of food and shelter."

"I remember one day, I remember it very well. We had just had our meal, a little vegetable cooked with chillies only, no fish or anything of the kind, and a little rice in a small bowl. I sat under a tree near a lamp-post. After that, using my arm as a pillow, I went to sleep on the verandah of a house. The others of our group too managed to sleep wherever they could find space, on this or that verandah. Next morning, we would resume our journey.

"In the morning we were passing in front of the house of a Chairman when some of his followers stopped us and said that the Chairman wanted us to wait for some time. We all – 25 to 30 of us – stopped. I was told that the Chairman wanted to see me inside. I was sure this was not right. Why should the Chairman call *me*? I was afraid. Everyone waited. I proceeded slowly towards the sitting room of the Chairman. I cannot recollect the location of that place now. My freedom fighter brothers were disappointed that I could not tell them the name of that place. He was later killed by freedom fighters."

"I was escorted to the Chairman's sitting room. The Chairman, who was quite dark, was lying on a bed with his legs stretched out. He was wearing practically no clothes. There was a long bolster pillow by his side. There were two other persons beside him, one was pressing his legs and the other his arms. On seeing this, I felt very uneasy. What sort of a man was he? He said, 'You are my grand daughter's age. So I am addressing you as a child. Do not be worried. As Chairman of this locality, I have a sense of responsibility and cannot allow a young girl like you to wander about in this way. You had better stay here. I will inform your father and arrange to hand you over to him.' I was terrified. But I soon got a grip on myself. This was surely a trap. He was trying to tempt me into a trap. This whole place, his appearance, the surroundings, his sycophants around him, all made me feel that he was a cheat. All along I had this very bad feeling about him. I made up my mind that I would not stay there. If I were separated from my companions, I might be trapped here. And how would my parents know where I was? I would never be able to communicate with them again. I would be in a prison for the rest of my life. The women in our group suggested that as this was a chance for my survival, I should accept the offer and stay there. But I told them, 'You should understand that I can't leave you and stay here. Please wait for me. I am going to go with you.' While all my companions waited, the Chairman ignored their presence. He singled me out and asked his followers to take me inside and give me food. I seemed to have turned into a puppet in the hands of the Chairman. Hungry as I was, I ate the food laid on the verandah. After I finished, I went and stood at the door of the room where the Chairman was. I sought his permission to leave. His sycophants warned me that I would be in trouble if I proceeded further. I was in a tight corner, unwilling to stay on, but unable to leave either. I said, 'All right, let me speak to the people with me.' It was about 2 pm. The whole issue had been dragging on since eight in the morning."

"God puts people into difficulties but also shows ways of resolving them. All of a sudden I saw a driver of the sugar mill passing that way. He was Nurul from Sylhet. I knew I could trust him, so I approached him and said, 'Nurul, I need your help.' I told him everything. Fully alert now and very much in my senses, I requested Nurul to do some acting and tell the Chairman that he had been sent by the superintendent of the mill to look for the wife of Mr. Kibria. He had found her here on his way to the mill. So, he was going to take her back. He did exactly as he was told. The Chairman then called me and asked me if I knew him. I replied, 'Yes, he is our driver.' The Chairman said, 'Well, it's getting dark now. Spend the night here.' I replied, 'If I stay the night, everyone in my group is going to stay too. You know, all the men and women.'"

I asked Fatema why her companions did not ask the Chairman why he was trying to detain her. Fatema said, "They were all too afraid to question him. Everyone had someone or the other fighting in the Liberation War. Also, their minds at that moment did not seem to be functioning properly. They said to me, 'Things are very well for you. You will stay in the Chairman's house, eat at his place, and he will arrange your safe passage.' But I didn't think like them, maybe because I was of that age."

"We were accommodated at night in an adjacent school building and supplied with rice. Some of us cooked. I requested the driver to keep awake at night. He seemed to have guessed the reason. He assured me, 'I'd rather die than let any harm come to any of you. Rest assured, I'll stay awake.'"

"With dawn we were free to leave the place. We resumed our journey. It was on the third day after my husband had been taken away that we had this encounter with the Chairman. I do not remember the date. I remember only the incident."

"After we started that day, a very wealthy farmer stopped in front of our procession. He owned a number of sugarcane fields, and was a big farmer and supplier. He addressed me, 'Everyone resents you, they look on you with angry eyes. I know your husband. You're now passing by my house. Please come and have a meal in my house.' We didn't have anything to eat that morning. Yet I did not feel like accepting his offer. But the others said they would because they were all hungry. We entered his house, a large one with a number of rooms. There were a few more buildings, but there was no one around. The man told me, 'Stay in my house or in any of the other buildings.

Wherever you like. You all can stay as long as you want, or forever if you wish.' He then told us to bathe. I had a torn blouse, and no other change. So I replied that I did not wish to have a bath. He assured me that there was no problem about clothes. He opened a wardrobe and showed me saris and blouses. He said that his wife was not there at the moment; she had gone to her father's house. 'You can choose anything you want from here and wear them after a bath.' I replied, 'No, I don't need anything because I'm not going to have a bath. I don't feel like having a bath.' We stayed on for the whole day and had lunch. After lunch he suggested that I stay on. I said, 'I will not stay.' I decided not to stay because I didn't like it when he showed me his wife's clothes."

"We started again that evening. We found shelter in a mason's house. He was humble and apologetic. 'I can't accommodate you in a house as big as that one. They are rich and moneyed people and I'm poor, but you're welcome to stay in my house.' We accepted his offer. It was a mud hut, with the roof slanting so low that one had to enter it with one's head bent. There were three rooms. I decided to stay here rather than in the previous houses, because I had a feeling that I might be prevented from leaving. Maybe they had no bad intention, but I was suspicious. Though I was now without shelter, without any place to stay, I did not feel tempted to stay in the other places."

"So I stayed in the mason's hut. During the day time he used to go around to different houses. He would describe our plight to people and collect rice and lentils for us which we cooked into *khichuri*. The three rooms that comprised his household stood in the midst of a field, without any fence. There were no trees around his house as is typical in a village. So people used to walk through the place. We huddled together in these three rooms. Sometimes we stayed on the bamboo platforms above the ground. Our host used to go out early in the morning in search of food for us. We stayed there for a few days."

"I asked my host to look for someone, if possible, from Noakhali. One day he found one such person. He was a teacher in a madrassa, a religious school. He visited me in my host's house. He knew my ancestral home and my grandparents. He said he would try to accommodate me in the house of one of his students. He arranged my stay in a house where there was a couple, both teachers from

Jagannath College. They had no children at that time. I am sorry I cannot remember their names or their address."

"Till this day, I did not, or rather have not been able to, narrate all this to anybody, because whenever I try to do so, or even think about these things, I start feeling unwell. I have developed a heart problem. I feel my heart thumping abnormally on the left side of my chest, but without any pain. You know, just like some people's eyelids flutter involuntarily, my heart does the same. Then I press my heart down hard with my hand for some time. In spite of this tremendous strain on my heart, I have been able to survive this far, and continue to work. My memory is still relatively good. Even my father did not expect that I would ever become mentally fit again."

"Now let us go back to 1971. The professor from Noakhali sent a bullock cart the following day for me. Bullock carts were the normal mode of conveyance in that region. Our group of 35 split up. Most of them walked, and only I and another woman, Halima Khatun, with her two small children, rode in the cart. Since both of us intended to go on to Noakhali, we separated from the rest. We went to the professor's house where we stayed for quite a long time, about two months, June and July. During these two months we had no communication with our families. It was not possible. We could not send letters. There was no other means of communication. We felt as if all our near and dear ones were lost."

When we asked Fatema if she had tried to trace her husband, she said, "No, I didn't. My husband was taken away on a Wednesday. Next Wednesday when I was staying in the mason's house, my husband appeared in my dream. It was past *asr* (afternoon prayers). The sun was about to set. I seemed to see in my dream my husband's smiling face in the western horizon. I woke up from sleep. And it was on that day, that is, the Wednesday following my husband's being taken away, that I burst into tears. Before that I had been unable to cry. I hadn't even felt like crying. But that moment I felt that my husband was dead, that he was gone forever."

"I remember with horror the day when my husband was arrested and taken away from me. No one has ever heard about it from me nor have I narrated it to any one, because no one would be able to understand how dreadful and terrifying that moment was. When the soldiers entered my room, all our neighbours had shut their doors and windows for fear of their own safety. When my husband was being taken away, I was so overwhelmed that I did not know whether to cry for his safety, or for mine, or to try to defend myself. That terrible moment has been haunting me for years. The soldiers took me into our room and broke the locks open and took out our things. It might seem incredible today that I was able to escape from them before they could do me any harm."

"The young men in our group who supported the freedom struggle had gone into hiding. Some of them brought back stories that everyone had been killed and that dead bodies were floating in the lake. All the corpses were in fact in the lake, Gopal Sagar, inside the office compound. Some men from our group secretly ventured out to search for their relatives' corpses. They confirmed that they had seen my husband's dead body. Most of the bodies had not been buried. Dogs had dragged the corpses to the front of the office building and were feasting on the bodies. No one was able to do anything because the area was under Section 144. I have never been able to tell all this to my son, who is now a fourth-year student of Mechanical Engineering at BIT (Bangladesh Institute of Technology) in Chittagong."

"After that I stayed on for about two months in the house of a young man, who was the student of the *madrassa* teacher from Noakhali. Afterwards, the teacher arranged to send me to Dhaka with an elderly man. He arranged a ride for me up to Daulatdia *ghat* in a bullock cart. From there I reached Dhaka by steamer. After I reached Dhaka, the teacher arranged our stay in the house of another of his students in Narayanganj. We stayed there for two days."

"At that time an uncle of mine – he was married to my mother's sister – was an Accounts Director in EPIDC (East Pakistan Industrial Development Corporation). I was able to remember they lived in Magh Bazar. I used to stay in their house during my earlier visits to Dhaka. The elderly gentleman with whom we had travelled informed my uncle and I went to my aunt's place. My uncle, in turn, contacted my relatives. It was the end of August. As soon as my father came to know about me, he and my elder brother came to Dhaka. We left uncle's house and went to Chittagong by plane, because road communication was practically at a standstill. Any road journey was risky. The army patrolled all the highways. I stayed in my elder brother's house in Chittagong and then from there I went to my mother. My child was born on November 3. I was staying with my mother at the time of my confinement."

"I stayed with my brother for about 15 to 20 days. But I was not happy there and wanted to go back home. But I did not want to live at my father's place. I told my father and my brother that I wished to go to my in-laws' home. I sent a message to my husband's elder brother who was working in the Railways at Chittagong. When he came, I told him everything. I cried and begged him to take me to their house, arguing that I could then have the honour of being a daughter-in-law in their family, whereas staying with my father would mean that I was still a daughter. My husband's brother simply listened without saying anything. I could not make out whether he was silent because of the sad memory of his brother, or at the thought that I was a burden. After that he left, never to appear again."

"I did not mean to go to my brother-in-law's house in Chittagong. My intention was to go to my father-in-law's home in Noakhali. As my father-in-law was not alive, my brother-in-law was the guardian of the family. My husband was the youngest son. I thought that, as a daughter-in-law, I was entitled to a place in my father-in-law's house, even if I had not been formally welcomed as a bride into the family. I was also keen on going there because I feared that my father might want me to get married again. I was capable of earning my livelihood as a school teacher. But, far from taking me along, my brother-in-law never even enquired about me again. We talk about gender equality but that is just a big sham. The hard fact is that it exists only on paper. No one came for me. I seemed to have been forsaken totally. On top of that, I was cursed as an ill-omened woman who had brought misfortune to the family, had caused the death of their son."

Fatema pointed out that her child's rights were denied. Despite a claim on his paternal property, her son was deprived of his share. She naturally expected that as his father was dead, the boy would deserve some compassion but he didn't. Fatema believed that the property factor led to her being ignored."

"Nevertheless, I brought up my son as well as I could. When we learned I was pregnant, my husband encouraged me, 'Don't be nervous. It won't be at all difficult for you to bring up your child. You're educated. You can be a teacher in a school and look after the child.' I remembered his words of encouragement and mustered the necessary confidence to bring up my child. During all these long years no one has bothered to enquire about what happened to me that day or later on, and how I passed my days."

"I loathe the empty words of praise for the martyrs of the Liberation War, and the show of respect to them. Only the DC (Deputy Commissioner) of Noakhali, who later became a Secretary to the Government, enquired about me when I met him in January 1972 for the job of a Social Welfare Officer."

"The job had been announced over radio, sometime in January 1972. I had added a few lines in my application, stressing my plight as a widow and my desperate need for a job. That probably led to three interview cards being issued in my name. My father, who did not want me to work, did not give me the interview cards, but hid them from me. My niece found out and told me about this."

"I then sent another application for the job. I was then staying at my father's house in Noakhali. I told my father that I wanted to go to Dhaka. But he told me there was no point as the date of the interview was over. I insisted on going, since they had been good enough to send me the interview card three times. Accompanied by my maternal cousin, I came to Dhaka for an interview at Segun Bagicha. At that time Mr. Abdul Awal happened to be the Executive Director of the Women's Rehabilitation Foundation. When I approached him, he initially rejected my application on the ground that the date of the interview was over. But when I told him that I was badly in need of a job, he advised me to get a minister's recommendation. At that time Begum Badrunnessa Ahmed was the State Minister for Education. I went to her residence at Dhanmondi. She behaved very kindly with me and recommended my case."

"I had reduced a lot after childbirth and must have looked awful. The Minister, perhaps looking at my poor state of health, took pity on me. She wrote, 'The applicant needs a job. A job might save her from possible ruin.' I had not mentioned the word 'save,' but my face and appearance probably led her to grasp my plight. When I came back to Mr. Awal, he agreed to give me a job at Bogra for taka 500 per month. He asked if I would agree to take it. I replied, 'Why only Bogra? I am prepared to go outside Bangladesh if I have to. I need a job desperately.' Then a person in army uniform who was sitting there intervened and pointed out that there was a vacancy in Noakhali. I did not know that a branch of the Women's Rehabilitation Foundation had been opened in Noakhali. Mr. Awal wrote a note for the DC Noakhali."

"When I met the DC with that note, he asked me how my husband had been taken and whether I had been able to see his dead body. I think he felt sorry for me. That was the only time I mentioned that I had not seen my husband's dead body. He asked why I had taken the trouble of going to Dhaka. He seemed very sympathetic and said, 'I could have done something for you, if you had come to me.' I replied, 'I didn't know that.' That very day he issued me an appointment letter. That was in March 1972."

"I joined started working in the Social Welfare Office. I did not know then that I was working under the Ministry of Social Welfare. Mr. Awal was our Executive Director-in-Charge. At a later stage I was absorbed into the Women's Rehabilitation Foundation under this ministry. There was a District Women's Rehabilitation Office at Noakhali. I was placed in the hospital branch where women raped during the War of Liberation had their babies. I carried three such babies to Dhaka and handed them over to the office there. Our work was to carry new-born babies to Dhaka. A house had been arranged in Dhaka for the purpose. I do not know where the place is located. A transport was provided to take the babies there. I had to collect the babies from their mothers. The mothers were not allowed to keep their babies, even if they were unwilling to part with them. Any mother wanting to keep her child was refused permission. I too asked for a baby once, but was not allowed to have one. I was told. 'What are you going to do with it except bring it up to be a domestic help?' The decision was not to keep the baby with its mother, and so it used to be separated from its mother immediately after birth. However, a mother was shown her baby before it was taken away. An unmarried *birangana*, named Helen, wept a lot when her child was being taken away. She too was not allowed to keep her child. As she was an unwed mother, the child would have been a liability for her. Eleven such children were born in that hospital. Some women gave birth to stillborn babies. Some had abortions. I do not know whether the husbands of these women who had been raped cared to enquire about their wives, and if not, why not. Anyway, that was the concern of the hospital."

"My father was a school teacher. I had six brothers. My brother said, 'Forget the past. Forget what has happened to you. Take admission in the University and continue your studies.' But I had a feeling that I was going to die, or commit suicide. I had a constant urge to commit suicide. I couldn't imagine that I would ever have a job or a family life. I could not ask anyone for anything. How could I say I needed clothes? My family too couldn't continue to provide for me. After my child was born, my mother reminded my elder brothers about the obligations they had towards me, but they did nothing. In a way that did me good, as it made me feel that they were avoiding me. I felt it was my fault, not that of my brothers. It was because of what had taken place that these things were happening. I suffered psychologically. Why should I have to ask for what my son needed? Why should they pay for my son's needs? Why do I have to ask people for money?"

"However, as the son of a martyr, my son was entitled to get a house from the government. At times, I had a feeling of remorse that I was depriving my son of things to which he was entitled. By this time, my son had come to know many things, though not in detail. My son consoled me, 'You've done well in not asking for anything.'"

"I told him, 'I've tried to keep your head high by not asking for anything from my brothers, and from others. If you feel sorry that I haven't applied for a house, I can still do it, and also arrange money and a scholarship for you. My feeling was that if you did not like all these, it might have been difficult to renounce them later. But if you now feel that I've deprived you for what you are entitled to, and if you desire to enjoy the bounty of the state, even now I may be able to get a house for you.' He appreciated my reply, 'You've done well. I never got the affection of my father.'"

"I have been able to manage somehow. No one can accuse me of having deprived my son. I have closely guarded his rights. After his birth I felt like dying. I wanted to commit suicide. Now I realise that I needed to live for his sake. Previously I used to think about committing suicide every day, and waited for night to kill myself. My father helped me greatly through this terrible period. He was always at my side and offered prayers constantly. He kept a close vigil over me at night, said a lot of prayers and blew holy words on my body and my face. I used to sleep with my mother and sometimes with my sister. They understood that I was in a terrible frame of mind. So, they kept a constant vigil on me."

"One day, I wrote a suicide note saying that no one was responsible for my death. I did this lest my father be accused of killing me and be arrested. I used to devise various plans of how to kill myself. Once I thought of hanging myself together with my child with a sari. Then the possibility that he might die and I might survive made me stop. I thought of other methods. I thought of tying the child to my waist and jumping into a pond. To ensure that in the process I would definitely drown, I thought of tying a pitcher or a heavy object to my body. Again, the thought that my son might die and I might survive stopped me from carrying out my plan. Such plans and random thoughts kept haunting me. I preferred darkness to light. I did not like people talking. I preferred to be alone."

"The job that I got saved me. State Minister Begum Badrunnessa Ahmed was hundred percent right in her observation that a job would save my life. But for the job, my state of mind might have led me to a point, God alone knows where! I might have committed suicide. No amount of guarding me or keeping vigils would have saved my life.

"At one stage I planned to draw up a list of the names of those *al-badrs* and *razakars* who had collaborated with the Pakistani army and denied us shelter in their homes. It was 1972 and I was working in the village hospital of Noakhali. I had trained girls in the method for collecting data. We collected data relating to the number of people who had died in each family. This included also *al-badr* and the *razakars* who had pronounced that killing Bangalis was sanctioned by religion, that it was not a sin. Such traitors who were killed came to be considered as 'martyrs' subsequently. Since no separate list of such people has been prepared, about one million *razakars* must have been included in the list of three million martyrs. The martyrs' list thus includes both *shaheeds* like my husband and collaborators like the *razakars*. A separate list for *shaheeds* must be prepared excluding all collaborators. If a *razakar* who was killed after the war is termed a *shaheed* by his family members, and if they can obtain an allotment of a house from the Government as easily as a *shaheed* family, where is the distinction between martyrs and collaborators? I do not object to their getting a house from the Government, because the children of *razakars* are also sons of the soil, and they may argue that their fathers were *razakars* but they aren't! Thus their getting houses from the Government may be fair enough. But if the son of a *razakar* who has been killed as well as the son of a freedom fighter who has been killed both get houses as the sons of *shaheed* families, where is the difference?"

"I had hoped that a distinction would be made by compiling two separate lists, with two separate identities, no matter if the privileges and opportunities were similar. But it is ironic that one person should get a house because of his love for the country, while another gets it because he was against the liberation of Bangladesh. That is why I have no desire to apply for a house because my husband was killed in 1971. I just cannot make such an effort. Any thought of doing this makes my heart beat fast and my head ache. Suppose I had been provided a house by the Government and was for the time being happily staying there, since I do not have the ability to build a house in Dhaka, the next moment I would have a completely opposite feeling when I realised that I had got this house because my husband was dead, because he had been killed by the army and because he had become a *shaheed*. This grief would torment me each and every day, all through my life. My conscience has held me back from asking for a house. It would be impossible for me to make an application for it. My conscience would prevent me from staying in such a house. Even knowing fully well that I could not build a house in Dhaka, and that it is foolish to ignore the chance of owning a house, I cannot reconcile myself to the idea. I am not speaking for anyone else, I am speaking only for myself. I have seen with my own eyes how my husband was tortured. Can a house wipe out those painful memories? Is a man's life negotiable? The very idea of such a negotiation torments me. I would never be able to justify this. When I imagine myself a rich person, content with owning a big house in Dhaka, the picture of my husband being kicked mercilessly and being dragged away would flash before my eyes, and remind me that my husband's suffering and death were the price I had paid for my house. I wanted to have a share of his pain. I also resisted re-marriage because I didn't want to forget his memory. But subsequently I was forced to marry. His son is his memory. I hold my son in my arms as a memento of my late husband. I have preferred to sacrifice a house rather than suffer the pangs of repentance every minute of my life. That is how I console myself. I take great pride, as does my son, that my husband and his father has been a martyr for the country. We lose that pride if we accept anything in exchange for that. Can there be any substitute for life?"

"You cannot imagine the extent of the mental agony I went through. My husband's body had been eaten up by dogs. After one year, I went to Gopal Sagar along with my younger brother and came across my husband's shirt. I was sure it was his. When I reached the side of the lake, I found it practically dry. On touching the shallow water we saw that shirts, pants and vests were scattered throughout the pond. I pulled at a shirt lightly and it came out easily. I was certain that it was my husband's. He had been wearing the shirt that morning. Bullets had pierced through the material in a number of places. The shirt was made of tetron. So, although the seams had come apart, the material was intact. I washed the shirt and carefully preserved it for quite some time. Later on, someone, maybe my father, took it away and hid it, and I could not find it again. I also visited the place where we had been staying, but could not find anything. Everything had been looted."

"My father intended to give my son a piece of land, measuring 48 decimals, in Noakhali, bought with his pension money. He wanted to have it recorded in my son's name. Someone pointed out that though his paternal uncles were indifferent to him now, they would not only start taking an interest in him when they found out that he was the owner of a piece of land, but would also start conspiring to obtain legal guardianship of him as a minor, so that they could get possession of the land. So my father had the land registered in my name. Later on, he obtained a loan and built a one-storeyed house on it. The house was rented out to a Government office. The office invested money and built a second floor and adjusted the amount from the monthly rent."

"My father did not like my working. He felt it was an insult to him. He thought that if I went to work, people would say, 'That old man sends his young daughter to work. Her husband is dead. Even then he sends his young daughter to work.' My father used to pay great importance to female education. He said that he had sent me to Comilla so that I could go to college. But now he said, 'It hurts my prestige that you work. I wouldn't have let you work even if you had discontinued your studies.' Still, he could not stop me from working. My office was very near my home. Father used to sit in my office from morning till afternoon. He used to say, 'Why don't you give me a job? You won't have to pay me anything.' My reply was, 'You're working all right. You come in the morning and go in the afternoon! That's your job!' Father replied, 'No, you need to recognise it formally.' My father was a teacher, and he used to speak as though I was his mother and he was my child. I used to feel uncomfortable at his sitting in my office."

"At that time my work was of a different nature. My responsibility was to provide relief, distribute blankets and clothes. These things were received officially and distributed as relief materials. I liked working very much and faced no problems. I liked working and put in a lot of hard work at the office. After I got the job, my desire to commit suicide waned to a large extent. Then an urge developed in me to educate my son and earn money. I wanted to buy biscuits and milk for my son. I bought a tin of biscuits for him as soon as I got my first salary, and also a stove and oil. So long I had been silent about my needs. After I was employed, I started managing things for myself. Before the job, I was depressed. I used to feel as if I was drowning in an ocean without any hope of survival."

"After I got the job, my father behaved like a small child. 'Everyone will criticise me if you work,' he said. 'Better get married. If not, at least don't go out to work.' I tried to be far-sighted and rational. If I did not get married or take up some employment, who would look after me in future when my parents were not around? Then I would be a burden on my brothers. Their wives would be busy with their own family affairs and would consider me a burden on them. If I could not stay with my brothers, where would I go? These thoughts made me feel that I had to stand on my own feet; I had to be self-sufficient. These considerations led me to marry my aunt's son in November 1973. My mother being the eldest daughter was a dominating personality in my grandfather's family. She told my aunt who was her younger sister, 'Before my daughter was married, you wouldn't have dared to propose your son as a groom for my daughter. Now I am proposing my daughter as a bride for your son.' My present husband had just joined a job, as a Postal Inspector."

"When I was staying in my father's house, relatives used to come to see me. My reaction was why should they come to see me? Why should I arouse their sympathy? Why should they come and look at me? Some of them suggested that I should wear white clothes as I had become a widow. White clothes were bought, and I wore them for some time. But my father objected, 'I can't stand you wearing these kind of clothes. Wear normal clothes, not a widow's garments.' He was quite firm and said, 'My daughter is not going to wear any white clothes.' My father was deeply concerned for me."

"My mother had a kind of mania about cleanliness. As a child if I ever sat on my mother's bed, she would have all the bed clothes, right from the pillow case, washed again. She had her separate plate and glass. So we used to avoid her. I used to be very close to my father from childhood. Mother used to try to console me after my husband's death but was unable to utter any word of consolation. Some people find it difficult to do what others can do easily. No one could beat my father in conversation, in persuasive talk. My brothers would rarely come near me. Maybe they were uncomfortable and could not find words to talk easily with me. Now I realise my father was a source of great strength for me."

Fatema Kalam is now a well-established government officer living in a government apartment in Azimpur. Her husband works in the Postal Department. At present she has three sons and one daughter. All of them are students. Her daughter is a second year student at the Home Economics College. Her eldest son is a student at BIT (Bangladesh Institute of Technology) in Chittagong, the middle one is doing his B.A., while the youngest son is studying in a private university. The family revolves around Fatema Kalam, but deep down in her heart she guards her anguish. Whenever she comes face to face with it, she cannot control herself. She loses her strength and self-control. She suffers acutely. There are thousands of women like Fatema in Bangladesh. How much have we cared to know about them? How much have we done to protest against those responsible for causing such torment to them? This is a question that we ask ourselves, ask our fellow citizens, ask all those who have been and who are now at the helm of affairs of the government.

Barisal

Introduction

Salma Chaudhury

According to Mintu Basu,[1] a journalist, "On the night of March 25, most probably at about one or two o'clock at night, there was an announcement over the loudspeaker that we had been attacked by the Pakistani military and we must be prepared." 'From an interview with lawyer Tapan Kumar Chakravarty we learned that the Pakistan army attacked Barisal on April 26. Mintu Basu adds, "As soon as the Pakistan military entered the town, they started looking for *mukti joddhas*. They caught Hindus and Awami Leaguers and tortured them. Many were shot immediately. The soldiers also destroyed and burnt houses of those who they believed supported the Liberation War. There was also considerable looting." According to Tapan Kumar Chakravarty, "The Pakistan military converted the city schools into *razakar* camps. All the Hindu temples were destroyed or vandalised, as well as some mosques."

Mintu Basu points out that on April 18 the Pakistan Air Force attacked Barisal. Around 11 in the morning their planes shelled the police lines, the marine workshop, the steamer ghat and other areas of the city. Two persons were killed and countless injured. After this attack, Barisal was emptied of people. About three in the afternoon, paratroopers were dropped from helicopters on the outskirts of the city near Taltoli. Meanwhile Pakistani gunboats started moving towards Barisal from Khulna and Dhaka. Khulna was attacked from all sides late that night. Kazi Maqbul Hossain, a journalist, said in his interview, "The largest army camps were in Sher-e-Bangla Medical College, WAPDA office, and the colony. People were brought here and killed. After they were shot, their dead bodies were flung into the river." Mintu Basu also wrote, "For one week the Pakistanis controlled the entire town. During this time they killed indiscriminately."

---

[1] Mintu Basu's account as well as the accounts of the others that follow have been taken from *Muktijuddhe Barisal:Pratyakshadarshi O Angshagrahankarir Bibaran* (Barisal During the Liberation War: Accounts of Eyewitnesses and Participants), edited by Moidul Hasan (Dhaka: Mowla Brothers, 2003).

At the beginning of June, Pakistani soldiers started fanning out into the countryside. They anchored their gunboat on the banks of the river near Banaripara and cut down shrubs and trees in the area, specially guava trees. They burned down all the houses. Mintu Basu writes, "They shot people indiscriminately: children, old people, women, farmers, everyone. They shot 15 to 20 people in one minute. They burned down all the Hindu villages in Mehendigram, randomly shooting as they went. A lot of ordinary people were killed in that firing. The greatest atrocities, torture and rape, were committed in the river port of Patar. The Pakistani soldiers burned down all the houses there. The roads were covered with ash. They killed everyone in the area. Everyday they would tie 5 to 7 persons with a rope, line them up and shoot them down. The corpses that were washed on to the sand bars would be pushed into the water at high tide so that they could float away. Many women's bodies had their breasts chopped off."

At Jhalokathi, 15 to 20 guava orchards were chopped down ruthlessly. There were 36 Hindu villages in the area. The residents of these villages, men, women, youth, as well as the elderly, hid among the water hyacinths in the ponds. The schools had been turned into camps, behind which were the killing fields. The corpses were flung into ditches behind the schools to be devoured by dogs and vultures. Not one corpse was treated with dignity. The Pakistani soldiers ransacked the wholesale fish market at Govindopur, firing at people indiscriminately and looting the shops. They loaded the gunboat with their spoils. They killed 300 people in one day in the market at Kalaskathi. They attacked the Gandhi ashram and killed four orphans there. The *mukti joddhas* were active in Barisal city from the beginning and put up some resistance. However, until July they could not take effective action. Towards the end of September, after being trained in India, the *mukti joddhas* returned to Barisal. They set up a camp at Jubilee School in Mehendiganj. Two hundred youths received training there. The freedom fighters sank the Pakistani gunboat at Kalaskathi. Quite a few Pakistani soldiers were killed in the incident. On August 26 the freedom fighters attacked Rajapur Thana and liberated it. They also attacked Bakerganj Thana on October 19. There was a 20 feet high wall round the place. The freedom fighters were able to capture the place only after a 36-hour fight. Bakerganj

Thana was liberated on December 7. Four freedom fighters lost their lives in the action. Banaripara was liberated only after the third attempt. The freedom fighters also attacked Sarsina, killing a number of *razakars* and Pakistani soldiers.

Shikha and Monica from the Bhimruli area of Jalbari Thana participated in the Liberation War. Most brutal atrocities on women took place in Kubiyana and Gaba, two predominantly Hindu villages.

Sheela Devi

Tale of a Woman Freedom Fighter

Suraiya Begum and Zobaida Nasreen

We first met Sheela Devi (a pseudonym) on 11 May 1997. It was not easy to persuade her to tell us about her experiences in 1971. It was only after a great deal of persuasion that Sheela finally agreed to meet us and tell us her story. However, even after agreeing to the interview, she refused to let us record what she said. Accordingly, we were obliged to sit down every evening and write out what we remembered from our visit.

Sheela was a moody woman. In a good mood she would talk at length; in a bad mood she would not say a word. Sometimes she would flare up without the slightest provocation. She was paranoid, always afraid of eavesdroppers overhearing what she told us. She would say there were spies everywhere, enemies all around her. At such times she would clam up and we could make no progress. Sheela's narrative was disjointed and she would move randomly from one incident to another. She would often talk about unrelated things. Those who knew Sheela believed that she was not quite right in the head.

Sheela could sew well, so people gave her a lot of tailoring to do. There were often people in her house. This created a problem because, when there were other people around, Sheela would refuse to speak about the Liberation War or about 1971. On several occasions we had to return frustrated from our visit.

When we met Sheela, she was about 42 years old. She often wore shalwar kameez. It was apparent that in 1971 she must have been fairly attractive. Here is Sheela's story, put together from the disjointed fragments of information that she gave us over a period of three months.

"I belong to a Brahmin family. My name is Sheela (pseudonym). We were four sisters and two brothers. One brother and one sister are dead. Like most other Brahmin families, our family was also fairly conservative.

"My father was an allopathic doctor. We were fairly well off, and I had a pleasant childhood. We brothers and sisters used to sing and dance. We used to have great fun together.

"In 1971 I was to appear for the Matriculation examination. At the time I was friendly with a Muslim boy. He was also a freedom fighter. I don't want to tell you his name – you will understand why after you hear my story."

"In April 1971 a distant maternal uncle of mine got me involved in the war, despite the vehement objections of my family. I could draw very well. And the man I loved was also a freedom fighter. That is why I also wanted to fight in the war. In the beginning, my work was to prepare food for the freedom fighters and to carry messages back and forth. Two of my friends were also involved in this work.

"Some time in June or July, I started to work in the *mukti joddha* camps, drawing maps for the freedom fighters. Our task was to draw maps of places where the freedom fighters would be carrying out their operations. Before the start of any operation we girls would visit the place and check it out carefully. We would also point out the houses of *razakars* to the freedom fighters. I knew the *razakars* whose houses we pointed out, but I will not disclose their names because some of them are still alive. My friends and I would stay in the freedom fighters' camp. This was in May. One of us would cook; I would draw maps. Afterwards we would go around with the freedom fighters, showing them the houses of *razakars*."

"The Pakistani army had set up two camps in our area. In the meantime, Sher-e-Bangla Fazlul Haq's son had joined the Pakistanis. As a result there was no military action on Chakhar. I was very courageous. Along with the freedom fighters I would go close to the Pakistani camp. The Pakistanis had cleared the forested areas and had chopped down the guava trees.

"I continued to participate in the fighting. In the midst of this I suffered a great tragedy. [After saying this Sheela Devi was silent for some time.] I will not be able to tell you what it was. I will never tell anyone about it, never.

"After the war ended, I did not return home but tried to see the man I loved. I met him and I spoke to him. I asked him to marry me. He said, 'I have just returned from the war. And, moreover, my family will not accept you.' The sky seemed to fall on me. I took shelter in the house of a friend.

"A month later, some freedom fighters whom I knew tried to take away two *razakars* from the neighbourhood where I had taken shelter. I tried to prevent them. I was very angry at the freedom fighters at the time. I told them that I knew those two. Though they were *razakars*, they had not harmed women. I told them they could not take the *razakars* away. The freedom fighters knew me and released the two *razakars*. I will not disclose their identity, as I don't wish to harm those whom I once helped.

"After a couple of months I left for India. My relations were reluctant to give me shelter knowing what had happened to me. [She never once used the word "rape," referring to her experience as *durghatana*, accident or misfortune.] I stayed in the home of one of my acquaintances and took a sewing course. I returned to Bangladesh briefly for two months, staying with my friend, to appear in the Matriculation examination. I returned home finally in 1974. No one from my family had even looked for me. They were angry with me because I was friendly with a Muslim boy. My misfortune had alienated them from me even more. They believed that I was in India.

"My younger brother too was in Kolkata in 1972. When I told him about the cold reception I had received from our relations, he told me not to stay in India.

"In 1974, I returned to Bangladesh. This time I was quite alone. I tried to see my lover again, even though he had rejected me once. He told me he had joined the Shorbohara Party. He told me to join as well and advised me to sacrifice myself for the people. I listened to him. Before joining the Shorbohara Party, I passed the Intermediate examination.

"In 1975, after the assassination of Sheikh Mujib, charges were brought against the two of us under the Arms Act. He was arrested. A warrant of arrest was also issued for me. Freedom fighters were intimidated and tortured. Towards the end of the year, I managed to flee and come to Dhaka. It was a very bad time. People were afraid of each other. No one knew whom to trust. Can you imagine this situation? Unless you have had experiences like mine, you will never understand."

"I had no relations in Dhaka, but a stranger befriended me. The woman I introduced as my aunt is not really my aunt, but a woman who gave me shelter. This woman, who became like a mother to me, looked after me for seven or eight years. I used to do sewing in her house as well."

"I approached Faizul Haq to help lift the charges against us. He was then a minister under President Ziaur Rahman. In 1971, he had sided with the Pakistanis. Nevertheless, in my desperation, I was forced to seek his aid. He managed to vacate the charges and I was released from jail."

"I was still staying in my aunt's house when I went to meet him. He was grateful that I had been able to arrange his release and agreed to marry me. I was overjoyed, thinking that my life would change for the better. But a couple of months after our marriage, he took me back to my aunt's house. His family was pressurising him to give me up. I had given him all the money I had saved through my sewing. I had converted to Islam. Because I wanted his family to accept me, I had even learned to read the Quran. But his family refused to accept me. He came two or three times to Dhaka after that, but he did not take me back with him."

Commenting on Mr. Faizul Haq, Sheela said, "Yes, Mr. Faizul Haq is a minister today, but he helped me in 1977. In 1975, after the assassination of Bangabandhu, I was accused in an arms case. To avoid arrest, I fled to Dhaka. In 1977 I took this job. Mr. Faizul Haq helped to have the case against me dropped. The two *razakars* whom I helped save after the Liberation War were his followers."

When we asked her why she had saved the two *razakars*, she touched her head and said that her head was paining. In other words, she did not want to talk any further.

Continuing her story, Sheela said that she had taken up her present job in 1977. "After I started working, I rented an accommodation. But I was unable to stay there. I moved to the house of my friend Jyotsna's father (a pseudonym). I stayed there for several years because I felt afraid to stay alone. I used to imagine that people were following me. I tried to go back to my husband, but he beat me twice and threw me out of the house. Still, from time to time, he would come and ask me for money. He got married again.

"I was staying at my aunt's place at the time. Even after his second marriage, I tried to go back to him a couple of times, but every time he beat me. In 1985, I left my aunt's place and moved into staff quarters. At that time my younger brother, who had gone to India, came to stay with me. He was the only one of my family who had kept in touch with me. Nowadays he stays with me. For these 25 years after liberation, I have tried to commit suicide but I haven't succeeded."

"When people ask me about 1971, all I say is that I was a freedom fighter. I do not want to remember anything else. I am still very afraid. In the middle of the night, I continue to wake up in fear. Anyone else in my place, would have died long ago."

After coming to Savar from Dhaka, Sheela stayed in the house of Jharna's father. Jharna's father calls her "Sister". Sheela had to leave Dhaka because her aunt was transferred. She had wanted to take Sheela with her, but it was not possible for Sheela to leave Dhaka because of her job. Sheela Devi went on, "I started to stay at Jharna's place and asked her to look for a place for me. Even after I had found a place, Jharna's father persuaded me to stay on for a further three months. He was a very good man. The day he died, it seemed that my sewing machine also stopped."

"I didn't have any children. But I tell people that I had a son who died. If I hadn't said this, people would have thought that I was bad, inauspicious. Women who live alone arouse curiosity and gossip."

"I am not in touch with my relations. At the beginning I had no connection with them at all. At present I meet them occasionally, but I am closer to those who gave me shelter when I was in trouble. One of my sisters got married after the war. Another sister got married a short while later. I didn't attend the marriage of either."

"In 1985, my younger brother returned to Bangladesh. In fact, I had sent him a letter when he was in Kolkata. After that we kept in touch. It was through him that I was able to contact the rest of my family."

"One of my uncles stays in India. Of course he is not really related to me. I took shelter in his house for some time. He did a lot for me. Sometimes strangers are better than one's relations. He still sends me clothes and other gifts from India. After the war was over, my own relations refused to take me back. Can you imagine that I was all alone in Kolkata? That was when uncle gave me shelter. He still keeps in touch with me. Acquaintances have been closer to me than my real family. After my brother died, I did not go to meet my sister-in-law. I do not like her. I didn't even go when my sister died."

We met Sheela Devi's younger brother. We learned that he had spent some time in India. In 1985 he had returned to Bangladesh and since then had been staying with his sister. He told us, "Occasionally, Didi gets very upset. On these occasions she behaves quite abnormally and talks somewhat disjointedly. The Liberation War has affected her badly."

He told us that Sheela had sat for the Matriculation examination in 1971. At that time she could sing and dance very well. She could also draw. After the war she stopped singing and dancing. He said, "Former President Abdur Rahman Biswas had invited me to sing at a function. I declined the invitation. Thinking about it now, I believe I made a mistake. Everyone took some advantage or the other. We suffered so much during the war. My sister's life turned upside-down. Is it wrong for us to take some benefits?"

Sheela Devi had three sisters and two brothers. One brother had died some time ago, and a sister had died shortly after getting married. Sheela's mother died on February 18, 1984; her father died later that year, on December 16. Talking to us, Sheela Devi said, "My family now consists of just this one brother. I don't have much contact with my sisters. I don't want to go back home."

About her sewing she said, "My mother could sew very well. But I really learned to sew in 1972 after I went to India and took a sewing course at a vocational college."

When we asked her why she had returned from India, she did not reply. In fact, she was quite irritated at our question.

When we asked Sheela about her two companion freedom fighters, she said, "One of them is a nurse at a medical college. The husband of another was also a freedom fighter. Two years after the war he was killed by anti-liberation forces. At present she and her son are in quite a miserable condition. I keep in touch with both of them."

Suddenly she glanced at the door. "I have been talking to you with the door open. Wait a minute. Let me close the door. There are enemies all around me."

From time to time, Sheela Devi would look terrified and start talking to some invisible person. She would say things like, "No, no, you will not go anywhere alone. There are enemies all around us. I don't trust anyone. If people hear you talking about the war, if they see the two of us conversing together, both you and I will be in trouble." At other times she would say, "I am going to take revenge twice: against the Pakistani army and against my husband." At other times she would say, "I think everyone is a *razakar*." Once a certain gentleman came to visit her. Pointing to him, Sheela Devi whispered in our ears, "He is a university teacher but belongs to the Jamaat. He is a *razakar*. Didn't I tell you that we are surrounded by enemies? He comes to my brother to learn singing. This is a pretext, to ensure his own safety."

Jyotsna also got a job in 1977 along with Sheela. Sheela and Jyotsna cook and eat together. Sheela's brother told us, "Jyotsna Apa and we eat together. In the beginning Sheela Di would not eat with others. After I returned from India, I found that she was eating with Jyotsna. Previously she would not eat food that had been touched by Muslims."

One day we went to visit Sheela and found her busy in the kitchen. Her younger sister's husband had come to visit so she was cooking. She had to cook separately because her brother-in-law would not eat food cooked by Muslims. Sheela Devi's family were Brahmin, so they observed certain taboos. Her brother-in-law had come to invite Sheela and her brother to his daughter's marriage. He wanted to take his brother-in-law back with him. Sheela Devi would not go. When we asked why not, she replied, "I don't go back home. There might also be problems if I go. That's why I won't go." When we asked what problems, she said she would tell us later. She was going to present her niece with a red *katan* sari. She said she would send it later.

However, Sheela Devi did go back home for a few days at the time of her niece's wedding. On returning to Dhaka, she informed us that she had gone home; it was not to attend her niece's wedding but to arrange the marriage of her younger brother. She had managed to find a suitable bride for him. Her brother-in-law had objected to the match because the girl's family was giving no dowry. Sheela Devi said, "I told my brother, 'I don't want you to say anything about a dowry.' The wedding will take place in our village, but I will not go to the wedding. I will send everything from here." When we wanted to know why she wasn't going to attend the wedding of her younger brother she said, "Among us Brahmins, 'inauspicious' (অভাগী) women are not supposed to attend weddings."

When we had first met him, Sheela's brother had told us about a young freedom fighter from their area who had been killed. He wanted to keep alive his memory. While we were talking, Sheela Devi listened to us with her head bowed. She didn't join in the conversation. However, when someone said that even people who had not fought in the war were eager to get certificates that they had been freedom fighters, Sheela Devi suddenly raised her head. "Who is a freedom fighter?" Agitatedly, she added, "I too am a freedom fighter."

During the course of our conversation, we discovered that in March 1997, Nari Pragati Sangha had given a reception to women freedom fighters. Sheela Devi hadn't gone. She said, "I have some problems, so I don't go to these functions."

We had to go several times to Sheela Devi because there was little continuity or coherence in what she said at each sitting, and what we did get was often disjointed and fragmentary. One day she said, "I am not going to work much longer. Once my brother has somewhat settled down, I am going to take revenge. I will become another Phoolan Devi and kill the *razakars* one by one as well as several freedom fighters. Do you think that all freedom fighters are good? I myself have seen freedom fighters turn into dacoits. That is why I will become Phoolan Devi and take revenge. Yes, and remember, do not trust men. They are very bad. They can harm you at any time."

Another day we went to Sheela Devi's place and found her watching television. She asked, "Do you want to see the movie? There are a lot of similarities between movies and real life." That day Sheela Devi was wearing two gold chains. She explained the chains, "I'm saving money. Didn't I tell you that I would save my money and become another Phoolan Devi? At one time I was associated with the Shorbohara Party. Not any more. My fires have not gone out. I will take up arms again. Only, I can't do so at this time. My brother will get into trouble if I do. However, I *will* take revenge."

Sheela's brother was a music teacher, so there were musical instruments in the room, a harmonium and a *tanpura*. Sheela said, "At one time I too used to sing. I don't any more. Tell me, can people sing after the music of their life has stopped? There was one song I used to sing a lot after the war, Rabindranath's '*Sahena Jatona*' (This pain is unbearable). Whenever I wanted to commit suicide, I would sing this song."

When we asked her about her sewing, she said, "I learned how to sew from my mother. She could sew well. She could also sing and paint. We learned all this from our mother when we were children. At night, we would sit in the courtyard and sing with her. Our house would be full of guests all the time. What a wonderful atmosphere our house had at that time! And see what it has become! At present there is nothing. I remember the days of my childhood quite a lot. But all my memories after eighteen or nineteen are sad ones. I haven't seen the face of happiness since then.

"It was with great difficulty that I found this present job. In 1977, after hearing about what had happened to me during the war, the foreign director of the organisation gave me this job. I didn't have to go through an interview process.

"I know everyone who was responsible for my tragedy. They belonged to my area. But I will not disclose their identity because I am afraid of them. My life is over, but I do not want any harm to come to my brother.

"I tell you, I will take two revenges: against the Pakistani army and against my husband."

Sheela Devi's neighbour, Jahanara Begum, told us, "I have known Sheela for twelve years. I know that she is a *birangana*. My husband told me that something had happened to her during the war. At first I thought Sheela was not married. Afterwards I learned from her that she had been married, to a Muslim youth."

Another of Sheela's neighbours, Shima, said, "I have known Sheela Devi for about 14 years. Everyone is fond of her because she helps people in trouble. She reaches out a helping hand to everyone. I have heard that she has been given a job because she is a *birangana*. Everyone is very fond of her. She is a very good person. Even though she doesn't always talk sense, she helps people."

The director of the office where Sheela worked also acknowledged her as a *birangana*. When we visited Sheela's office, we saw that she had very cordial relations with everyone.

Regarding the *mukti joddha* certificate she said one day, "I have a certificate. But I will not show it." Afterwards, however, she said it was a *birangana* certificate.

Sheela did not like to talk about what had happened to her. She explained, "I do not want to remember the war. I have nightmares when I try to sleep. And to whom will I say these things? I feel everyone is an enemy." She added, "I am afraid of nightmares, very afraid."

Sheela refused to provide any information about others. For example, she didn't tell us anything about the woman she called *Khala*. All she said was, "One day I'll take you to *Khala's* house." She didn't want to give us her husband's name. She also did not volunteer information about her child who had died, and about whom we had learned from other sources. When we asked her about her child, she denied that she had had a child.

Sheela tended to introduce people as relations. For example, she introduced Zobaida Nasreen as her cousin. She would do the same with others of whom she was fond. At the most difficult time of her life, Sheela had had to live without the support of her family. The only way she had been able to survive was by creating relationships, through the kindness of others. At present too she lives alone, and it is with the help of these relationships that she manages to survive. This was her legacy of 1971. The Liberation War changed her life, uprooted her from her moorings, her relations, her society, her religion. In fact, it alienated her from the world around her. Hurt, stubborn, angry, Sheela Devi is fighting still. The 1971 war is not over for Sheela Devi.

Sherpur

Introduction

Manzurul Ahsan Bulbul

"Hills, rivers and paddy constitute the life of Sherpur" is a popular saying that gives Sherpur its identity. The forests of the Garo Hills in the north of the country bordering the edge of the Meghalaya state of India are rich in *gajari, shaal, tomal, teak, chambal* and pine trees. The land is fertile with numerous rivers flowing down from the hills into the forest. Bountiful crops grow around the year which makes Sherpur self-sufficient in food. Sherpur district with an area of 1,355.53 sq km., is composed of five upazillas (sub-districts): Sherpur Sadar (HQ of the region), Nalitabari, Nokla, Sribaradi and Jhinaigati. On the north of the district stretch the Garo Hills and across the border is the Tura district of the Meghalaya province of India while on the east lies the district of Mymensingh. On the south and west are the river Brahmaputra and the district of Jamalpur.

While this district abounds in a wealth of fish varieties, it is also a predominantly agricultural region, surplus in food. Eighty percent of the population is, directly or indirectly, involved in agricultural work. Nearly all the *robi* crops (winter crops) including rice and wheat are produced here. Sherpur is also noted for its production of sugar cane and jute, the golden fibre. Most of Sherpur sadar, Sribaradi and Nokla are big *char* areas (land formed by sand deposits after the flood water recedes). This vast *char* area is a fertile ground for growing vegetables, potatoes and sweet potatoes.

The Garo Hills extend over a large area of Nalitabari, Sribaradi and Jhinaigati upazillas. The green forests of *mohua, gajari, shaal, tamal, teak* seem to stretch to the horizon and reach up to the sky and present a beautiful sight. The Ghazani Recreation Centre has been set up in Jhinaigati upazilla at the foot of the Garo Hills, so rich in natural beauty. Besides the Tourist Centre at Modhutila in Nalitabari upazilla, there are excellent surroundings for developing attractive tourist resorts at Panihata, Baromari and Khalchanda.

Sherpur was made a separate district in 1975: the 61st administrative district of Bangladesh.

Sherpur played an important role in our independence movement. There was only one wireless office (station) in the whole of Sherpur region, in Jhinaigati. Bangabandhu Sheikh Mujibur Rahman's Declaration of Independence at midnight of March 25 (i.e, March 26) on the wireless was detected at this station. Wireless Operator Mohammed Zaman, on receiving the message, hurriedly sent words through his office peon to the local Awami League leader Abdul Mannan Master and other leaders. The leaders rushed there and collected the copy of the Declaration from the wireless office, and assembled at the Awami League office. Soon the news spread and hundreds of freedom-loving students and others gathered to hear the Declaration. Awami League leader Abdul Mannan Master read the Declaration first, after which it was sent to Sherpur. By now, the premises of New Market were overflowing with frightened and confused multitudes. The next Programme of Action was announced from here.

April 1, 1971: A Training Centre was set up in the camp at Rangtia Kumbhipata in Jhinaigati Thana close to the Indian border. Twelve student leaders of Sherpur were trained in the first batch in the Training Camp here.

April 26, 1971: Pakistani invading forces, firing indiscriminately, entered Sherpur. They indulged in kidnapping, looting and killing. They set up their Operational Headquarters at Noyanee in the Zamindar's (currently, the District Officer's office. That day, two students named Mostafa and Bulbul, bread vendor Ahmed Ali, Subrata Bhattacharya, the priest of the temple of Shonee (a Hindu deity) and many others whose names remain unknown, became martyrs. That day, the Pakistani forces also raided the village of Jhaugora, and lined up businessmen Chouthmal Karua, Nipu Saha and Mahendra Dey and eight others who had take refuge, and mercilessly shot them. Within a week the invading forces set up their camps in the border outposts and the thana headquarter.

May 7, 1971: The Pakistani forces undertook an indiscriminate mass killing at Jagatpur 14 kilometres away from Jhinaigati Upazilla sadar.

May 25, 1971: Nakugaon of Nalitabari Thana and Dalubazar of India became red with rivers of blood. A large number of people of India and Bangladesh including nine from the Indian BSF (Border Security Force) were killed by the Pakistani raiders.

June 30, 1971: In the village of Tontur in Nalitabari Thana of Sherpur district seven brave freedom fighters laid down their lives in a frontal fight against the Pakistani raiders.

July 6, 1971: After a successful operation in destroying the Katakhali bridge and the Teen Aanee ferry of Sherpur district, Nazmul Ahsan, Mofazzal Hossain and Ali Hossain became martyrs in a face-to-face fight against the Pakistani raiders, and many more were wounded. In addition, the inhabitants of the village of Rangamati were subjected to inhuman torture because they had provided shelter to the freedom fighters.

July 25, 1971: Sohagpur is a village in the Kakorkandi Union of Nalitabari Upazilla. On July 25 (10th Shrabon in the Bangla calendar), a ghastly holocaust occurred in this village. On this day, the Pakistanis massacred 187 innocent people. All the male members were herded into one single locality and killed. Today the village is called *Bidhoba Para*, the neighbourhood of widows.

The contribution of Sherpur to the War of Liberation is enshrined in the battles of Nokla and Narayangola, and linked to different incidents of mass killing in the village of Surjodee.

At long last, December 7 dawned on Sherpur as the day of deliverance from the clutches of the invaders. On this day in 1971, the Allied Forces of the Liberation Army and the Indian Army freed Sherpur district from the occupation of the Pakistani raiders. That day of glory is still enshrined in the memory of the freedom-loving inhabitants of Sherpur.

Amirjan Bewa

Widowed and Childless in 1971

Suraiya Begum

The liberation struggle in Sherpur district was led by the brave freedom fighter Colonel Taher. The Pakistani forces were defeated in the battle of Dhanua-Kamalpur. They retreated towards Jamalpur and Mymensingh, and Sherpur was liberated on December 7. The victorious freedom fighters entered Sherpur through the border at Nakugaon.

Amirjan Bewa lived in Kalakuma village under Nalitabari police station of Sherpur district. During the Liberation War, her husband, Abbas Ali Sarkar, her eldest son, Idris Ali, her two daughters, Feroza Khatun and Rasheda Khatun, and her husband's brother, Kalimuddin, were brutally killed by the Pakistani army and their Bihari collaborators. Her son, Idris Ali, died fighting the Pakistani forces.

I first came across a news item about Amirjan Bewa in the daily *Sangbad* on December 2, 1996 and immediately arranged to visit Sherpur. It was the monsoon season. We went by microbus to Nalitabari, 30 kms away from Sherpur, and from there to Hatipagar. There was only a mud track from here so we took a rickshaw. After travelling for about four kms, we reached the banks of the turbulent Bhogai river. It had been raining for two days and, as we reached the banks, the downpour turned torrential. We had to wait in a roadside shop for about an hour. The swollen river had strong currents and it was with great difficulty that we crossed the river in a boat. We walked about a mile before reaching Kalakuma village. Accompanying us were the local district correspondent of *Janakantha* and a local freedom fighter named Mostafizur Rahman Mukul, who introduced us to different cross-sections of the people. Without his help Amirjan's interview would have been very difficult.

We had to walk some distance to reach Amirjan's house. It was a small hut with a *dochala* roof and a small courtyard in front. As there was not enough space inside for us to sit, a bench was placed outside in the courtyard. We were exhausted after our day's journey. A wave of excitement spread over the people of the neighbourhood because we were visitors from Dhaka, presumably linking our visit with some prospect of help. Amirjan was a frail woman of about fifty, but looked much older. She was wearing a dirty sari without a blouse, with one end of her sari covering her head. She personified poverty. Amirjan Bewa, the mother of a freedom fighter, a wife who had lost her husband, a mother who had lost three sons and a daughter in the war of independence, stood before us like a huge question mark on our conscience!

Amirjan Bewa was living a hand-to-mouth existence; often she had nothing to eat. She had a small bit of land which produced a small amount of grain that her sons harvested. She had received no grant from the state as a member of a freedom fighter's family. She had applied several times in 1972, 1984 and 1995 to the Freedom Fighters' Welfare Trust but in vain. No action had been taken by the government to aid her.

We reached Amirjan's house at about four in the afternoon. On seeing us, a big crowd gathered, and we had to interview her in these circumstances. We also interviewed her sister-in-law Shahar Banu, who lived next door. Shahar Banu was the widow of the brother of Amirjan's husband. Their interviews are given in detail below.

In 1971, Amirjan's eldest son, Mohammad Idris Ali, was a student of Class X. He went to India to join the War of Liberation and trained in Dalu Camp. His sector commander was Colonel Taher. In August 1971 Idris, along with a few friends, went to attack the Telikhali BDR Camp under the Haluaghat police station in Mymensingh district. While advancing, they failed to notice the presence of the Pakistani soldiers in the bunkers. As soon as they peered into the camp to gauge the situation, the soldiers saw them. Realising they could be killed, Idris flung a grenade at them. The explosion killed Idris as well as some Pakistani soldiers. Idris Ali's body was blown to bits, and could not be recovered. The villagers who witnessed the fight narrated to Amirjan later how her son had died a hero's death.

Amirjan's home was close to the Indian border. Dalu Bazar in India was only half a km. away from Kalakuma village, separated by the river Bhogai. The Pakistani forces had set up a camp at nearby Telikhali. Terrified of the army, Amirjan, along with her husband and children, started for the Dalu refugee camp on the 7th or 8th of the month of *Shraban*, that is, about the third week of July.

Amirjan spoke in her local dialect and her narration was often jumbled, irrelevant, fragmentary, repetitive. There were many gaps in her account which we filled in with information from neighbours. The following account by Amirjan of the incidents that took place on that fateful day when her husband and two daughters were killed has been recorded and transcribed by us.

"We were going to cross the river Bhogai to reach the other side, that is, the Indian side. With my husband, three sons and three daughters, I was walking along the banks of the river. My husband was carrying our youngest daughter on his shoulders; our eldest daughter, was carrying our youngest son. She was married, but, because of some problems with her in-laws, we had brought her home. She had no children. Our two other sons and daughter were walking with me. We reached a point where the river was shallow and we could wade across in 10 to 15 minutes. We stepped into the knee-deep water. However, there was a strong current. I could not swim, so I held on to my husband's waist. Other people too, from Kalakuma as well as other villages, were trying to cross the river."

"The Pakistani army had their camp at Telikhali. We had not noticed earlier that they had bunkers along the riverbank. As we were wading across the river, the Punjabi soldiers suddenly started firing at us. There were no shrubs or bushes where we could hide. We tried desperately to escape the hail of bullets. As we reached mid-stream, a bullet struck my husband and split his head open. He bled profusely, reddening the water all around. I felt as though my fingers holding on to his waist were being severed. I could hold on no longer and released my grip. I seemed to be losing my senses. Our daughter, who had been perched on my husband's shoulder, was also hit by the bullet that struck him. She was blown to bits. I saw them both die before my very eyes."

"Bewildered and desperate, we tried to scramble to safety, wondering how we could escape the volley of bullets. My sons, though very young, were able to wade through the knee-deep water. I held on to them tightly. My married daughter, who was carrying my youngest son, got hit too. The bullet splinters did not spare my little son either as we discovered later. They have left scars as you can see even now. But I did not know at that time that my daughter had been hit. Everyone was frantically trying to swim across, running and splashing in the water."

"When we reached the other side, people helped to pull us out of the water. We could not find either my husband or my youngest daughter. Three or four persons helped to carry my eldest daughter out of the water. I was almost senseless then. They brought us to a place under a big banyan tree by the side of a jungle. There was no army there. By that time my daughter was almost unconscious. After a while she started vomiting blood. A bullet had pierced her chest. This caused her to vomit blood again and again. The Pakistan army just killed people right and left. They destroyed my family."

"As we were already in India, my eldest son, who happened to be in the Dalu camp nearby, came to know of the incident and rushed to see us. He arranged for transport and took my daughter and son to a city hospital near the Turag. We were left behind. I did not see my daughter again, alive or dead. We heard that she died the following morning at ten. We stayed on in the refugee camp in India. Hundreds of others from Bangladesh also took shelter there."

The river Bhogai flows east of the Nakugaon border. The Bangladesh villages lie along the eastern side of the river. Bangladeshi villagers can enter the Meghalaya state of India by crossing the Bhogai. That is what people from Bangladesh did in 1971. One Pyar Mahmud of this locality continued Amirjan's story.

"Hundreds of people on the Bangladesh side had raised structures along the river bank and had been living there for years. Now lots of people who wished to cross over to India came and took shelter there because the Pakistani army had not reached that area. The army came on April 23. They led a three-pronged attack. One of their groups proceeded along the eastern border of the Bhogai into India. They made a sudden raid on the Indian army and, after killing a few Indian soldiers, returned to Bangladesh. They also fired at random and killed many of those who were fleeing across the border towards India. Amirjan Bewa's husband and daughter were among those killed. A countless number of people died that day. The Bhogai turned red with the bodies floating in the water."

"That day when the army returned after the massacre, the people of the area crossed the river and hid in the Kantabari canal behind the Hatipagar camp. Except for seven or eight male members, all the others had fled into Dakshingaon, leaving the whole region empty. After continuously firing for an hour, the army captured three Indian soldiers and a civilian whom they set free after a few days. But that day they ruthlessly killed whoever came in their way between Hatipagar and Nakugaon. All this happened on the 7th or 8th of *Shraban*. That day we all left our homes, our cattle, everything, and took refuge along with our wives and children in Beltali village in Master Sahib's house."

After Pyar Mahmud stopped, Amirjan continued.

"We stayed in India for four days, practically without food. We couldn't even feed the children except on some lentils and water drained from boiled rice. When our children were almost starving to death, we started begging from some Bangladeshis who had taken shelter in India. From one woman we took some of the water in which she had soaked stale rice, and from another a few grains of salt. That is how we somehow fed our children."

"Meanwhile, my father-in-law was looking frantically for us. After about four days he found us in India. He brought us back to Bangladesh. Although we had gone through immense hardships in crossing the border, we could not help returning to Bangladesh as my father-in-law was terribly anxious for the children and wanted to take them back."

"After our return we passed our days in great distress. My husband possessed a small holding and ten acres of cultivable land. That had been enough for us. But now I had small children to look after by myself. I was forced to sell some of the land to survive. My father-in-law was an invalid and was unable to work. My husband had a brother but he was killed by the Biharis, and his other brothers soon deserted us, fed up with my constant wailing. They never bothered about us again.

"My eldest son, Idris Ali, had joined the War of Liberation as soon as it started. He was undergoing training in India. From time to time we would hear about his whereabouts. Twice after his father's death, he came from India to see us and console us. My other sons were too young and could not earn anything. So the only solution was for me to sell bits of land. But before that we left for Dakshingaon. At that time it was being said that nothing north of Nalitabari would remain intact. Hearing this we moved to our village in Trishal in Mymensingh. We left our landed property behind. My parental home was in Assam. My eldest daughter had been staying in Trishal, and there were other relatives too. We went to the house of my daughter's in-laws along with my children and parents-in-law. The place was small and food was scarce. They somehow managed to get some rice and lentils for us from different people. Neighbours used to contribute. We moved from one house to another every month. We hadn't sold our land at the time."

"When the country became independent, we returned home to find the place had been ransacked and burnt. No one was living there. We had to somehow manage by selling our land, bit by bit. Those who lived nearby bought up this land. In this way, my husband's share of the ten acres of land – he was one of five brothers – got sold. Besides my husband, another brother died in 1971. He had gone to the funeral of a relative in the neighbouring village of Tantur. He was shot and killed there."

"The government gave me two calves in two years, and the *mukti joddha* Shangshad (Freedom Fighters' Trust) gives me a sari every year in the month of *Chaitra*. We were photographed by the government authorities a number of times. Our hopes were raised but nothing happened. Our petitions went unheeded. I have suffered immensely. I have lost everything. I am hanging on to life just for the sake of my children. I have gone begging (in a choked voice) for a morsel of food, just to feed my children."

Amirjan's son Shamsul Huq, who was about forty at the time of the interview, recalled some of the incidents that had taken place that day.

"I was then about 10 years old. We had started out at noon. The villagers had a feeling that an army raid was imminent. No one advised us to flee, but from the trend of their conversation we felt that we had to make a start. One of my brothers had already left for India. We sat on the river bank to cross over to India. At that moment we heard that the Punjabi soldiers were heading north. As soon as we heard that, we fled along with my parents, brothers and sisters. When we were midway across the river, there was a great rush of water but we continued to brave the current. Then the Punjabi soldiers started firing. Their bullets hit my father in the head and also my younger sister, blowing her head to bits. The current was strong and it swept away my father's body. But I was able to lift my sister's body. I saw that the bullet had gone through her head. I put her body down, on the Indian side of the border. We were in a Hindu area and it was not possible to bury her there. So I lowered my sister's body into the water and let the current take her away."

"Then I started looking for my elder sister. I found her gasping for breath close to a hole by the riverside. With the help of my younger brother, I lifted my sister and brought her ashore. She had been hit on the left side of her chest. She was bleeding but not too much as she had already lost a lot of blood. Then she started to vomit blood. Blood gushed out of her throat. My elder brother, who was in India, rushed to us in a frenzied state when he came to know about the incident. With our father and a sister already lost, and this sister's life hanging by a thread, he made hurried arrangements to move her by minibus to a hospital near the Turag. She died in the hospital. We could not bury her and had to leave her behind."

"My brother Idris stayed with us for 4/5 days. We took shelter in a Garo house, but we did not have enough to eat. The Indian Government did not help at that place. Only those who were able to work or who had carried money with them were allowed to stay. After staying there for 4/5 days we returned to Bangladesh. We suffered here too. Pakistani army raids were a regular feature as were clashes between Pakistani soldiers and freedom fighters. We witnessed such a fight and a heavy exchange of fire one day. After the fighting stopped, my brother Idris came to see us. He acutely felt the loss of our father and sisters. He wept constantly and kept looking at mother."

"After that, we started for Tantur, thinking that the war was over. Idris Bhai carried our younger brother on his shoulders. In that village my cousin sister's brother-in-law had died. On our way to that place we heard that my uncle had been shot by the Biharis. My brother nearly died of shock. He hurriedly left us at home and returned to India. We went to Tarakandi village in Nakla police station, but we were not allowed to stay there for long. Our relatives did not want us to stay there. They were worried about their own security. We were a freedom fighter's family and hence a danger to anyone who gave us shelter. We left for Trishal where we came to know that our elder brother had died fighting."

After independence Amirjan Bewa started anew her struggle for survival. During the time of the interview, one of her three sons was employed as a guard in the Koirabazar branch of Rupali Bank in Jamalpur, another was a tailor and the third was a carter. The family passed their days in extreme poverty. All the sons were married and had children. They all betrayed signs of poverty and deprivation, even though Amirjan belongs to a family which participated directly in the Liberation War. The family's history is a tragic one, of losses and irreparable damages. The Liberation War deprived Amirjan of her husband, three of her children, her husband's brother, and with them, her peace, her happiness, and her financial security. There are thousands of Amirjan Bewas like her scattered all over Bangladesh. They sacrificed everything they had so that a new state could be born.

Kalimuddin, the brother of Amirjan's husband, too was killed in 1971. His wife Shahar Banu lived next door. We talked to her to find out what exactly had happened.

On the day of the incident, Kalimuddin had gone to his son-in-law's house in Tantur village. His son-in-law's brother had died, and he had gone to attend the funeral. The Biharis of that locality were already angry with Kalimuddin because his nephew Idris (Amirjan's son) had joined the Liberation War. The Biharis got hold of him at the graveyard and took him to the bank of the Bhogai river. Earlier, people had identified Kalimuddin as Abbas's brother and Idris's uncle to the Biharis and they waited for him at the graveyard. The Biharis then took him to the river bank and shot him with three rounds of bullets. His daughter's house was not far from the place. As Kalimuddin lay dying, he asked for water. But before he could take a sip, he succumbed to his injuries."

Shahar Banu said, "My mother-in-law's sister, who lives in the area told me what had happened. I immediately rushed to the spot. When I saw what had happened, I screamed and screamed. I did not know where he was hit, with how many bullets, or how it had happened. My children were small then, the youngest one only seven months old!"

"After my husband's death, I passed my days with my three sons and two daughters in great uncertainty. My elder daughter and her husband left for India. They neither informed us nor took us along. I had to sell some of my husband's land to save the children from starvation. Then I went to Trishal in Mymensingh. I had a few relatives there. I eked out a living by husking paddy for people, working as a domestic help, and sometimes plastering people's floors with mud. How ironic! When my husband was alive, we had been reasonably well off, with our own household. We harvested our own rice and stored it for the entire year. After my husband's death, I first set foot outside my home, something I had never done before. I had to do this, or else how could I have provided for my daughters and my three sons? I had to work hard for them. Many suggested that I should re-marry. I didn't. I only wanted to bring up my children well. I put my full faith in God."

"After independence we returned home. I again sold some land to feed my children. We spent a few years here and then went back to Trishal again. I managed to get one of my sons employed in a house, and another elsewhere for taka 300 a month. When my sons grew up, they felt they should come back home. My eldest son returned without telling me. My son-in-law arranged jobs for my sons here and suggested that they should end my suffering and bring me here too. That is how I came here."

"After independence we have not asked for anything from the government. Who will take the initiative? My children are simple and naive. They have not asked for anything nor has the government granted us anything."

She continues to feel the tragic effects of her husband's death. She often sees him in her dreams. She often remembers him, even when she is busy with her work.

Shahar Banu continues, "The Liberation War was necessary. But my husband was killed by Biharis."

We asked Shahar Banu, "Have you forgiven the Biharis and the Pakistan army?"

She did not answer this question, but stated that she resented the Biharis immensely. She has never been to the meetings held every year in honour of freedom fighters, nor has anybody ever invited her to these meetings. She said that initially after independence, she used to get things like milk, clothes etc, but not any more.

We asked a local man at Amirjan's house why he had joined the Liberation War. He replied, "The news spread that the Pakistani soldiers were catching people and killing them right and left. People in large numbers were fleeing to India across this border. They were saying that the soldiers were raping women. So we left our homes along with our wives and children. We joined the Liberation War because we heard Mujib's speech: 'The struggle today is the struggle for freedom. You have to fight with whatever you have.' We were young then. There were not many radio sets around. Committees were formed everywhere to organise resistance. We practised marching. We made our start by organising camps within Bangladesh."

"When we reached the border belt of Nakugaon, we saw Meghalaya on the other side. On either side of the border there was a graveyard, the Indian one in the north, and the other one in Bangladesh. The former was well laid out with a monument and flower beds around. There were soldiers on guard. In short, that place honoured the martyrs of the Liberation War. The graveyard in Bangladesh was a marshy lowland, about one *bigha* wide, on the eastern side of the road. It was full of weeds. A faded signboard on a bamboo pole identified the place as the graveyard of the martyrs of the Liberation War."

The local freedom fighter, Mostafizur Rahman Mukul, commented about the Bangladeshi graveyard, "The Pakistani army massacred a large number of people and set fire to their houses. The day following this havoc, young people of the area took up arms and joined the Liberation War. Fifty or sixty of those who were killed during this period are buried in this graveyard.

"Idris, who died at the battle of Telikhali, and others who fell in the same battle, were brought and buried here. We used to consider this area a liberated zone. Consequently we used to arrange the burial here of those who died fighting in Telikhali and Baromari. Later on, as freedom fighters became more active in this zone, the Pakistan army ventured into this place less and less. So, this was a convenient place for us to bury the freedom fighters who died fighting."

"Three years ago the Deputy Commissioner laid the foundation stone for a monument in honour of the martyrs, but there has been little progress. We are planning to start a tree-planting programme from this year. That will beautify the place. With that in view I have brought a few *krishnachura* saplings. I have also brought a raintree sapling to plant here. If the government does not help, we will raise a monument, like the one in India, with the co-operation of local freedom fighters."

Editors' note: Amirjan Bewa passed away in February 2004. We deeply honour her memory. It is our earnest prayer that her endurance and sacrifices in 1971 will not be forgotten.

Binapani Saha

The Many Faces of 1971

Suraiya Begum

Acompanied by my assistant researcher Farhana, her cousin's husband Mannan, a businessman, and his friend, Jafar, went to Sherpur. We went to an old single-storeyed house in the market place. Mannan guided us to the house. We entered a small sitting room where there were two chairs, a bookshelf and a bed. A floral embroidery along with several pictures of gods and goddesses hung on the walls. The house belonged to one Nibaron Chandra Saha who had been shot by the Pakistan Army in 1971. When we visited the house, Binapani Saha, Nibaron Chandra Saha's wife, and their eldest son, Gautam Chandra Saha, were there. We had come without any prior notice.

We were received by Gautam Chandra Saha. He was about forty years old. He is a businessman and the adjoining market belonged to him. His income came from the rent he received from the market. We sent word to Binapani Saha who was in an inner room. While waiting for her, we started talking to Gautam Saha because we had to return to Dhaka the same day. Gautam Saha had been a young boy of 12 or 13 years in 1971, and our discussions revolved around his memories. His mother joined us shortly afterwards. We recorded what both of them narrated. As the mother spoke, she looked at her son to endorse facts, and to check whether she was correct. At times her son looked to her to fill in the information he lacked. Their collective narration forms the content of this story which is of a distinctive nature. It has its origin in March 1971.

Gautam Chandra Saha started as follows:

"I was about 13 years old in 1971, and a student of class six. By mid-April, the 1st or 2nd of *Baishakh* of the Bangla calendar, people from the adjoining districts had started taking shelter in our area. They were coming from regions like Jamalpur, Mymensingh, Tangail,

Muktagachha, etc. Thousands of people, mostly Hindus, were gathering here at the temple near our house because the Bangladesh border at Chichingora is about 50 kms away. The Indian state of Meghalaya is on the other side. The refugees believed that India would open its borders for them. They took refuge at the Kalibari temple too. They kept gathering there in order to cross the border and take shelter in India. Most of the people in the refugee centres were Hindus, though there were also Muslims, Awami League leaders. They stayed with the local leaders. We saw all this. We didn't go to the Kalibari temple. We stayed in our house. We intended to go to India as soon as the border was opened."

"The Awami League leaders contacted the relevant persons on the Indian side to help the flow of people from here, since the Pakistan Army was gradually closing in. When the army reached Dhanbari, Awami League Leaders held a meeting to discuss what was to be done. Muslim League leaders of the locality also joined in the discussion. They met at my uncle Mongal Chandra Saha's house nearby."

"At that time my father had a Marwari partner, Chotmal Karwa. My father had been doing business in jute in this region for a long time and he was well known and influential. The centre of the jute trade was in the village of Jhaugora, three kms away. Although we had no house in Jhaugora, people there used to respect my father, because that was where we purchased our jute. My father thought that if at all he had to leave his home and hearth, he would rather go to India than to the village. The villagers of Jhaugora wanted to give us shelter. They said, 'Come with us, we will try to help you.' But my father had no intention of going there. However, Chotmal Karwa wanted to go to the village. He tried to persuade my father to do the same instead of going to India."

"My father did not want to go to the village but Chotmal Karwa was bent upon going there. He decided to send his family to the village and told my father to do the same. My father was undecided. I remember a little of what happened the day we finally went to the village. That afternoon we were playing a game of *dariabanda* in the field in front of our house, which is now a market place. After he saw Chotmal Karwa's family leaving for the village, my father was disturbed. He came home and lay down on the bed. My maternal grandparent's home was very close to ours. My maternal uncles were big businessmen, and one uncle was a specially important person. When I was returning home in the evening after playing at our grandparents' house, I noticed people were somewhat uneasy. They were whispering about possible places where they could take shelter. The whole atmosphere was tense and fearful, with discussions of where to flee. I came home. My father was lying on the bed. One of my paternal uncles suggested to father that since Chotmal Karwa had sent his family to the village, and since we were all in different places and could not be accommodated together in one place, it was better for my father to accompany his Marwari partner. When my father did not reply, my uncle took hold of his arm and pulled him out of bed. Leaving his bed, father went to my maternal uncle's house, taking me and my elder sister (then studying at the higher secondary level) to seek his advice. When we reached the place, we found it full of people. Top-level leaders of the Awami League, the Muslim League and the Communist Party were discussing the situation. Although the Muslim League leaders were supporting Pakistan, they were confused. That is why they too had gathered there to discuss the situation. The local Muslim League leaders, Mr. Alauddin and Mr. Zia, were at the meeting."

"My uncle had business dealings with the people who attended the meeting. He was very busy attending to all that was being discussed. We waited there to meet him but he had hardly any time to speak to us; he only looked at us. After waiting a long time, my father at last went inside to speak to my grandmother. She told my father, 'We ourselves aren't sure where to go.' Referring to Chotmal Karwa, my grandmother said, 'He is an intelligent man. If he has gone to the village, you too should do the same.' We returned home, but then again went to my uncle's house along with my elder sister, because we were still unable to take a decision. We wanted to get my uncle's opinion in this matter. By that time the Pakistani forces had reached Dhanbari. That night around 8 or 8:30, we returned home. We saw that our Marwari friend was there at our house. Informing my father that he had sent his family to the village, he enquired whether my father would like to send his family with him."

"It was the 7th of *Baishakh* (that is, April 21). My father asked my mother to pack as we were going to leave the place. She packed a bag of rice, with about 20 kg, from the stock that we had for the whole year. We also took four suitcases of clothes. We left through the back door and took a rickshaw. The garden in front of our house was an open space at that time. A large number of refugees had assembled there. As it was difficult for the Pakistani forces to cross the river Brahmaputra without any ferry service, people thought this place was relatively safe and hence crowded here. We left for the village accompanied by father. He intended to return to Sherpur after we reached the village, but his Marwari friend advised him to avoid travelling at night and suggested that he go the next morning. My father made a mistake in going to the village. That very night all the Hindus of this area and people working for the Awami League and for independence who were a target of the Pakistani forces were able to cross the border and go to India. After a midnight meeting in Sherpur, the border was opened. All the people in the locality crossed the border. They carried rice and lentils with them. But we were away in the village at that time and could not cross over."

"My grandmother knew that we had left for the village, but my maternal uncle did not know that. There were trucks and transport at his disposal. All these were utilised for everyone to go to India, but, as we were in the village, we were left behind. My mother was the youngest among her brothers and sisters. She was known as Bina. After reaching India, my uncle asked about his sister, 'What's the matter? Where's Bina?' and my grandmother replied, 'They have gone to the village.' My uncle immediately sent Jamsher, the truck driver, with the truck to our village to take us to India. But Jamsher did not contact us, thinking that if he went back to India with the truck, my uncle would keep the truck in India. So he did not contact us. We were left in the dark about all these arrangements, because we were then at Jhaugora village."

"My father returned to Sherpur the next day, the 8th of *Baishakh*. He found the area empty and returned to the village again. The Marwari made sure that Father stayed close to him, rather than to my mother. The people of Jhaugora village were divided about us. One section supported us and the other were against us. Those who were against us belonged to the Muslim League. They wanted to take away everything we had. The other section supported us. Almost every day the former group came to attack us but they were prevented by those villagers who supported us. Eight to ten days passed in this manner. My mother was in a state of great tension, my older sister was grown up, studying in college. The two groups in the village even had gun fights over us."

"One day there was a fight among the 24 or 25 people who had taken shelter in the house where we were staying, many belonging to different families. This led to the death of a person belonging to the Muslim League."

"By that time, about six or seven days after we had left for the village – the Pakistani soldiers had already reached Sherpur. All those days my mother had been urging my father repeatedly to go to India as the others had done. But our Marwari friend always managed to keep my father away from my mother, we just could not understand why. He was my father's business partner and was much older. My father was always respectful towards him, and did what he was asked to do. He was obliging and somewhat afraid of the Marwari, we simply could not understand why. My father was a very soft-natured man. He was a non-smoker; he did not chew betel. I never saw him quarrel with anyone in his life. When my mother tried to persuade my father to go to India, his Marwari friend used to get scared. Then he would take my father aside and talk to him."

"While this situation was prevailing, I came to Sherpur accompanied by one of our employees to take some provisions out of our annual food stock. While we were heading back for Jhaugora village, and were about one km away from the village, we were attacked by dacoits. They took away our foodstuff at dagger point. That day one of our uncles was coming to Bangladesh from India. He was the one who had advised my father to go to the village. When my uncle was at Sherpur, he saw the homes of those from Sherpur being looted. At that time there was a gunfight between the looters and the freedom fighters. A stray bullet hit my uncle in the back. We heard about it when we returned to Jhaugora village. On hearing this, we wanted to return but one of our employees, said 'You can't go because there is a lot of trouble on the way and your uncle has been shot.' We had great difficulty in attending to uncle, with no doctors nearby and with so many other problems. We had to arrange to take him to a hospital with the help of two or three of our employees. I wanted to come to Sherpur, but was again prevented. Had I been able to come here, I might have been able to communicate with the freedom fighters and made arrangements to go to India, but that was not to be.

"The Muslim League leaders carried the dead body of the person killed during the fight with the Pak forces. We did not see it ourselves but heard that Dr. Bodi had taken the lead in this. Earlier, we used to hear from my father and from our Marwari friend that Dr. Bodi was taking part in anti-Bangladesh activities. He was the same age as my father but he was against us. My father was a big businessman. During our stay in the village it had been arranged that we would be ensured security in exchange for some money. Dr. Bodi had opposed this."

At this stage Nibaron Chandra Saha's wife, Binapani Saha, entered the room. She supplemented Gautam's narrative. Binapani Saha said, "Dr. Bodi's house was in Jhaugora village. One day, accompanied by a few others, he came to see my daughter, not to bring any marriage proposals, but, as he said, just to see how big our daughter, who was studying in the college, had become."

Gautam said that he had learned from his father that the officer-in-charge of the Police Station then was Mr. Siddique. "Mr. Siddique had taken Rupees 7,000 from my father and our Marwari friend. This was security money for guaranteeing our safety. We do not know whether Dr. Bodi took any share of this money, but there was some discord between the two. Meanwhile they carried the dead body of the person who had been killed in the fight to the Pakistan Army and complained, 'There are freedom fighters here who have killed our man belonging to the Muslim League.' Immediately after this, on the 26th of *Baishakh*, the Pak Army, under the command of Major Riaz, conducted an operation here."

"Meanwhile my father had decided to leave this village and go to another. A cart was ready for us. But since his Marwari friend did not want us to leave the place, he assured my father that as long as he was there Father had nothing to fear. He did not support the idea of going to India. We heard a story about his reluctance to leave the place. It was rumoured that the house where Chotmal Karwa lived in Sherpur belonged to an Indian Marwari named Rakhi Marwari. Chotmal Karwa had been his employee. When Rakhi left for India, he left his house under the care and supervision of Chotmal Karwa. Chotmal's concern was that if he went to India, Rakhi would claim the house from him and he would not be able to keep it. That is why he feared going to India. All this was hearsay but we were not sure how far it was true. All we knew was that we may became the sacrifice at the altar of his wishes. We were unable to leave the village."

"On the 26th of *Baishakh,* the Pak Army entered the village with jeeps and two truckloads of soldiers. We came out of our house at 3 o'clock after lunch. All the men were reclining on long wooden benches under the trees. Standing by the water tap, I noticed a green jeep stop some distance away and khaki-clad army personnel get down."

"I ran to the house crying, 'The Pak forces are here!' From a quarter mile away they started encircling us. I screamed at the sight and entered the house, shouting, 'The Pak forces are here. We must flee!' Hundreds of Hindus, Muslims, men and women, started fleeing in the opposite direction. The scene resembled the one in the movie *Arunodayer Agni Shakkhi*."

Binapani Saha said, "I was not able to flee. I was in the kitchen and had just sat down to eat. My husband rushed in and told me to get up, saying that the Pak forces were there. I became so puzzled that I did not know what to do. In a daze I picked up the pot of cooked rice and then the bowl containing the lentils, without any purpose. The children all slipped out of my mind. His father kept telling me to hurry up. When I came out of the kitchen, I saw the children who had attempted to flee being turned back by the Pak forces who were shouting 'Go back! Go back!'"

At this point Gautam took up the narration. He said, "When we were fleeing in the opposite direction, we noticed a large number of people on that side. We didn't realise that these were the Pak forces chasing us from the rear. They had been lying on the ground. When we were running, we saw them stand up. We did not realise up to this point that they were after us. Ahead of us was a fair-complexioned army officer holding a sten gun in his hand. His eyes were red. It was about 3 pm. Nasir, a collaborator from Khorompur, was there with Major Riaz. We learned his name later. They were ordering all of us to turn back, 'Go back, go back.' We returned towards our house. We were like fish clustered in one place when a net is cast. All of us assembled in a verandah. That is how we were caught. We understood that Major Riaz was the leader when we saw all the soldiers saluting him."

"He assembled all the Hindu and Muslim women in one room. There were two rooms, one was a kitchen and the other a store room for fuel and other articles. He assembled the women in the second room. He enquired, 'Who are the Segun?' meaning the Muslim women. After that he separated the Muslim women from the Hindus. There were a few more Hindu families in that village. Two or three Hindu families had accompanied us from Sherpur. The house where we had taken shelter also belonged to a Hindu gentleman named Hemendra Babu. The major got all the Muslims of the village together, brought them along, and made them sit in a row. Hindus, both rich and poor, were made to sit in another row. The ladies were kept inside the room, and the men outside. After this Hindu-Muslim segregation, the rich were separated from the poor. The local collaborators who helped in the Hindu-Muslim segregation were Syed Ali Chairman, who is still alive, Faju Munshi and Masud, the nephew of Dr. Wadud, the ophthalmologist. I knew the latter three. Nasim too was there, not in the forefront, but in the background. The three mentioned above took the lead along with Major Riaz. These three actually tried to kill us. While the people were being segregated, I ran into a nearby house and climbed up to the roof to hide. Though the house was made of jute sticks, I climbed up to its delicate roof for shelter, following my instincts for survival as all human beings do. However, I soon realised that my lone survival would be meaningless if my father, mother, brothers and sisters and all were killed. I knew it would be difficult for me to survive if all the others were dead. All these thoughts brought me down from my hiding place. I saw my father lying on a bed with his hands under his head. He too might have thought that when all were outside, why should he be alone in the room. Even if he were in the room, he would have soon been found out and would have been tortured even more. So my father went out and joined the others sitting in the row."

"After the Hindus and Muslims were divided into two groups and made to sit in rows facing each other, the hands of the Hindus – there were about 14 of them – were tied behind their backs. They were made to sit on the wide verandah – and in the courtyard. Six of them were released later by the Pak forces. Then the Pak forces asked the Muslims to loot the Hindu houses. Some of them did not want to do so. One of them, a bearded old man, refused point-blank. I do not know his name. He said something in Urdu which I did not understand. I understood this much that he was refusing to do what the soldiers were asking him to do. He was kicked in his back and started bleeding from the mouth. Another group indulged in looting and took whatever they found in the houses. Even the wooden posts supporting the roof were chopped down. The house we were staying in was also ransacked. Hundreds of villagers joined the looting. It took hardly five minutes for a house to be ransacked."

"Meanwhile, a hot exchange of words was going on in the verandah between Chotmal Karwa, the Marwari, and Major Riaz. The former was speaking in Hindi and the latter in Urdu. The Marwari was hot-tempered and imposing like a leader. He was the only one arguing with Major Riaz. My father was sitting listlessly on the bench with his head drooping. I was there too along with seven or eight boys of my age including the Marwari's son, Kalidas. He is still alive. All of us were made to sit in a row facing the soldiers. My mother approached Major Riaz, fell at his knees and implored, 'Please release my son, please release us.' The soldiers seemed undecided about keeping us in custody. They kept releasing us and taking us back into custody. They did so two or three times, and made us again sit in a row. At one stage, the Marwari's eldest son was forcibly taken behind the house at gunpoint. There he was beaten blue. He was rather big and plump. We could hear the dull thuds of the beating from the back of the house. There were two or three gun shots too but these were blank fires. The Marwari gentleman's wife was asked to go and see her dying son. Meanwhile, the Marwari was being beaten. The soldiers had sharpened bamboo rods which they poked at his stomach as they talked. The pointed ends pierced his body, causing him to bleed profusely. But the Marwari did not stop arguing. He was being beaten because he had weapons; these were personal ones and licensed. At one stage we sensed that Major Riaz would not kill us. This is what we felt. At that point he was looting whatever clothes we had. He was telling us repeatedly 'You have guns. Surrender them.' I told him we did not have guns, we had money. 'Okay, bring that,' he said. I asked my mother, 'Do you have any money? They will release father in exchange for money.' I told Major Riaz, 'Please release my father. We will pay you whatever money we have got.' I told my mother, 'Please give him whatever money we have.' Earlier, the Marwari had come into the house and had handed over to Faju Munshi, Syed Ali Chairman and Masud a large amount of money in shining bundles of fifty rupee notes that belonged to my father and the Marwari. These had been hidden in a red piece of cloth. My mother also had some money consisting of one-rupee notes in bundles of hundred. My father would occasionally give my mother bundles of one-rupee notes. My mother kept these bundles away safely. She had 18 such bundles that is, eighteen hundred rupees. The money was hidden in a petticoat in the kitchen. I brought the bundle and handed it over Major Riaz. He tore the petticoat open and Masud took out the money. Then Major Riaz asked me my father's name. I replied that his name was Nipu. It was his nickname. Major Riaz assured me that he would set my father free. I begged whomever I saw to let my father go."

Binapani Saha said, "Major Riaz was then standing near the door of the kitchen where all the ladies were. He did not move from that place; maybe he was trying to protect them from the lustful eyes of his men. So he was standing in front of the door."

In reply to my question whether Major Riaz abused the women, "Not at all," was Gautam's reply. He was the only person at the end who returned to Pakistan. Gautam was all praise for him. As he was describing Major Riaz, Gautam's face glowed with praise, "He was about 27 years then and very handsome. He was from Baluchistan. Later on, we got details of his family. We had developed a good relationship with him which I will describe later. So, I am going back to what I was narrating."

"The Siri flowed through Jhaugora village. They took all those people whose hands were tied, including my father, to the other side of the river. The Marwari was tortured badly, and also his son. The latter was shot at, but the bullet missed him. All, including the Marwari's employee Gopeshwar Babu of Kaliakoir, were beaten, then tied up and taken to the other side of the river. Fourteen of them were taken away. I followed them. When Major Riaz was taking them away, I was a hundred yards behind them. I had no clothes on my body except the black shorts I was wearing. I was following them to identify my father. Then Masud remembered that I had fallen on Major Riaz's knees begging for my father's life. He realised that if I kept pleading, my father would be released. Masud who had a 303 rifle in his hand, struck me on the back with a cane, and said, 'I will shoot you.' I got scared, lay down on the road and started crying. Meanwhile, they started shooting the captives one after another, on the bank of the river. The last two were yet to be shot, my father and the Marwari's younger brother. The Marwari himself had been shot from behind and killed earlier. The river was knee-deep. All of the victims were made to get down into the water with their backs to the riverbank. They were shot from behind and fell face down into the water. The last to be shot were my father and the Marwari's brother. Suddenly, remembering that one of them was to be set free as requested, Major Riaz called out, 'Who is Nitu?' I had said my father's name was Nipu but Major Riaz mispronounced it as 'Nitu.'"

"The Marwari's brother perhaps realised that my mother and I might have fallen on Major Riaz's feet begging for my father's life. My father remained silent as he was not Nitu. He had been abused badly – a person who had never been struck even mildly, had been tied up, held by his hair and kicked. He must have felt terribly insulted. He hung down his face, silent and speechless, perhaps out of revulsion and shame. Even when Major Riaz was enquiring who was Nitu, my father did not bother to clarify that he was Nipu, and not Nitu. Then that Marwari fellow took advantage of the situation and cried out, 'There is no Nitu here, I am Jitu.' Major Riaz released him and asked him to leave. He then shot my father dead. After that the Pak forces left the place."

When I asked Gautam whether that Marwari gentleman who survived said anything later, he replied "No, he didn't. I heard everything. When the Pak forces left, I ran to the spot. When I looked down I saw the knee-deep water red with all the blood spilled from those who had been shot there. I found my father nearest the bank, which indicated that he was the last one to be shot. When I turned my father on his back, I saw his internal organs spilling out of his chest, shattered by 303 bullets." Gautam pointed to the left side of the chest to show how his father's chest had been ripped open. "His arm hung limp. My father gasped faintly and became silent forever. When my mother came along with my elder sister who was not well and asked where my father was, I pointed to his dead body and said, 'There he is.'"

"When I looked up, I noticed thousands of onlookers on the river bank, asking us to leave the place. My mother and I saw that my father's tongue was hanging out of his mouth. I started removing the sand sticking to his tongue. My father was a very handsome man. Crazy with grief, I kept caressing his eyes fondly and the nails of his feet. Then the villagers repeated their request, 'Please leave the place, otherwise the Pak forces will come back.' They pushed us away from there. The Pak forces did all this killing a quarter of a mile from the house where we had taken shelter. The local people asked us again and again to leave the place, otherwise they feared they would be killed. The six persons that they released were from poor families. The Pak forces, had, however, also killed a couple of young persons from poor families."

Binapani Saha continued the narration. "After that we started running towards the village. We did not head towards the house where we had taken shelter because people from that house too were lying dead. All of us belonging to Hindu families ran for shelter from one village to another. I have eight children, all of whom were quite small, the youngest being two years old. My eldest daughter was 16 or 17 years at age. We also had a maid. There were the family members of the Marwari as well, his wife, three sons and two daughters. Again there was the family of the local Brahmin priest and two other Hindu families. We were all bewildered and were running about aimlessly. At times we approached a house at random and asked for water to quench our thirst. The Pak forces had gone back after completing their operation which lasted an hour and a half. We were running from around 4.30 in the afternoon. We were moving about aimlessly, as the places were not known to us. The villagers too did not come forward to help us. We seemed to be running around in circles, coming back to the same place more than once. In this way, we came to a house which was known to my husband, through his jute business. He used to go there at times. There was a fierce storm and torrential rain at that time. We were given shelter in a thatched hut. We were to sleep on the floor. How could we sleep? We had not washed, we had not eaten. At midnight the landlord came and requested us to leave the place. 'If the Army knows that Hindus have been given shelter here they will come and torture us.' I gathered courage and said, 'Where can we go at dead of night? We will leave the place soon.' We were more than dead, and there was danger everywhere. We stayed on in that house that night and left at five in the morning. We had no adult men with us, only young children. This son of mine was then in class six. That morning we took a mud road, avoiding the paved road. We came across a gentleman named Billal, a member of the Awami League who was from Rangpur. He had come to this area because of the turmoil in the country. He took us (all 24 of us) to his house and put us up in his cow shed, emptying it of cattle and goats. That village was known as Bhatchhala. Billal was not very well off. There were some kind people in the village who collected rice and lentils from different houses and provided us with utensils and *kanthas*. We stayed on like this for six or seven days. Billal was a good man. He gave us rice and lentils that he had got by begging. Billal also managed to get some milk for my young daughter. I would not have survived without his help at that time. At the same time, there was no dearth of cruel people there. They kept harassing us. We were being guarded against them by Billal and others."

"One day, the house of a rich Hindu Brahmin of that village was looted. When the house was being robbed, we heard loud noises. It appeared as if someone was breaking down the house. I said, 'That house is being robbed. It is time for us to think of leaving this place.' A villager named Abed Mia, who had been in Sherpur before, recognised me and offered to take Gautam with him, assuring me that he would bring him back in the evening with clothes. You can well imagine my frame of mind at that time. Gautam was certainly going to die of starvation staying with me, so I handed over my son to Abed Mia. Five to seven persons too went with him to Sherpur. Meanwhile a few middlemen helped the Marwari family to cross over to India. I did not know anything about this. The Marwari family was living in one room, and we in another. They crossed the border at night. Dusk had fallen, but my son had not returned. When he did not return even till late at night, I became very worried. The middleman said to me, 'If you want to go to India, come with me.' But I did not have the courage to do so. I had three grown-up daughters with me. My son was still in Sherpur. How could I go? If midway, the middleman tried to do some mischief, what could I do? I said to him, 'No, I won't go. If we have to die, we'll die here.'"

"Next morning I went to Boyra. On the following day those who had taken Gautam came to Boyra to look for me. They suggested if I was willing to go to Sherpur, they could arrange it. I thought that in that village I had no place to stay and no one on whom I could depend. In Sherpur, I could at least stay in my own house. So I agreed and said I would go. But it was no easy matter going back to Sherpur. An office of the Peace Committee had been set up there. Permission from this committee and the police station was necessary. So there were a lot of problems."

"Although these persons were somewhat crooked, at that time they did a lot for us. Otherwise I could not have survived."

"Next day these persons took us to Sherpur. However, we could not get into our house straightaway because it was occupied by other people. So we went to the house of Mr. Alauddin, a Muslim Leaguer. We stayed there for about an hour, and then moved to Mr. Bashar's house, adjacent to ours. We stayed in Bashar's house that night. Two persons were occupying our house. When my son went to our house, the trespassers addressed him aggressively. They said, 'You son of a *malaun* (non-Muslim)! With whose permission have you come here?' My son recognised one of them as the friend of my sister's son, Ranjit. I went there and introduced myself as Ranjit's aunt. They appeared to soften a little."

"We stayed in Bashar's house for two or three days. After that I gathered enough courage and went to our house. Bravely I said to the occupiers, 'You have occupied my house but I am the owner, and I am here. How can you continue to stay here?' There were two men with their families staying in our house. I made one of them move out and started living there. After three or four days, I made the other family move out too. This is how I took re-possession of my house. With my four sons, four daughters and the helping hands, we were ten in all. I told Abed Mia, who had brought us here from the village, 'If the major comes here, point him out to me.' I was no longer afraid of death."

"They did not take me to the major. So I took two rickshaws and started for the major's place with my children. The office of the Peace Committee was on the left of my house. When I reached the place, I was not allowed to get down. The major's jeep was near the godown. I turned back the rickshaws and headed in that direction. Again I was not allowed to get down. I halted my rickshaw and waited. Later on when the major and a few others came out to wash their faces, they noticed our rickshaw covered with a piece of cloth for *purdah*. They must have realised that there were women in the rickshaw. After some time we were called in. We entered a hall room. The major appeared before us and asked us to sit down. I was too afraid to sit down. He then addressed us in Urdu, 'Sit down, Ma. Do you want to say something? Why have you come here?'"

Gautam said, "At that time a few Muslim Leaguers, Mr. Khalil, Professor of English of Sherpur College, Mr. Sardar and Dr. Jamal were sitting there. Dr. Jamal was not a collaborator. They wanted to kill him. But when his wife introduced herself as having studied in Karachi, a brother-sister relationship with Major Riaz developed. That explained Dr. Jamal's presence there. In addition, there were other Muslim League leaders also, because the Muslim League was a strong party in that area. Now it is the stronghold of Jamaat. In this Bajitpur Union, during the 1970 elections, few votes had been cast in favour of Bangabandhu. It was held by Qamruzzaman, the former Joint Secretary of the Jamaat."

Binapani said, "In reply to the major's question, I said in Bangla, 'You had given me your word that you would release my husband, but instead of releasing him, you killed him.' He replied, 'No, Amma, I set one man by the name of Nitu free.' I said that that was a different person. He said, 'If I find him I will shoot him.' Then he asked, 'How are you passing your days?' I replied, 'By begging. Now either kill me and my children, or else look after us.' Then he said, 'Very well, Ma, please go back today. I will see you tomorrow.' Then we came back home."

"The next day about 10 or 11 in the morning Major Riaz came with his men. At that time the house had practically no gate or even doors or windows. Abed Mia, the carpenter, wanted to repair the gate. He was seated, in fact, right at the gate. My daughters were going next door to have their baths. My youngest daughter came running into the house saying, 'Mother, Mother, the military are coming again.' Saying this, she and Gautam ran into the latrine in the thicket in front of the house. I had overcome my fear of death long ago. So I went and stood at the door. I had forgotten about Major Riaz's promise the day before."

"Two soldiers entered the house with major Riaz. The Major sat inside and I stood by the door. He said, 'Okay, Ma, tell me all you have to say.' I told him, 'My children are all small. Either kill me or else look after us.' I spoke in Bangla but he understood. There was a Haji Saheb who acted as our interpreter. When Gautam understood that they had not come to kill us, he came forward."

"I had heard that things from my father's house had been seized and taken to the local police station. I told Major Riaz this and requested him to give me back some of those things. The things taken were rice, pots and pans, clothes, etc. The major pointed at Gautam and said 'Ma, I'll take him along. I'll give him whatever I can.' I noticed the soft attitude of the major. He resembled my niece's husband, and I told him this too. Anyway, the major took Gautam to the police station in his jeep."

"After they left, many of our neighbours came and said, 'What have you done? You have given your son again? They'll kill him.' I thought, 'Well, if they kill him then so be it. If he stays with me, he will die without food anyway. How can we survive? I don't have any money. How can I look after this large family?'"

Gautum said, "After I 'came back from the latrine where I had hidden, Major Riaz pulled me towards him and made me sit on that *chowki*. There were tears in his eyes. After a while, he asked me to go with him. I was not frightened to go with him. Since I had seen him cry, I was no longer afraid of him. Moreover, when he came out to the jeep, he took Haji Saheb as well. So I was not frightened. I think I was bare-bodied then as well, just wearing a pair of shorts. The major held my hand and helped me into the jeep. Then he let the driver go and drove himself. Haji Saheb sat behind. First Major Riaz went to the hospital and visited some patients. Then he headed towards the police station. On the way, he placed his hand on my back and said, 'Does your brother-in-law look like me?' Riaz was speaking in his own language. I looked minutely at Riaz and realised that he really looked like my brother-in-law. The only difference was that Riaz was very fair and my brother-in-law was fair for a Bangali. I said that there was a resemblance."

"Major Riaz then drove to the police station. He took me towards the lock up where the accused were kept. I shivered at the sight of the lock up. I used to be terrified of the police. I was scared that he had brought me to be locked up. I did not know that things from my grandparents' house were kept at the police station. All the accused stood up at the sight of Major Riaz. He told them to sit down. Major Riaz was very good looking; people liked him a lot. He also had a good character, though I did not know this until later. He said to me, 'Take, take,' but I did not take anything. I then picked up one thing timidly. I had heard that those who took too many things were beaten. If I took too many things, I might be beaten. Major Riaz gave me one pitcher, two glasses, a few brass plates. He took me to another room. There were clothes there. In this way, he gave me a sack of clothes, a sack of pots and pans, five sacks of rice, and 100 rupees. He put me on a rickshaw and sent me home. The money was handed to Haji Saheb who came to our house with me."

"Major Riaz lived in Ahmednagar Camp, three miles from Jhenigathi. After that, whenever Riaz came to Sherpur, he used to visit us. He used to come to Sherpur every day on office work. He used to see my mother quite often. He enrolled us one by one in school and my eldest sister in college. He used to call my mother 'Ma' and we used to call him 'Nana.' In this way we passed nine months."

"Once some Muslim Leaguers said that if we wanted to stay, we had to become Muslims. One day, the religion teacher at school, Maulana Momtaz, made a number of us wash and do ablutions near the Marwari's house. Then he taught us to say Muslim prayers. He said that we had to say our prayers in this way. My name was changed from Gautam to Tafiruddin. Dulal was the same age as me and he was renamed Dabiruddin; the first letter of his own name was used to make his new Muslim name. Later, we were never asked whether we said our prayers. One day, Mother told Major Riaz that her son had been made a Muslim. On hearing this, he laughed. After that we had no problems because we were treated as Major Riaz's 'grandchildren.' On the contrary, people were frightened of us."

Binapani said, "The major used to come and ask about our welfare. I was quite young then and I had grown-up daughters. He used to say, 'Ma, does anyone ever look at you with lustful eyes? Just tell me and I will gouge out his eyes.'"

"Once Major Riaz ordered 300 green coconuts to be bought for his camp. At that time, my brother's garden had a lot of coconut trees. Jamaat leader Qamruzzaman went with eleven men to my brother's house and just cut off the coconuts from his trees. I told Major Riaz about this. He was furious and later scolded the men thoroughly. My son had gone there. Major Riaz said to his men, 'Why are you like this? We have come to fight a war. Why should we take other people's things? Why do you do this instead of fighting the war?' Later Qamran (Qamruzzaman) who had taken the coconuts was made to go to my brother's house to apologise."

"After some time, Major Riaz could not come regularly to ask about us. Six hundred maunds of rice had been confiscated earlier from my brother. Major Riaz arranged for 100 maunds from those 600 maunds to be sold. He gave the money to Abed Mia and told him to set up a shop with it. Abed Mia would run the shop. That arrangement would help Abed Mia, and the income from this would also help meet our financial needs. The shop that you see in front of our house today is the same shop that was set up at that time. The profit from the shop met the needs of two families. Major Riaz used to come from time to time to see how the shop was doing."

Gautam said, "Major Riaz wanted to take me to Pakistan twice, and I also agreed to go. We had forgotten then that he had ordered the killing of our father. We could not think of him as a murderer. In our opinion he was not to blame. "

We asked Binapani whether she considered Riaz a murderer. She replied unhesitatingly, "No. The major said, 'The people of your own country are themselves greedy. We don't know where Jhaugora village is, who are Awami Leaguers, who are Hindus. Your people themselves have shown us everything.' We had developed a very good relationship with Major Riaz. Towards the end, he did not wear military uniform when he visited us, he used to wear civilian clothes. If we had not been befriended by Major Riaz, we could not have been saved from the demons in this country. Even the local people had become our enemies."

Gautam said, "Major Riaz told his family in Pakistan about us. He told them how he had wrongly had someone killed. His family invited us to go to Pakistan. Twice he attempted to take us. The situation was such that I almost went with him."

We asked Binapani Saha, "Did you also want to leave for Pakistan?"

Binapani said, "No, no, I would not have gone."

Gautam said, "One day Major Riaz came to give Ma a sari. It was a printed sari. Ma had stopped wearing printed saris. She had started wearing white saris because of her widowed state. Perhaps Ma told him, 'I can't wear that.' The sari had a boat print. My two younger brothers jumped up and exclaimed, 'Ma, Ma, see the boat design!'[1] Major Riaz was standing in front. He started to laugh and said, 'This country will be independent one day. It will be independent.'"

Gautam said, "Major Riaz even told General Niazi that he was taking care of a Hindu family. I was made a member of the scouts. Biju Bhai was the scout leader. On August 14 Niazi came to Charpakkhimari and we went there. Niazi came to Sherpur Park as well. The day he came to Sherpur Park, we scouts went to welcome him. Major Riaz gave me a torch-like thing to hold saying, 'Keep it in your hand.' When the helicopter carrying Niazi came near, the Major took the apparatus from my hand and clicked it and at once a strong beam of coloured light darted upwards. Directed by this light, the helicopter descended. Major Riaz went forward and escorted the General from the helicopter. He introduced the people gathered there and Niazi shook hands with them. He shook hands with me too. The Major introduced me as his grandson." Gautam flashed a proud smile. "I shook hands with General Niazi."

Gautam continued, "Major Riaz was so good that people of this area piked him. When he used to come to our house, he used to leave the jeep some distance away, near the Peace Committee office or in front of the Town Hall. It was usually a market day and he knew that if he brought his jeep, it would inconvenience the crowd on the road. Lots of people wanted to give him all kinds of food items, but he never had anything. Only at our house he used to eat my mother's home-made *monda* or drink green coconut water. And he used to eat home-cooked food made by Dr Zaman's wife. People used to leave their green coconuts at our house for Major Riaz."

"Once Major Riaz took leave to go to Pakistan. He left Major Ayub, who was in charge of Bakshiganj, in charge of our area. Major Ayub was a tyrant, and people used to be afraid of him."

We asked Gautam what the freedom fighters thought of their relationship with the Pakistani major. He replied, "There were two types of freedom fighters. Not all freedom fighters had the same attitude. That we, a Hindu family, were being looked after by the Pakistani forces was also reported to the Indian Army."

---

[1] In 1971 boat was a symbol of victory. In the 1970 's election Awami League won a landslide victory with this symbol.

"Towards the end of November or early December, Major Riaz went bird hunting in the hills. He loved shooting birds. There he was shot at by freedom fighters. The bullet hit his leg. He left on his jeep from Jhenaigothi towards Jamalpur. It was winter and I was standing at the corner of Khorompur crossing, eating *pitha.* I noticed the Major driving his jeep past the place at very high speed. What I did not know then was that he had been shot. Later in the afternoon I learnt that he had been hit in the leg. Dr Zaman went to Jamalpur and treated him. I have heard – though I did not hear it from Dr. Zaman – that major Riaz had asked about us. He stayed in Jamalpur for four or five days and then left for Pakistan."

"In the meantime, those who were against liberation were preparing a list of persons they meant to kill, and my name was on the list. On December 6, at dawn, the Pakistani forces retreated towards Jamalpur with 108 trucks and jeeps. We saw very early in the morning, militia dressed in black jumping into the last of the trucks. By the morning of December 7, the last remnants of the Pakistan army had left. Sherpur was liberated on the same day, on December 7. In the afternoon we were standing in front of my maternal uncle's house lest it be looted again. At that time some people came and said, 'Let us go to India. The freedom fighters are on one side, the Pak army is on the other side. When fighting starts between these two forces, we are going to be killed. Go and tell your mother that some of us should take our families and go together towards Jamalpur.' We could not make up our minds about what to do. It was 11 or 11:30 at night, but we still could not decide whether we should go to Jamalpur or stay where we were. At around 1 pm we heard that the freedom fighters had arrived but they were not shooting. Then about seven or eight of us went forward with the flag, the one that had the map of Bangladesh, along with a white flag and shouted 'Joy Bangla.'

"On that day (December 7) eleven freedom fighters came to Sherpur. They were not local boys but had come from Rangpur. This became a bone of contention with the local freedom fighters later, as both claimed they had entered Sherpur first. Those who had come from Rangpur were sturdy and well built; they had fresh garlands around their necks. Their *lungis* were raised above their knees and tied between their legs like loin cloths. As they entered, they blew whistles. In this area, there had been a fight on December 3 in Dhonia

Kamalpur. The Pak forces retreated on December 6, and the freedom fighters came on the 7th."

When asked how many Pakistani soldiers had been killed in the war, Gautam replied, "In this locality no one in Major Riaz's forces was killed. His camp was in Ahmednagar and there was no fight there. Major Riaz was not shot while fighting, he was shot on a bird shoot. A battle had taken place in Kamalpur with Major Ayub. He died in action. Major Ayub was the number one person in this region. The battle in Kamalpur had been fought under the leadership of Colonel Taher. The Pakistani camp at Kamalpur was very well fortified and that is why the battle there had been furiously fought, but the Pak army was defeated. On the 7th, the freedom fighters entered Sherpur, and on the 8th the local freedom fighters came. On the third day of the liberation of Sherpur, perhaps it was December 10, a Thursday, when the Indian forces came and questioned my mother about Major Riaz."

In this connection, Binapani said, "Our relationship with the Pakistani major was seen by some freedom fighters as simple and straightforward. But others did not take it well. Especially those who were very young could not see it in a good light. They indicated that we were in some kind of immoral relationship. They wanted to say that we were collaborators. They did not try to understand our problem. They kept saying 'Why didn't you go to India? Why not? The Marwaris went, why not you? You must have been involved in treacherous activities.' These people later tried to add my son's name to the list of collaborators prepared by the Ghatak Dalal Nirmul Committee (Committee for Eradication of Murderers and Collaborators)."

Gautam talked about all the problems they had to face after Sherpur was liberated. He felt a great deal of anger towards the freedom fighters and the politicians of that time. He said, "I don't want to do any politics now. Once I used to be active in the Chhatra League (students' wing of the Awami League). The local Awami Leaguers feel that those of us who stayed on in Bangladesh during the Liberation War are all traitors and criminals. They have even tried to present a distorted view of liberation. All of us who stayed back have suffered a lot. I was made to do forced labour by the Pak forces – piling bricks. When they heard that I was Major Riaz's 'grandson' they quickly released me and gave me a banana to eat.

Lots of things like this took place. My father was killed, and I feel a lot of anguish and anger about it. One of those who helped to kill my father was made the secretary of the orphanage in 1972 by the then local MP, Anisur Rahman (who later became the district governor.) My father's killers are roaming around in front of my eyes. No one says anything to Faju Munshi, Dr. Wadud's nephew. Major Riaz told us everything about the people who pointed out to him the Awami League leaders and the Hindus. If the major had wanted to, he could have killed all of us that day. We are alive in exchange of my father's life. He treated us like human beings and saved us. He killed one and saved nine. I did not like the local Awami League leaders. I felt that they were not loyal to the ideals of liberation, they only pretended to be interested. I feel that the real objectives of liberation have not been achieved."

Gautam showed an overwhelming partiality towards Major Riaz. He refused to regard Major Riaz as a murderer. When he was told that Major Riaz not only killed his father but a whole lot of other innocent people, he replied, "It's not right to say that Major Riaz killed a lot of people." We argued, perhaps he did not kill people himself but he gave the orders to kill them. To that Gautam said, "No one had gone and met him before. After my father's death, Major Riaz did not kill any more innocent people. When there was a battle with the freedom fighters or with the Indian army, that was a different matter."

"Major Riaz himself never killed any innocent people. But unknown to him, a lot of innocent people were killed by people like Qamruzzaman. Qamruzzaman had a camp and he had his student body. He was the chief of Al-Badr and Al-Shams (collaborators) of the Mymensingh region. He was also party chief of the Mymensingh Islamic Students Organisation. As a result, he was extremely influential here. He killed a lot of people. He starved people to death. When Major Riaz was not in the area, he used to catch people from the villages and shoot them at night under the bridge on the Siri river. In this way, he held captive the local Commissioner Majid, intending to kill him. Kajal, a footballer, was singing the song 'Joy Bangla, Banglar Joy' in the library. He was taken by these collaborators and killed near the Siri bridge. All these were outside the knowledge of Major Riaz."

Gautam added, "Major Riaz never took part in any abuse of women. But I was quite young then and so did not know much about these things. Others in the locality told us that the collaborators were involved in this. We also hear that women were supplied to the Pak forces by the Al-Badr and Al-Shams. There is no evidence of Qamruzzaman's involvement in supplying women but he was involved in killing people. Qamruzzaman was acquainted with Major Riaz, but they weren't close. Here the local collaborators were Syed Ali Chairman, Faju Munshi, former Muslim League MP Dr. Samadul Haq and others. After independence these collaborators were jailed. However, when Bangabandhu declared a general amnesty, these people were all released."

We asked Binapani Saha, "How did you find out that it was Major Riaz who had ordered the killing of your husband?" She replied, "We were still in the village after the incident. We enquired about it. Besides, Abed Mia, who was a Muslim League follower, was there. He said this area was under Major Riaz's command and the operation was undertaken by his orders. The day the Pak forces were returning after the operation at Jhaugora, they kept distributing clothes to people on the way. They proceeded from Jhaugora to Sherpur Park and then gave speeches there. Moreover, after we came to Sherpur, the Muslim League leaders talked of Major Riaz. They described his appearance. Then we were confirmed that this person was Major Riaz."

Binapani was asked whether she had any anger or resentment against Major Riaz. She answered, "No. I have no anger. The one who was destined to leave us has gone. After that if Major Riaz had not helped, if he had not cared about us, where would we have been? I was young then; I had three grown-up daughters. If he had not looked after us, we would have been completely destroyed. After getting to know Major Riaz, we started to feel safe. The major told us, 'If anyone looks at you with any bad intentions, just tell me. I'll post two soldiers near your gate.' Besides, he helped us with rice, clothes and money. If we had not received this kind of support and kind behaviour from him, we would have harboured a strong resentment towards him. But because he behaved so kindly, I think I have a soft corner for him and have developed an affection for him. I have forgiven him."

We noted that Binapani Saha harboured no feelings of resentment against Major Riaz. But, we asked her, did she have any resentment against the other Pakistani soldiers?

"That will remain," she replied.

Did she think it was a matter of fate?

Binapani responded, "Yes, it is partly a matter of fate. It was written in my fate, so it happened."

Gautam added, "We were not supposed to go to the village."

Binapani agreed. "Yes, we were not supposed to go to the village. We had always thought that we would cross the border and go to India."

After independence, neither Gautam nor Binapani had any communication with Major Riaz because they did not know his address. However, Gautam has a strong desire to meet Major Riaz again. Even Dr. Zaman who had treated Riaz was unable to give them his address. The family could not reconcile themselves to Major Riaz's sudden departure after being shot. This was apparent from their feelings for him.

The explanation for their strong affection for Major Riaz might be that the family strongly believed that the major had wanted to set their father free and it was owing to some confusion that Nibaron Chandra Saha was killed. That is why they were compassionate towards the major. Above all, when the major started looking after the family, their day-to-day contacts created a bond between them. Due to their relationship with Major Riaz, this Hindu family was able to survive during those tumultuous days.